SOUTH JERSEY TOWNS

SOUTH JERSEY TOWNS
History and Legend

WILLIAM McMAHON

RUTGERS UNIVERSITY PRESS

New Brunswick **R** *New Jersey*

© 1973 by Rutgers University, The State University
Manufactured in the United States of America

Eighth Printing, 1993

Library of Congress Cataloging in Publication Data

McMahon, William H.
  South Jersey towns, history and legend.

  Bibliography: p.
  1. New Jersey—History, Local.   I.   Title.
F134.M16   974.9'9   78–163961

ISBN 0–8135–0718–9 Paper

The history of a nation is only
the history of its villages . . .

Woodrow Wilson,
Newark, 1895

CONTENTS

ACKNOWLEDGMENTS

Many people assisted in the preparation of this book. I am especially indebted to those who allowed me access to private family papers and to those patient, devoted guardians of the heritage of the past in libraries, museums, historical societies, churches, schools, and company, city, county, and state offices.

Among those who contributed in the form of letters, interviews, photographs, maps, and special research on my behalf were the following: Arthur E. Armitage for information on Collingswood; Ray Baker on Pleasant Mills and the "Kate Aylesford house"; Bush Barnum of the Glass Containers Manufacturing Institute for information and pictures on the Mason jar; E. G. Bowman of RCA-Victor for early pictures and articles on the Victor Talking Machine Company; G. Edwin Brumbaugh on the Batsto restoration; Shelley Budnick, county farm agent of Ocean County; Paul Burgess, of the Chelsea Title Company, who clarified many early grants; Frank Butler for notes and stories on Cumberland and Salem counties; Howard Chapelle, curator, Division of Transportation, Smithsonian Institution; George F. Cleary, editor of the *Gloucester City News;* Sam A. Christopher, editor of the *Ocean County Daily Times* of Lakewood; John L. Cole on Bordentown Military Institute; Dr. Kurt D. Degener for records on Renault's Egg Harbor; Henry Denmead for data on Mays Landing; Karl Dickinson, Cape May Museum, on early families of the Cape; Raymond Dixon, Cape May County Historical Society, on early Dennisville and Cape May County; William Fennan, former manager of Steeplechase Pier, for information about Sousa and the Floradora Sextet; Daniel Fenton on Millville holly; Loren D. Flood, Vineland historical writer; Dennis Gallagher on the Seabrook Farms enterprises; Mrs. Ralph Goff of Ocean View for personal experiences in upper Cape County; Dr. Maurice Gordon for a search of state medical records; Frank Gravatt on early days of Atlantic City piers; Charles Green for secrets of the Pines and Pleasant Mills; Leda Greene, librarian of the State Department of History in Des Moines; William J. Haffert, Sr., on Cape County storms and Sea Isle City; Morgan Hand II for trips along forgotten Jersey Cape trails and recollections of the Stone Harbor Railroad; Edward Hazelton of the Stratford Township Historical Society; Earl Higginbotham, county engineer in Mount Holly, on bridges; Harold R. Hirshlond, curator of Mount Holly's Prison Museum; John W. Holmes for notes on Medford Lakes; David Jackson, last surviving seaman of the *Sindia,* for his recollections; Marshall A. Joyce of Pitman Grove for reintroducing me to scenes of my childhood; Howard R. Kemble, Haddonfield newspaperman; Charles F. Kier of Hammonton for information on the Lenni-Lenapes and other Indians of South Jersey; Mayor Frank Klein of Ship Bottom for tales of Long Beach Island; Vincent LaManna, former mayor of Sea Isle City; Jack Lamping of Toms River for information about the Tuckerton radio tower and Revolutionary War activities in Ocean County; S. C. Loveland, Jr., for his letters about the Great John Mathis and the John Mathis Society; Merill S. Lufthouse, historian of the Church of Latter Day Saints, Salt Lake City; Professor Fred R. McFadden, Jr., of Copping State College, Baltimore, on the Jersey Devil; J. C. MacDonald, New Jersey Department of Conservation, on Finn's Point and Fort Mott; Richard Magnell on the background of Haddonfield; Carig C. Mathewson, Jr., on the postal history of South Jersey; Ken Matthews, executive secretary of the Greater Lakewood Chamber of Commerce; Mrs. Katherine Mattson, assistant borough clerk in Swedesboro; James Mecray of Cape May on first days of the Ford agency and Henry Ford's racing days; Charles B. Miller, of the First National Bank of South Jersey, on Hammonton, Atlantic, Gloucester and Camden counties; Mrs. Herbert (Pauline) Miller of Toms River on the naming of that town; Mrs. Mary Molek, curator of the Eldridge Reeves Johnson Memorial Collection, Delaware State Museum; Mrs. Jonathan Moore on Bridgeton's Nail House; John D. F. Morgan, Camden County Historical Society, on Long-a-Coming and Indian King Tavern; Mr. and Mrs. Fred Noyes on the Towne of Smithville; Steve O'Keefe on the Coopers of Camden; Mrs. Ruth Penn, Forked River Historical

Society, for her research; J. E. Pfeiffer for his notes on South Jersey glass and Mason jars; Mrs. Mary Pietroski of Lawrence House, Burlington, for original material; David W. Poinsett, supervisor of Historic Sites, New Jersey Department of Environmental Protection; Mrs. Delia Pugh on Shane's Castle; Kenneth N. Scull for his findings on the West family of Atlantic County; Hazel Simpson, curator of manuscripts, Gloucester County Historical Society; J. Horace Sprague, Barnegat Historical Society, for his research; Francis A. Stanger, Jr., on Bridgeton; J. A. Starkey for his personal notes on Smithville and Batsto; Mrs. Catherine Stevens on Beesley's Point families; W. W. Summerill of Penns Grove on old Salem County houses; Reynold Thomas of Harvey Cedars for priceless old photos; Mrs. Irma L. Tilton, Hammonton, on Atlantic, Gloucester, and Camden counties; Joseph L. Truncher, New Jersey State Department of Environmental Protection, for his personal findings on Batsto; Emilie Webber, daughter of salt hay king Charles Webber of Green Bank; Emmett Welch on early day minstrels in Atlantic City and Philadelphia; Frank H. Wheaton on Millville glass; Joseph Wilson, editor of the *Hammonton News*, on upper Atlantic County; Eric Winberg for research on Batsto records; Raymond Wood, New Jersey Development Council, for statistics on industry; Captain John L. Young on early real estate in Atlantic City and the Million Dollar Pier; Adrien B. Hommell of Sussex and John B. Snyder of Madison for catching some errors in the first printing.

A special thanks to Mrs. McMahon for her assistance on some of the research problems, to Charlotte Carlson for the maps, and to Roberta Blaché for the index.

SOUTH JERSEY TOWNS

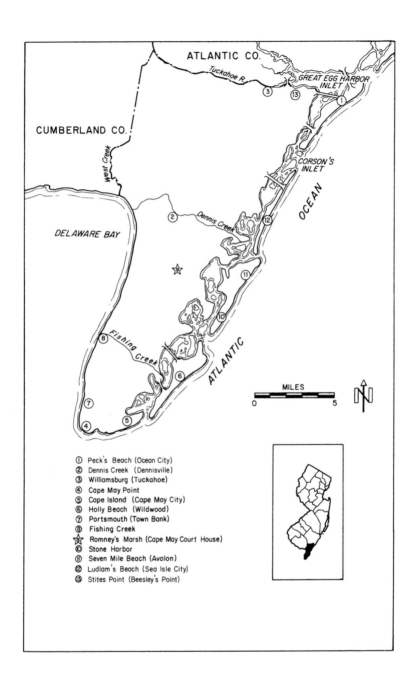

CAPE MAY COUNTY

ATLANTIC CO.

Tuckahoe R.

GREAT EGG HARBOR INLET

CUMBERLAND CO.

West Creek

CORSON'S INLET

Dennis Creek

DELAWARE BAY

OCEAN

Fishing Creek

ATLANTIC

MILES
0   5

N

① Peck's Beach (Ocean City)
② Dennis Creek (Dennisville)
③ Williamsburg (Tuckahoe)
④ Cape May Point
⑤ Cape Island (Cape May City)
⑥ Holly Beach (Wildwood)
⑦ Portsmouth (Town Bank)
⑧ Fishing Creek
☆ Romney's Marsh (Cape May Court House)
⑨ Stone Harbor
⑩ Seven Mile Beach (Avalon)
⑫ Ludlam's Beach (Sea Isle City)
⑬ Stites Point (Beesley's Point)

THE JERSEY CAPE

Long before the arrival of the first European explorers on the shores of the New World, the southern tip of New Jersey, now known as Cape May County, was inhabited by the Kechemeches, a band of the Lenni-Lenape Indians.

In the spring of 1524 Giovanni da Verrazano, a Florentine navigator in pay of the French, sailed along the Jersey coast, followed a year later by Estevan Gomez, a Portuguese who made a rough chart of the mouth of the Delaware River.

On August 28, 1609, Henry Hudson, an Englishman employed by the East India Company of Holland, sailed the two-masted vessel *De Halve Mann* (*Half Moon*) up the Delaware River and took possession of all adjoining lands in the name of the Dutch. He continued his explorations up the coast to what was to become New Amsterdam.

On March 27, 1614, the States General of Holland issued an edict for the encouragement and promotion of the New World lands described by Hudson. In the wake of the edict Holland merchants outfitted a fleet of five vessels to follow the Hudson trail with the New Amsterdam territories as its target. Cornelius Jacobsen Mey, a Hollander, was navigator of one of the vessels said to have cruised the coastline in the vicinity of the Delaware Bay.

In 1616 Cornelius Hendricksen, another Hollander, landed his ship *Reckless* on the tip of New Jersey and did some trading with the Indians he found there.

It was not until 1620 when Mey returned as captain of his own vessel, the *Blyde Bloodchap* (*Glad Tidings*), and chartered the bay and river for several miles inland that the Jersey Cape entered the pages of history with a definite designation. Captain Mey made sure there would be no doubt as to his presence by naming the bay (Delaware Bay) New Port Mey, the Jersey Cape itself Cape Mey, and the cape on the opposite side of the bay (now the state of Delaware) Cape Cornelius.* He named another jutting piece of land further south (on the Delaware side) Cape Henlopen.

Mey made a second voyage in 1623 with a group of refugees known as Gallois, who had fled to Holland, where they were called Walloons. Thirty families sailed with Mey in the ship *New Netherland* and were landed at Fort Nassau on the Delaware River. Mey became the first director-general of the territory claimed by the Dutch. He returned to the Netherlands and spoke of the New World in glowing terms but never attempted another voyage.

On May 5, 1630, Samuel Godyn and Samuel Blommaert, directors of the West Indies Company, were authorized by Peter Minuit, then director-general of New Netherlands on the Delaware, to start a colony near the Jersey Cape. They purchased a tract of land 12 miles long from ten Indian chiefs, members of the Lenni-Lenape. This project never materialized.

On December 5, 1632, Pieterzen De Vries arrived at Delaware Bay aboard the *Walvis* (*Whale*), to launch a whale-fishing industry. Two years later this was an admitted failure, and De Vries attempted to establish another economy based on grain and tobacco. This also was unsuccessful.

In 1638 whalers from New England came to the cape and were more successful than the Dutch, a whaling industry flourishing for many years at Town Bank.

Under the 1664 grant from Charles II to his brother the Duke of York, much of West Jersey (now called South Jersey) came under the rather loose designation of Eyren Haven (Egg Harbor), with several mapmakers changing boundaries according to their own whims. Eyren Haven shows up as part of the Dutch province of New Netherlands in the Mey maps. When the English took over in 1664, many of the Dutch spellings on West

---

* Mey soon became May, the spelling used widely today for the areas named by the Dutch captain. On the Vischer map published in Amsterdam about 1651, the spelling May was already in use, while on the Van Derdonck map of 1656 the tip of the New Jersey cape was noted as Port May.

Jersey maps changed and Eyren Haven became Great Egg Harbor.

Cape May County was created November 12, 1692, from land held by the West Jersey Society. It embraced all of South Jersey to a point about twenty miles up the Maurice River and then easterly to the most northern point of the Great Egg Harbor River. (In 1694 Egg Harbor was attached to Gloucester County and in 1837 it became part of Atlantic County.)

In the original act of establishment, Cape May County courts were restricted to cases involving values not over 20 pounds, making it necessary for residents to continue traveling to Burlington and Salem for more important legal matters. This was protested, and on May 12, 1697, the Assembly placed Cape May County courts on the same footing with other tribunals in the state.

Also in 1697 an act important to the new county was passed by the Assembly. It called for a road between Cape May and Burlington. Records show that progress on the road was slow. In 1706 Shamgar Hand and William Goldin, commissioners for the county, were just completing the layout of a road from Egg Harbor to Cold Spring and from there to Town Bank, a project completed in 1707.

On April 2, 1723, the county was divided into three precincts (now called townships)—Upper, Middle, and Lower. The census of 1726 showed 668 inhabitants in the county. In 1745 a courthouse was built at Middletown (Cape May Court House), and court was held in May of that year.

The Bank of Cape May County was established in 1853. Five years later a toll road from Cape Island to Cape May Court House was completed. In 1855 the first county newspaper, the *Ocean Wave,* was published on Cape Island.

BENEATH THE BAY

Tales of cities beneath the seas have long fired the imagination of writers. Seldom has truth approached the fiction. One of the exceptions is the story of the original whaling settlement of Cape May County which now lies beneath the waters of Delaware Bay. There is evidence that such a place existed; that it disappeared and is still there under the waters is likewise a fact.

Around 1640, when the great whales began to feed southward along the Jersey coast and in Delaware Bay, the New England whalers followed. They established camps on Long Beach Island, Brigantine Island, and at a place near the tip of the cape where they later built a group of houses and a high lookout tower which was known at various times as Portsmouth (after their New England home port), Cape May Town, New England Village, and Town Bank.

A piece written by the Rev. Daniel Hughes, dated March 25, 1894, and now in the possession of the Cape May County Museum, credits William Penn with creating the name of Town Bank and once having had a home there. But Mr. Hughes gives no authority for his statement, and a study of dates makes the truth of this assertion unlikely. According to records of New Castle, Delaware, William Penn was granted land by the crown in 1681 and in late October 1682 arrived and took possession of his grant at New Castle. Philadelphia records show that Penn founded his colony there in 1682. This would seem to leave little time for a stay at Town Bank, although Penn may have visited the settlement on his second trip to England.

Mr. Hughes calls the Penn house "substantial," and says it was next occupied by Thomas Forrest, who lived there until his death. When two of his nephews arrived from England to settle his estate, the house was sold to Daniel Stillwell, who moved the structure to his plantation called Higbee Beach.

For many years the house was known to fishermen of the area as the Hermitage Hotel. Its last days were spent as a fishing shack; it was finally torn down in 1940.

Efforts of historians to find a drawing of the old building have not been successful. Karl Dickinson, curator of the Cape Museum and a recognized historian, has never been able to pinpoint the original location of the so-called Penn house, although the legend about it is often repeated and accepted as truth by the natives of the cape area.

The exact date of the establishment of Town Bank is also subject to debate. Dr. Maurice Beesley, early historian, says there is no proof that the lower cape was settled before 1683, when Caleb Carman was appointed justice of the peace and Jonathan Pine constable. Bancroft's *History of the United States* talks of Cape May Town or Town Bank as having been settled forty years before the Beesley date. Records of New Haven, Connecticut, concerning the whaling industry, contain the line: "It is probable that from 1640 there was sheltering and resting places at Town Bank for the whalemen."

A study of old maps at the Cape Museum shows the original shoreline of 1605 several hundred yards farther out in the bay than the 1648 shoreline. A map made in 1951 by Russ Lyons tends to show the town as it appeared in 1726, with a number of dwellings penciled in in still a third indent of the shoreline. This map shows these dwellings gone by 1868, while the Town Bank line of today is even farther inland, a creek and two ponds seemingly having disappeared after 1868.

By 1695 the original settlement of Town Bank was beneath the bay. And the indiscriminate killing of the whales at the mouth of the Delaware so depleted the herd that by 1700 the whale was gone from bay waters. Many of the whalers returned to New England. Others moved farther inland and took up fishing, trapping, and log mining.

But the name Town Bank was preserved in the new village built on more secure ground near the tip of the cape directly across from where the original settlement disappeared into the waters of Delaware Bay. It is a community of private homes, many of them summer cottages.

PIRATE SAILS

There is something about the Delaware Bay region of the Jersey Cape that conjures visions of pirate ships in the off-shore waters, buried treasure among the sand dunes.

Oddly enough, such impressions are backed by a scattering

of historic lore and fact. One such fragment is a report by pirate
Captain Shelley, on May 27, 1699, to his consignee Mr. Delancie
at New York. Shelley was anchored in Delaware Bay and reported he had just arrived from Madagascar with a cargo of
fine muslin, calicoes, elephants' tusks, and opium.

That pirates were giving the government of West Jersey much
concern is attested in a report of Colonel Robert Quary, judge
of the Admiralty in Pennsylvania, to the Lords of Trade, dated
June 1, 1699, in which he stated:

There has arrived sixty pirates in a ship from Malligasco [Madigascar].
They are part of Kidd's gang. About sixteen of them have quitted the
ship and are landed in ye government of West Jersey at Cape May.*
The rest are still aboard ship which lies at anchor near ye Cape of this
government, waiting for sloops from New York to unload her. She is a
very rich ship. Ye captain of ship is one Shelley of New Yorke, and the
ship belongs to merchants of that place. The goods were all purchased
from the Pyratts of Malligasco. I seized of these pyratts two and conveyed them safely to Burlington goale in ye Province of West Jersey.

In a letter from Burlington dated June 9, 1699, Governor
Jeremiah Basse also attested to the presence of pirates at the
cape:

I went down to Cape May and took four persons suspected of piracy,
who confessed. They were committed to jail in Burlington. They had
a large quantity of treasure composed of Arabian and Christian gold,
amber, coral necklaces, India silks and other costly goods.

In another communication Governor Basse said that he had
been informed that Captain William Kidd, in a large sloop with
sixty hands, had been seen near Cape May. He said he saw the
sloop himself when he went after other pirates in the area and
would have made an attempt to capture it but it outsailed him.

A favorite legend of the Cape is that Captain Kidd buried

---

* The term Cape May in these early dispatches is a loose one and could
mean anyplace from the tip of the cape up to the Great Egg Harbor Bay.
In this case, it is safe to assume that the area referred to is on the Delaware
Bay side of the cape, possibly in the vicinity of Town Bank.

treasure at Cape May Point. Numerous attempts to find it have failed, but brave hearts still try. A large cedar at the point is known as the Captain Kidd treasure tree.

That the pirates were busy around the cape as late as 1722 is revealed in a dispatch from Philadelphia printed in the July 26 issue of the *New England Courant* of Boston:

On Sunday the 22nd arrived a small sloop, Jonathan Swain, master, from Cape May by whom we have advice that a Pyrate Brigantine and Sloop have been cruising on and off both our capes for about three weeks. They several times sailed up the bay.

There were many official complaints to Burlington that settlers of the cape area were hiding pirates from law officers. The pirate crews were said to have spent freely and paid cash for provisions, which may have accounted for this alleged leniency on the part of the settlers.

"THE LIGHT ON OLD CAPE MAY"

In an old collection of American sea chanteys I came across one popular with the square-rig sailors about 1900—"The Light on Old Cape May." It was sung to the tune known as "Bigelow" and went like this:

> The wind it blew from Sou'sou'east,
> It blew a pleasant breeze
> And the man upon the lookout cried:
> "A light upon our lee!"
> They reported to the captain and
> These words did he say—
> "Cheer up my sailor lads,
> It's the light on old Cape May."

According to Mrs. Corinne R. Swain of Cape May, the above version was sung about 1903 by her husband, a member of the Life Saving Service (later the Coast Guard).

"The Light on Old Cape May" has served ships at sea since 1744. The present lighthouse, the third, was built in 1859. Its beam is now elevated to aid air navigation as well as ships. (Lippi Photo)

The Cape May lighthouse now standing is the third structure to serve the shipping lanes at this spot. The first was built by the English government at Cape May Point about 1744 on the plantation of Thomas Hand at the same time one was ordered at Cape Henlopen on the opposite side of Delaware Bay. On old maps this lighthouse was designated as "Flash Light."

The second lighthouse was built of bricks in 1823 and brought down the river from Philadelphia. A number of these bricks are now in the Memorial Fireplace in the county historical museum at Cape May Court House.

The present lighthouse was constructed in 1859. A kerosene-wick lamp was used to illuminate the beacon. In 1910 an incandescent oil-vapor lamp was developed; it was in service until 1938. A 250-watt electric lamp was then installed in conjunction with 656 glass prisms and lenses to throw a beam for 19 miles to sea.

The lighthouse is 170 feet high, 27 feet in diameter at the base and 15 at the top. It is located about a thousand feet from the shoreline amid sand dunes and brush which make it an ideal subject for artists and camera enthusiasts.

In 1945, at the end of World War II, the federal government declared the Cape May light obsolete. The lens was dismantled and given on permanent loan to the county museum. Installed in its stead was a 36-inch rotating beacon equipped with a 1,000-watt electric lamp. The light is elevated $1\frac{1}{4}$ degrees to afford aid to air navigation. It has an intensity of 350,000 candlepower.

THE OLDEST RESORT

Mid-Victorian charm is the hallmark of Cape May City near the tip of the Jersey Cape. This atmosphere has been preserved not only in Victorian Village, the central part of the town, with its gas lights, horse-drawn car, strolling mall, and gingerbread architecture, but throughout the community itself. Even the newest building are required by law to follow Victorian lines.

Originally known as Cape Island, Cape May City bases its

claim as America's oldest seaside resort upon advertisements placed in the *Philadelphia Daily Aurora* in 1801 by Ellis Hughes, owner of a hotel tavern located between Perry and Jackson streets, who offered a single night's lodging for 7 cents. The advertisement added:

The subscriber has prepared himself for entertaining company who use sea bathing and he is accommodated with extensive house room, with fish, oysters and crabs and good liquors.

The Hughes establishment, named Atlantic Hall and described by some unfeeling scribes of the time as "a desolate barn of a place," remained the resort's only hotel until 1816.

There was apparently no rush of visitors in answer to early Hughes advertisements because of transportation problems. A sailing sloop carrying passengers first visited the waters of Cape May in 1809, but it had no set schedule. By the time Hughes opened his hotel the *Morning Star*, another sailing vessel under command of Captain Isaac Howland, was making weekly trips from Philadelphia during the bathing season only. Howland, an experienced fisherman, offered to take "gentlemen" out to the fishing banks for a day of sport. The ladies were left ashore at Cape Island.

In 1816 the new schooner *General Jackson*, Aaron Bennett, master, left Masden and Bunkers' wharf in Philadelphia for Cape Island every Tuesday, returning to Philadelphia on Saturdays. Captain Wilmon Whilldin, Sr., did much to popularize steamboat passage between Philadelphia and the cape, making trips on his *Delaware* between 1821 and 1827. The cost of the all-day trip was $5.

When the Whilldin boat began to make a stop at New Castle, Southern passengers boarded there adding to Cape Island's early popularity as a playground. An excellent history of steamboat travel to the cape was written by Robert Crozer Alexander of the Cape May County Historical Society and published in 1967 by the Cape May Geographical Society.

In 1816 the first Congress Hall, a frame building three stories high and 108 feet long, was built by Thomas H. Hughes, son of

Ellis Hughes of the Atlantic Hotel. It stood at what is now the northwest corner of Perry Street and Congress Place at the west end of Washington Street. It could house 100 guests. The maximum for room and board was $10 a week with guests served a diet of seafood and game. While Thomas Hughes contented himself with being a hotelman, his father served as sheriff of Cape May County and in Congress from 1829 to 1833. He died in 1839 and is buried in the Old Brick Cemetery at Cold Spring.

Today's Congress Hall, which dominates the city's Victorian scene, was built in 1879, a year after the original was destroyed by fire. The hall has been the vacation White House for six Presidents.

The Mansion House, built in 1832 by Richard S. Ludlam, is remembered as the first lathed and plastered house on the island. One of the unusual customs of early Cape Island was followed at the Mansion House. Simultaneous bathing by both sexes was prohibited at the beaches between the years 1839 and 1843. To make certain there were no embarrassing mixups, the Mansion House would fly a set of flags high above the roof—a white flag for the ladies, who were given the beach from 6 A.M. to 7 P.M. and from 11 A.M. to 12 noon, plus 4:30 to 5:30 in the afternoon; a red flag for the gentlemen, who could bathe from dawn to 6 A.M. and in the afternoon from 5:30 to 6:30. The bathing law was strictly enforced.

Among the famous guests of the Mansion House were orator Henry Clay and young congressman Abraham Lincoln.

In 1840 the Columbia Hotel, forerunner of several of this name, was added to Cape Island's ever growing list of hotels by builder George Hildreth. The Central and the New Atlantic hotels appeared in the same year. In 1843 the United States Hotel made its debut; A. W. Thompkins of Philadelphia was its builder.

On March 8, 1848, Cape Island was incorporated as the borough of Cape May, and James Mecray was named burgess. Thomas Hughes was high constable. By 1850 the borough was a leading resort of the Jersey coast, attracting Southern gentlemen and plantation owners from Delaware, Maryland, and Virginia. They brought along their finest horses to display in rides along the beach. Many spent the evening hours gambling

During the summer of 1869 the United States Hotel in Cape May City was headquarters for President U. S. Grant. Built in 1843, the building was among those destroyed by fire on November 9, 1878. The Merchants National Bank now occupies the site. (Courtesy of the Thomas Hand Collection)

at the Blue Pig, a casino operated by famous Northern gambler Harry Cleveland. Often a planter in a "game of honor" at the Blue Pig wagered his plantation on the turn of a card. The gambling house, long since gone, stood on a corner of the lot occupied by Congress Hall.

The resort remained a borough until March of 1851, when it was reincorporated as the city of Cape Island with a mayor, six councilmen, an alderman, and a recorder. The first council met on March 15 in the schoolhouse on Franklin and Lafayette streets. Isaac M. Church, a Baptist clergyman, was chosen mayor.

Most remarkable of early Cape May City hotels was the Mount Vernon, built in 1853 at Broadway and Beach Avenue. It was said to be the largest hotel of its time. A front section was four stories high, 300 feet long, with one wing three stories and 500 feet in length. The complete sections had 482 rooms, with something unique in early hotels—a bathroom for each room. The dining hall seated 3,000. A second wing was started but never completed. On September 5, 1855, the hotel was destroyed by fire. Philip Cain, one of the proprietors, and three of his family perished in the blaze. An anticipated capacity of 2,100 guests was never realized.

On April 12, 1861, Fort Sumter, in the harbor of Charleston, South Carolina, was fired upon by the Confederate forces, signaling the beginning of the Civil War and the end of Cape May's reign as a Southern bathing spa. The fine ladies and gentlemen who frequented its hotels and gambling casinos and trotted their thoroughbreds on the beach no longer came across the Delaware Bay from New Castle. Hotels were empty, the Blue Pig was shuttered, and an era vanished almost overnight.

On November 9, 1878, Cape May City's hotel section was swept by fire. The town's small fire-fighting force was unable to cope with the blaze. A trainload of firemen and equipment was rushed to the scene but arrived too late to be of help. When the fire was over, part of Congress Hall, the Ocean House, the Atlantic Hotel, the Columbia House, Center House, United States Hotel, and numerous private dwellings and mansions lay in ruins.

By this time the Delaware River had ceased to be a front

door to Cape May. The steamboats no longer called at its landings and the coming of the railroads brought a new type of visitor to its shore, the middle-class businessman and his family from Philadelphia and other Eastern metropolitan centers.

Cape May City was again hit by disaster in the hurricane of 1962, which swept away most of the beachfront, the boardwalk, and convention hall, and left the streets piled high with wreckage of homes and pleasure boats. The citizens and the officials of the city tackled the work of rebuilding. Disaster loans were secured, new bulkheading and jetties were built, a new larger and stronger convention hall was built on the site of the wrecked one, and the former boardwalk became a paved promenade.

In 1964 after years of controversy and planning, a ferry line linking the cape with Delaware became a reality. The Garden State Parkway was cut through from Beesley's Point to the tip of the cape. These two means of transportation brought new trade and life to the resort.

A planning board launched an ambitious program for the preservation of Victorian Village, with the result that today the city retains its turn-of-the-century charm (with modern conveniences) and has become a favorite family resort, with emphasis on bathing, boating, and fishing.

SEAT OF GOVERNMENT

Cape May Court House, county seat of Cape May County, is located in almost the geographical center of the county. It has been known as Shamgar Hand Plantation, Rumly Moch, Romney Marsh, and Middletown. Historians are at odds as to whether the name Middletown was applied to a specific place or the area in general which became Middle Township.

First settler Shamgar Hand purchased about 1,000 acres from the physician to King Charles II, Dr. Daniel Coxe, one of the largest landholders of his time in West Jersey. Hand named the area Romney Marsh from a village of that name on the Straits of Dover, Kent, England.

The horse car was the principal means of public transportation along the beachfront between Cape May City and Sewell's Point. (Courtesy of James Eadline)

The choice of the site as a county political center seems ideal from today's point of view. At the time it was chosen there was no such unanimity of thought. Proponents of Dennis Creek as the county seat were militant on the matter. They declared Dennis Creek was the logical choice because of its extensive shipbuilding activities, its big timber business, and its direct connection by water with Philadelphia. Dennis Creek business interests argued that because of its location it would some day be the industrial center of the county. Time has proven them wrong. Dennis Creek, now Dennisville, is a small community of beautifully restored homes.

A group from Goshen, today also a small group of houses, contended that their centrally located town was more suitable than the little inland village of Romney Marsh. The matter was put to a vote, and Romney Marsh became Cape May Court House and the county seat at the same time.

The first county court proceedings of records did not take place at Romney Marsh but at Portsmouth on March 20, 1693. In that year Timothy Brandreth was named sheriff of the county; he served until 1695. George Taylor was first clerk, serving from 1693 to 1697.

In December 1699, owing to increased court business, the Assembly appointed new circuit judges to hold court on February 20 and October 20 of each year: Shamgar Hand, Jacob Dayton, William Goldin, Samuel Mathews, and John Townsend.

In 1704 Governor Cornbury ordered general sessions of the peace held at the home of Shamgar Hand. Colonel Daniel Coxe was appointed judge in 1710.

Some point out that perhaps Daniel Hand had a deal in mind when he donated land for a courthouse in the same year that he petitioned for a license to "keep a house of entertainment" in the county. He received his license for a tavern in the village despite the opposition of the Baptist congregation. His inn became a landmark later known as the Union Hotel. It stood on the site of the present Title and Trust Building.

An interesting legend concerning the old Hand tavern was told me by historian Karl Dickinson. In the autumn of 1777, when the American cause was at low ebb, a stranger came galloping into the village of Romney Marsh and stopped at the Hand place. Days passed and he showed no inclination to leave. On one occasion in the public room he said he hoped to see the day when every rebel would hang high, and he invited all to drink to the health of King George. The tavern was a hotbed of Liberty Boys, so he had no takers. In fact, immediately afterward he disappeared. No one today knows what happened to the Loyalist stranger. But years later, when the tavern was remodeled, human bones were found cemented in a basement recess. They were never identified.

In 1774 the jail at the county seat burned to the ground; the freeholders were authorized to build a new one near the original site. The courthouse was rebuilt at this time and served the county until 1850. This new courthouse, which dominates the government buildings of the town, followed the classic designs of famed English architect Christopher Wren. Cost of the entire structure, including furnishings and a bell weighing 333 pounds, was $6,284.33. It was retired from original use in 1927, when a new brick building was constructed, but the 1850 structure stands today as a handsome, useful, and historic landmark.

The Hand family dominated Court House for many years, and its history is interwoven with that of the Dickinsons. Dr. John Dickinson, who moved from Salem to Cape May County in June of 1786, was one of the first active physicians of the county.

Cape May Court House today retains its county seat status. Within its limits are the Burdette Tomlin Hospital, Cape May County Library, County Historical Museum, the restored Jonathan Hand house, and Crest Haven, county home for the aged.

The town retains its colonial charm by careful preservations of buildings, both public and private, and by restrictions on signs and new structures that do not conform to the adopted pattern. A 106-foot flagpole on the courthouse lawn, flying the Stars and Stripes, can be seen for miles on any approach to the town.

QUAKER GUNS

The Quakers were in Cape May County as early as 1691 according to existing meeting records. Thomas Leaming, a whaleman, was among the first to settle in the area. A reminder of this early Quaker beginning is the meeting house at Seaville, which has been restored and is one of the historic sites of Shore Road. The structure, built in 1716, was known for years as the Cedar Meeting House.

One of the contributions of the Quakers to the history of Cape May County is the legend of the "Quaker guns." During the War of 1812, Reed's Beach on the Delaware River about three miles west of Cape May Court House was a spot favored by the British for filling water casks and restocking stores.

One night, according to the story, the Quakers who had long suffered British raids without protest gathered for a discussion of the situation. A day later the shoreline of Reed's Beach was bristling with cannons peeping out from the underbrush. The British discontinued their raids.

The "Quaker guns" were actually logs shaped and painted to resemble cannons, a trick credited to William Douglass, a ship's carpenter of nearby Sluice Creek. By this deception the Quakers were able to continue their creed of not taking up arms but saving their goods from those who did.

FIRST FERRY IN CAPE COUNTY

The original settler of what is now Beesley's Point on the south shore of Great Egg Harbor Bay was Irishman William Goldin, who supported the cause of King James II against William and Mary in 1690 as an officer in the battle of the River Boyne in Ireland, where King James was defeated. Forced to flee, Goldin landed on the shore of the Great Egg Harbor in 1691.

The area in which he settled became known as Goldin's Point, carrying the name until about 1717 and being so noted on old maps. Many writers of Cape May County history have used the spelling Golding. But an original deed dated 1717, in the Cape County museum collections, bears a signature spelled Goldin.

Rem Garrison was another early settler, he and Goldin having bought 1,061 acres of land. Following Goldin and Garrison to the upper part of Cape County was Hope Willets, a Quaker whose father Richard had fled religious persecution in his native Wales and later in the Plymouth Colony.

The settlement was known as Willets Point from about 1717 to 1750, after which it was called Stites Point, so named by Isaiah Stites, grandson of Henry Stites, one of the whalemen of the lower cape about 1689. Isaiah Stites secured considerable holdings in the upper cape region about 1750.

What is said to have been the first ferry in the area was established by an act of the provincial assembly in 1693 and ran between Job's Point (Somers Point) and Goldin's Point (Beesley's Point). Consisting of an open boat worked by sails and oars, the ferry was sometimes inoperative because of rough weather. It existed until 1762, when a toll bridge was built over Cedar Swamp of the Great Egg Harbor River, a short distance below Mays Landing.

A stone commemorating the ferry was erected at Job's Point by the Richard Bowen Division, Sons and Daughters of the Pilgrims on June 13, 1942. The tablet reads: "Near this site at Jobs Point was located Somers' Ferry established in 1693 to connect Somers Point and Beesleys Point." It is not accurate in that the site was called Goldin's Point at the time of the ferry.

Job Somers was the first ferryman, followed by Nicholas Stillwell, Sr., who purchased land at the point in 1748. Stillwell is believed to have been the first in the area to obtain a tavern license. His license is dated 1750, and his inn was located next to the ferry, in fact, in the ferry building itself.

The tavern continued in operation long after the ferry was

abandoned and passed through numerous ownerships. Thomas Beesley acquired the property in 1803 and three years later sold to Captain John Chattin. Around the turn of the century the place was known as the Beesley's Point Fishing Club. It was headed by Henry Clay, a Philadelphia political figure. In 1923 the property became a training school and has served that purpose ever since. The only part of the original building standing is a back kitchen.

During the years 1848–49 Richard Stites built a hotel across from the original tavern. This continued as an inn until 1906, when Henry Clay assumed title in addition to his fishing club. During World War I his daughter Mabel opened it as a Red Cross headquarters.

Following Miss Clay's death Norman Pullin, a Baptist minister, conducted church services in the rapidly deteriorating building. In January 1961 the old structure was destroyed by fire. A colonial-type tavern was built on the spot in 1963 by the Charles Harp family, who christened it the Tuckahoe Inn.

The point changed names with its principal land owners until the advent of Thomas Beesley, who officially registered the name Beesley's Point at Trenton and secured a post office under that name on March 3, 1851. Thomas was one of four sons of Captain Jonathan Beesley of the 1st Battalion of the Cumberland County militia, which fought in the Revolution. Captain Beesley was killed in a skirmish near Haddonfield, and each of his sons was bound out to a different family. Thomas, who was raised by Mr. Brick of Port Elizabeth, New Jersey, followed the sea, finally settling at the point.

Dr. Maurice Beesley, another of the ten children of Thomas Beesley and Rhoda Stites, made a name in the area by completing in 1857 a historical record of the county which is considered the most accurate ever compiled. He was a member of the Legislative Assembly from 1840 to 1842, first superintendent of public schools in the county, and one of the founders and directors of the New Jersey Historical Society. Dr. Beesley died on January 13, 1882, and is buried in the old cemetery in South Dennis.

A TALE OF 1776

Goldin's Point (Beesley's Point) on Great Egg Harbor Bay provided the setting for one of South Jersey's favorite Revolutionary War stories.

On September 19, 1776, as the story is told, the men of the settlement under Captain James Willets, son of pioneer John Willets, marched at dawn to answer Governor Livingston's plea for men to help defend Philadelphia. Even the young boys joined the ranks, leaving the women and children behind to guard the warehouses of salt which had been stored for use of the Continentals. While the march was intended to be made in secrecy, someone had relayed the information to the British.

Later in the day a British craft appeared in the bay. Young Rebecca Stillwell, daughter of Nicholas Stillwell, took command of the situation. Running to Foxborough Hill, the highest point nearby, she watched the ship through a marine glass belonging to her father. When a longboat was lowered from the craft, she decided it was not on a friendly mission.

Returning to the Stillwell house she cried to her sister, "Sarah, run up the flag!" To her mother, "Bring a fire brand, send for Rem and the horn!" The rest of the women gathered to help.

A cannon, 12 feet in length, which had lately reached the point in answer to a petition of the settlers for a weapon to protect themselves from possible invaders from the sea, was in position overlooking the bay—and loaded for just such an emergency.

Aiming the cannon at the oncoming boat, Rebecca lit the fuse. The charge passed over the heads of the oarsmen but near enough to halt their rowing.

At that moment twelve-year-old Rem Goldin set up a din with his grandfather's horn. Believing they were faced by a strong defending force, the British returned to their larger craft, which hove anchor and sailed out into the Atlantic Ocean.

Rebecca Stillwell married Captain James Willets, while sister Sarah married Captain Moses Griffin. Sarah gained her own nitch in local history when her husband became a prisoner of the British. She successfully enlisted General Washington's aid in a prisoner exchange which included her husband, who was in a ship in New York harbor.

The Ocean City chapter, Daughters of the American Revolution, is named for Sarah, while the youth chapter is named for Rebecca Stillwell.

DOCTOR ON HORSEBACK

Cape May County's first active physician was Dr. John Dickinson, born October 11, 1758, in Alloway, Salem County, in the ancestral home of the Dickinsons on a 500-acre tract deeded by John Fenwick to his granddaughter Ann Adams Dickinson.

During the Revolution the young doctor served as a surgeon's mate on two United States vessels, part of a fleet under Commodore Hazelwood, by whose direction he selected a house at Red Bank, New Jersey, and fitted it out as a hospital. For his services, General George Washington presented John Dickinson with a sword which is now in the county museum at Cape May Court House.

In June 1786 Dr. Dickinson moved from Salem County to Cape May County, where he set up a practice from Cape Island to Beesley's Point, traveling the country trails on horseback, sleeping under the open sky or wherever he could find shelter for the night.

Cash was scarce so his services were paid for with farm products such as salt pork, dried beef, fish, wheat, potatoes, and berries. At times the doctor resembled a peddler as he made his way home with various items tied to his saddle. For calls on main roads Dr. Dickinson secured a black rig like that used by most early American doctors. His was filled from time to time with sacks of potatoes or boxes of salted fish.

Dr. Dickinson served as county collector from 1805 to 1813 and was appointed colonel of Cape May Militia on November 25, 1806. The doctor and his wife Mary Powers Dickinson are buried in the old Baptist Cemetery at Cape May Court House.

His apothecary cupboard is preserved at the county historical museum, of which his great-great-grandson Karl Dickinson is curator.

CAYS OF THE CAPE

Off the mainland of Cape May County there is a group of island resorts that could be termed the Jersey cays. Resting on two of these islands, Five Mile Beach and Seven Mile Beach, are the resorts of Sea Isle City, Stone Harbor, Avalon, Townsend's Inlet, Corson's Inlet, and the various Wildwoods.

In 1692 Joseph Ludlam, son of Anthony, who came to this country from Yorkshire, England, purchased a strip of land he called Ludlam's Island, which he stocked with cattle and sheep. It is recorded that livestock roamed these islands as late as 1875 and that some of the first visitors were bitten by them.

Because of numerous wrecks in the area the government established lifesaving stations No. 33 at Ludlam's Beach and No. 34 at Townsend's Inlet. In 1880 the captains and crews arrived to live on the island nine months of the year. A lighthouse was erected at Ludlam's Island in 1885 and served until 1923, when it was replaced by an automatic steel tower.

Actual development of Ludlam's Island began in 1880, when it was purchased by Charles Kline Landis, who had established Vineland in Cumberland County. He christened his new development Sea Isle. On May 1, 1882, the community became a borough with Martin Wells as first mayor.

During the next few years many hotels were built, including the Continental, a five-story structure with giant parlors and the only steam-operated elevator in Cape May County. Never a financial success, it was demolished in 1921 after being closed for eight years.

An interesting note on the early houses of the island is that many of them were moved from the Centennial Exposition in Philadelphia, where they had been on display as the latest in architectural design.

One of the unusual beach buildings was the Excursion House,

Even the public buildings of South Jersey resorts were sometimes designed more for visual elegance than for the convenience of their patrons, who had to climb a flight of steps to get their mail at the first post office in Sea Isle City, built in 1882. (William Haffert, Sr., Collection)

built in 1882. It was a glorified grandstand from which could be viewed the horse and auto races on the beach. The pavilion was later enclosed and became the center of social activities on the island.

On July 27, 1893, Sea Isle greeted its first train. A trolley line extended the length of the island. In 1907 after studying the Atlantic City structure, Sea Isle built its first boardwalk. Washed out by storm in 1928, it was reconstructed. In 1944 a hurricane hit the Jersey coast, and the boardwalk disappeared into the sea. Again it was rebuilt, this time on concrete piers, and lasted until the storm of 1962.

A year later a new beachfront street was created upon sand dunes pumped in by U.S. Army engineers. The old boardwalk idea was discarded, and the structure became an asphalt promenade.

Fishing and boating have always been the top attractions of Sea Isle City in the summer months.

Sea Isle was incorporated as a city on April 30, 1907.

The longest of the Jersey cays in Cape May County is Seven Mile Beach. Here is found the highest elevation of land in the county, winds and waves having erected sand dunes thirty-five or more feet in height.

On this island are located Avalon and Stone Harbor, both family resorts. Avalon was founded in 1887 by a land company headed by Frank Siddall of Philadelphia. In 1891 the community located on the north end of the island was made a borough with Thomas Brady as first mayor. He kept this office until 1897, when he returned to New York.

Avalon is the site of a 953-acre marshland purchased by the World Wildlife Fund of Washington, D.C., in November of 1968 so that the land will forever remain in its natural state as a wildlife preserve.

The tract joins Cedar Island, owned by the State Department of Conservation's Green Acres Division. Cedar Island is the last stand on the Jersey coast of the osprey, often called the fish hawk. This bird was once a common sight in Cape May County marshes, where it built large nests atop trees and telephone poles. The bird has all but disappeared as a species.

Stone Harbor, on the lower end of Seven Mile Beach, was incorporated as a borough on April 3, 1914. It is a family resort with boating and fishing featured. Among its attractions for visitors is the 25-acre Stone Harbor Bird Sanctuary, nesting ground for American egrets, snowy egrets, little blue herons, night herons, and the Louisiana herons. Bird-watching posts are plainly marked; long-range viewers are available, and an Audubon official is on duty during July and August.

The next cay south was known as Five Mile Beach when Philip Baker and his brother Latimer of Vineland, New Jersey, visited it in 1869 and planned a family bathing resort. They found the island inhabited by herds of wild cattle; later settlers and merchants were to make bitter complaints of being chased by these animals.

The wild woodlands of the cay prompted the brothers to christen it Wildwood-by-the-Sea, the name by which its principal resort is known today. Except for official documents the resort is designated as just plain Wildwood, surrounded by Wildwood Crest, North Wildwood, West Wildwood, and so forth.

The lower part of the island was originally known as Holly Beach. In 1885 it gained town status with the election of Franklin J. Van Valin as mayor. At that time it had a population of 300 compared to Wildwood's 109 settlers. The first houses of Holly Beach were in the vicinity of Burk Avenue, a center for fishermen who brought their boats up on the beach and sold fish direct to the customers, a practice which was still prevalent as late as 1909.

Water was a problem for the first settlers as there were only a few good wells. Mrs. Jeanette D. Meech, an early resident of the area, had water sent from Vineland in bottles. She sold it for a penny a bottle at her store, in front of the Sea View Hotel, at Cedar and Pacific avenues.

In 1891 Gilbert H. Baker allowed the use of his beach pavilion for nondenominational church services, the first religious exercises on the island. The Baker brothers later that year donated land for a church which in 1896 affiliated with the Presbyterian church.

The borough of Wildwood was incorporated on May 1, 1896,

with Latimer R. Baker as mayor. At that time it had four streets, Cedar, Oak, Wildwood, and Pine. In 1901 the Rio Grande Road, from Rio Grande on the mainland, became the first highway into the budding resort.

On January 1, 1912, Holly Beach and Wildwood merged into the city of Wildwood and adopted the commission form of government. Frank E. Smith became the first mayor. With the completion of the Wildwood and Delaware Bay Shore Line on December 12 of that year, the first Reading Railroad trains ran into Wildwood.

One of the picturesque sights of Wildwood's Otten's Harbor, which extends along the line of Davis Avenue from Park Boulevard to its junction with the Inland Waterway, is the old racing yacht *Grand Atlantic,* which in 1905 set an all-time record for the Atlantic Ocean crossing under sail by winning the Kaiser's Cup in the time of 12 days, 4 hours, and 1 minute. The *Grand Atlantic* served as a navy ship in World War I and a coast guard vessel in World War II. In 1963 it sank at its docks and was underwater until the early part of 1970, when it was raised and restored.

In 1912 Wildwood adopted the Atlantic City Boardwalk as a model for a 50-foot-wide beach promenade on which are located several piers and a score of amusement rides.

SUNKEN FORESTS

On the wall of my study hangs a hand-carved whale from the Great Swamp of Dennisville, Cape May County. The history behind this piece of woodcraft involves one of the unusual industries of South Jersey—shingle mining.

The Great Swamp at the headwaters of Dennis Creek is perhaps the largest sunken forest in America. Stretching through both Dennis and Upper townships with outlets on Delaware Bay and Tuckahoe River, the swamp is about 17 miles in length. The soil contains black, peaty earth, composed of vegetable matter which when dry will burn. It is of varied depths, ranging from 2 or 3 feet to 20 or more.

This swampland gave birth to shingle mining. Miners roamed the marshes in the late 1700s and early 1800s with a progue, a slender pointed iron rod 6 or 8 feet long. This they would shove into the ground until it hit a submerged log. A small piece of the log was cut with a long saw. This was tested to see if the rest of the log was worth bringing to the surface from the muck in which it had laid, possibly for centuries.

In the second annual report of the Geological Survey of the state of New Jersey for the year 1855, Charles Ludlam is credited with counting 700 rings of annual growth in an old tree which was living when cut down in the Dennisville swamp. Dr. Maurice Beesley, early historian of the area, said he counted another with 1,080 rings.

The miners classified the logs. Trees blown down and in prime condition when they fell were dubbed "windfalls." Rotted trees which broke off and settled into the mud were called "brokendowns," the less valuable of the two. There was never a set rule in distinguishing these two log finds, the shingle miner working on a sixth sense which was his most valuable asset.

That shingle mining was a profitable business is attested by a report made in 1855 to the effect that "for the past five years the average number of these shingles, sent from Dennisville, is not far from 600,000 a year. They are worth from $13 to $15 a thousand. About 200,000 white cedar rails have been sent from the same place this year. They are worth from $8 to $10 a hundred."

In 1864 Robbins Swamp, a part of the general swamplands, was cut off and drained, enabling miners to investigate the bottom. It is recorded that 25,000 cedar shingles cut from logs of this swamp were used in the reroofing of Independence Hall, Philadelphia, for which John Anneley was contractor.

The discovery of asphalt shingles and other roofing materials plus modern machinery, which produced shingles at greater speed than any miner could hope for, brought the end of shingle mining in the Jersey Cape. Another factor was that the swamp shingles had a life potential of nearly a hundred years; building contractors felt they could make little profit from such a sturdy product.

Shingle mining as an industry has ceased to exist, but there are still excursions into the swamp by those interested in restoration of old homes in the area. One such excursion was conducted in 1963 by Lewis Albrecht of Cape May Court House, who, after purchasing a mid-1700 house at Swainton known as the Godfrey house, decided to cover it with hand-made shingles from the swamp.

Woodcarvers have pried some logs loose, but there are plenty left. The swamp itself remains a mute monument to a lost craft of South Jersey.

TWO FAMOUS SONS NAMED GRACE

Although in existence since 1710, when the first settlers of mid-Cape May County built cabins there, Goshen reached its peak of activity as a shipbuilding center around 1859. In that year the *John H. Wainwright* slid down the ways of the William F. Garrison, Sr., boatyard on Goshen Creek.

The Garrison yard was large enough to allow construction of two vessels at a time. Like the shipbuilders of Dennis Creek, the Goshen men sent their boats into the waters sideways. Wood used was from adjacent timberlands while the ironwork was accomplished in the shops of Page R. Douglass and Lambert Finley at Goshen.

A record of the Goshen shipbuilding activities shows that the following vessels were built at the Goshen landing:

1859	*John H. Wainwright*	1881	*Varuna*
1861	*William F. Garrison*	1883	*Anna Camp, Annie E.*
1863	*Rachel Vanaman*		*Blackman, Haddie*
1868	*William F. Cullen*	1884	*Roxana Hand,*
1869	*Edith B. Evermann*		*Carrie, Mary*
1871	*Samuel Carlton, Ella C.*	1886	*Pearl, Jane A. Smith*
1872	*Lida Babcock*	1888	*Lizzie C., Dart*
1873	*Sallie E. Ludlam,*	1889	*Gracie*
	Emma C. Babcock	1892	*Excel*
1875	*Advance*	1898	*Diamond*

Old sea captains of Goshen were Robert Baymore; William M. Burk; Enoch, Joseph and Thomas Camp; Thomas Coombs; James and William F. Cullen; Henry and Jesse H. Wesley; Libran C., Philip H., and Warren Grace; Samuel Hearon; John C. Malachi; Ezekiel High; Alex R. and Isaac Ludlam; George S. and Thomas Peterson; William B. Powell; Edward Price; Griffin Smith; Lewis S. Stillwell; Thomas H. and James Swain; John Thompson; Hugh, Maurice, and B. Frank Tomlin; John D. and Luke Vanaman; and David Warwick.

While shipbuilding was an important part of Goshen's past, her most notable contribution to history was made by two famous sons, both named Grace. If you pass along Bay Shore Road, Goshen, stop for a moment at the monument erected by school children of the area honoring the first Grace, John, who served in the Revolution. He enlisted on June 12, 1777, in Captain Samuel Flannagan's company 3d New Jersey Battalion, 2d Establishment, and fought in the battles of Brandywine, Monmouth, Bennington, and Yorktown. He carried a letter written by General George Washington to General Gates commending Grace as "a trusted scout." Grace was discharged on June 5, 1783; he died on April 11, 1835, and is buried in Union Cemetery, Dennisville.

The second Grace of note arrived on August 27, 1876, in the home of John W. and Rebecca Grace. John W. Grace was the proprietor of Goshen's general store and hoped some day his son would take over the business. As he grew older Eugene Grace worked in the store, but his sights were set far beyond the dusty roads of Goshen. Eugene Grace entered Lehigh University in Bethlehem, Pennsylvania, from which he graduated in 1899.

The sprawling Bethlehem Steel Company fascinated him. To aid in the payment of his college tuition, Grace worked for the company as a laborer. By 1906, with his school years behind, Grace became general superintendent of the Bethlehem Company. On April 1, 1913, he became president, serving until 1946. He was chairman of the board until his death on July 25, 1960.

Several times when financial troubles threatened the Goshen Methodist Church, which he had attended as a young boy, Eugene Grace came to the rescue. The Grace homestead in Goshen is now the church parsonage, so designated by Grace for as long as the church exists.

Goshen no longer has its shipbuilding industry; it is a community of homes.

THE GREAT STONE HARBOR RAILROAD

Today railroading involves a mass of facts, figures, computers, and charts. Not so in the busy, brawling days of the Stone Harbor road as sweating crews cussed and dragged the road across the meadows from Cape May Court House to the new beach island development of Stone Harbor.

The man who mapped the road through the woods and marshes in 1912 was Morgan Hand II of Ocean City, a young surveyor fresh out of Rutgers College with a lot of theories and no practical experience in railroading. Most of the facts of the following story of this railroad were supplied to me by Hand, who later became president of the Cape May County Historical Society.

The Stone Harbor Railroad was conceived by the South Jersey Realty Company of which David Risley was president and his brothers Howard and Reese directors. They considered the road necessary in the promotion of their newest real estate venture—Stone Harbor. The company had gone through a bad experience with a deal called Isle of Pines in the Caribbean, so when it came to the railroad the brothers were gambling for high stakes with low cards, inexperience, and little cash.

Standard rails supplied by the foundries were of 30-foot lengths. The Risleys learned there were a number of rails stacked on the meadows near Atlantic City. Once used by the major lines in their resort runs, these were considered "exhausted" and could be bought cheaply. Hand later discovered that the real reason for the bargain was that the rails were 45-foot lengths, which made for expansion, which could easily cause derailments in hot August days if a speed of more than 60 miles per hour was attempted. Since there was little chance of developing such speed on the 4½-mile stretch of the Stone Harbor road, the rails were purchased.

With no money to buy regulation ties, the company decided to cut its own, and a steam sawmill was rented and backed into the woods. Agreements were made for the amount of timber to be cut, but the crew was not careful about boundary lines. As a consequence, a group of irate landowners marched on the camp. The matter was settled with a lot of talk and promises (no money) plus a few rounds of corn likker. The result of this type of tie cutting was that the Stone Harbor Railroad was perhaps the only one in New Jersey with few ties the same length.

The further inexperience of all concerned showed up when, sight unseen, an electric locomotive and one passenger car, a former Philadelphia Rapid Transit double-tracker of 75 tons, was purchased from a West Virginia mine road. It arrived and was set in place and the first run planned for July 4, 1912.

The promoters tried to get President Taft to come for the occasion, but he was unavailable. Governor Woodrow Wilson of New Jersey, who was being promoted for the presidency, accepted an invitation to preside—until he learned he was to cut a ribbon on a 4½-mile track, whereupon he recalled urgent duties elsewhere.

Despite this setback the promoters decided to go ahead with the original plans. Stunt flyer Marshall E. Reid was hired to help attract a crowd. Several hundred persons in holiday mood arrived to cheer the maiden run.

Upon the firing of a salute, the big locomotive started down the track—and blew a circuit breaker at the powerhouse. Another power setup was quickly rigged, and the iron monster again rolled —as far as the first curve, where the engine jumped the track. Every time it was jacked up and placed back on the rails, it repeated the performance. The crowd drifted away. The Risleys conferred and decided to abandon the entire project. The engine was returned to the West Virginia Company, at a financial loss.

This should have been the end of the railroad, but lots had been sold on the beach, and those who had bought them and built there felt that without rail transportation their investments were lost. In the fall of 1920 a town meeting was held, and the Stone Harbor Railroad Company was formed with L. R. Lewis as president. Profiting from the mistakes of the prior operation, especially in the matter of locomtives, the new company decided to use a rail motor omnibus purchased from the J. G. Brill Company of Philadelphia. This odd-looking bus body on iron wheels measured less than 30 feet, with a 16½ foot wheelbase. It sported a double truck of wheels in front and a single axle-powered truck in the rear, with four speeds forward and four backward. While it was no luxury item, the company found it kept to the tracks. Traffic became so heavy a second car was purchased.

The following year six single-truck cars were added. Bought from the Washington Railway and Electric Company, they cost $250 each. The cars continued in use from 1921 to 1930.

Representatives of other small rail lines came to Stone Harbor to study the operation. They found the converted engine made 10 miles to a gallon of gas, cost about $150 a year to maintain, and ran the 4½ miles in fourteen minutes.

The Stone Harbor Railroad reached its peak in the summer of 1926, when it hauled 5,000 passengers per month. Excursions of the Reading Railroad were brought to Stone Harbor via the meadow line.

By 1926 the automobile began to make inroads, and profits declined. In April of 1930 the Reading Railroad bought out the Stone Harbor company, and continued the operation until 1932. A year later the road merged as the Pennsylvania-Reading Seashore Lines, and thereafter the Stone Harbor spur was used for freight only. Thus another chapter of Cape May County history came to an end.

SHIPS THAT REALLY WENT SPLASH!

"Dennis's Creek, part of Dennis's Creek township, Cape May County at the head of navigation of Dennis's Creek, 6 or 7 miles from Delaware Bay, 7 miles north from Cape May Court House contains from 30 to 40 dwellings, 2 taverns, 5 stores, and a tide grist mill. The town is built on both sides of the creek, extending each way, about half a mile. Ship building and trade in lumber are carried on extensively here. The country around it, above the marsh, is of sandy loam." That is how a writer described Dennis Creek (Dennisville) in 1834.

Dennis Creek, the name the village carried during its heyday, was settled in 1726 by two sons of Cape May County pioneer Joseph Ludlam: Anthony on the north side of the creek, Joseph on the south side.

Shipbuilding flourished there in the early 1700s and reached its peak in 1883, when eleven ships were in the stocks at one time. Because of the narrowness of Dennis Creek, boats had to be launched sideways.

The community's glory as a shipbuilding center was described for me by Mrs. Ralph Goff of Ocean View. Mrs. Goff was born in South Dennis and took part in many homecoming celebrations held when captains returned from the sea after long voyages.

A boat launching was the signal for a general picnic, with banners flying and bands playing. When the boats hit the water, according to Mrs. Goff, they created a wave that drenched all observers on the opposite bank. "These unfortunates," she recalled, "were mostly foreigners (visitors from other parts of the county) who had not been told the perils of Dennis Creek boat launching. At times it was a toss-up to tell which held the most interest, the launching or who got wet." Although she refused to admit it, Mrs. Goff gave me the feeling that the foreigners were placed on the off-side position just to add hilarity to the occasion.

Although it may now seem strange that ships were launched ten miles from the open bay, there were two good reasons for the procedure: Builders were close to their wood supply there, and the rushing tides nearer the bay completely flooded the area, making industry there impossible.

Among the ships of record built on the creek were the *J. G. Fell*, the *Harry Diverty*, the *James Diverty*, the *Eva Diverty*, the *Jennie R. Diverty*, the *Macrus Edwards*, the *Ella Mathews*, the *Gregory Matthews*, and the *Mary C. Carrow*.

Principal shipbuilders were Richard Leaming and Jesse Diverty, who were also prominent in the social life of the town. As can be seen from the above list, Diverty usually named his ships for someone in his family. He began his shipbuilding business in 1865 and launched more than thirty vessels.

During the War of 1812 there was a small log fort on the creek, but today there is nothing to show its former existence.

Packets made regular trips between Dennis Creek and Philadelphia. Ships that navigated the creek were mostly 3-masted, 350-ton craft which often had to be helped along by crews pulling ropes from the shore.

Mrs. Goff recalled that a sail down the creek was a major undertaking. If the wind failed, one spent the night on the creek. As the packets were not equipped with staterooms, everyone slept on deck. Mrs. Goff took many such trips with her father, one of the captains of the area.

Women of the village would give her lists of what they wanted from Philadelphia. "I shopped for most of the things in stores on Second Street, Philadelphia. Usually by the time I again got aboard ship I had to have several people help me with the bundles," she said.

Recollections of Dennis Creek as a post village have been provided by Walter Robinson of Delsea Drive, Dennisville, who said that the earliest mention of stagecoaches to the village that he could find was in the *Daily Aurora* of Philadelphia for June 13, 1801: "A stage starts from Cooper's Ferry on Thursday in every week and arrives at Cape Island on Friday. One leaves Tuesday from Cape Island, by way of Dennis Creek, and arrives in Philadelphia the following day."

The article also gave directions to "gentlemen who travel in their own carriages": "From Philadelphia to Glass-house [Glassboro] nineteen miles; Lehman's Mill, forty-one miles; Dennis Creek sixty miles and to pitch of the Cape eighty miles. Those who choose water conveyance can find vessels almost any time."

The community of Dennis Creek had the first postoffice in Cape May County, established on October 9, 1802, with Jeremiah Johnson as postmaster. On January 12, 1854, the name of the community and the postoffice was changed to Dennisville. On February 23, 1873, South Dennis had its own postoffice with Robert Hutchinson as postmaster.

The stage line was still operating in 1883. Alfred Cooper's *Cape May County Gazette* of February 17, 1883, stated: "The Dennisville stage is to be repainted. Travelers say it is now the best equipped line in Southern New Jersey."

Dennisville and South Dennis, communities proud of their many beautifully restored homes, are now part of Dennis Township, which also includes the 4,000 acres of Belleplain State Forest and fabled Lake Nummy, named for the last of the Lenape Indian chiefs of the area.

The oldest restored home in the village is the Belle Carroll house, built in 1800, and opened to the public once a year during the Cape May County Old Homes Tour.

AN EMPHATIC "NO!"

In the summer of 1849 a woman stamped her foot on the porch of the Mansion House in Cape May City, said "No!" emphatically, and possibly changed the course of American history. The incident also provides the substance for one of the favorite tales of the Jersey Cape.

Abraham Lincoln, "lame duck" congressman from Illinois, had wound up his duties in Washington early in the summer of 1849, and faced an uncertain future. Before he left the capital he appealed to old friend President Zachary Taylor for a position on a land grant commission, a post paying $3,000 a year which happened to be open at the time.

In Washington, Lincoln had become acquainted with John S. Irick, a wealthy farmer of Vincentown, near Mount Holly, New Jersey, who suggested to Lincoln that, while he was waiting for word from President Taylor, he escape the heat of the capital by spending a few weeks at "the southern resort of Cape May."

Irick and Lincoln, together with Isaac Field, an iron manufacturer of Fieldsboro, New Jersey, and wives, met in Philadelphia and took a Delaware River boat to the cape. Also on the junket was Henry J. Irick, then only sixteen, later a state senator from

New Jersey, who supplied the details of Lincoln's visit to the Jersey Cape resort.

On July 31, 1849, the visitors arrived at the cape, were driven to the Mansion House, and registered there. The Lincolns occupied room 24 according to the original Mansion House register still preserved at Cape May Court House. Lincoln signed himself as from "Phila."

While vacationing, Lincoln learned that his application for the commission job had been turned down by President Taylor, who instead offered him the governorship of the new Oregon Territory, created in 1848, which was then mostly a wilderness of desperate gunmen, gold prospectors, and Indians.

It is reported that Lincoln, pleased with the offer and with the message in hand, approached Mary Todd Lincoln, who was talking to a group of friends on the porch of the Mansion House. Mrs. Lincoln was not impressed with the prospect of exchanging Washington, D.C., for frontier life. She said, "No! I will not go to Oregon!"

Lincoln resigned himself to this opposition and soon returned to Springfield, Illinois, where he resumed his law practice and the career that led to the White House.

Cape May storytellers like to point out that a decision at the Mansion House later gave the nation a great president.

THE FIRST FORD DEALER

Between the years 1903 and 1905 the Cape May beach was the mecca for advocates of the new horseless buggy who raced their cars on a two-mile stretch of sand fronting a real estate development named New Cape May. The measured track extended from the lifesaving station east of Madison Avenue to Sewell's Point at Cold Spring Inlet and was known for years as Poverty Beach.

Pioneers who staked their prestige on a race on August 25, 1905, were Henry Ford, Louis Chevrolet, A. L. Campbell, and Walter Christie. Christie, a popular race driver of his day, was at

Henry Ford (second from left) in 1905, when he raced in competition with Louis Chevrolet, A. L. Campbell, and Walter Christie on a two-mile stretch of sand between Cape May and Sewell's Point named, prophetically, Poverty Beach. Ford had to leave one of his cars in payment for his hotel bill and enough money to get home. (Courtesy of Ford Museum)

the wheel of an 8-cylinder, 13-horsepower *Blue Flyer*. A. L. Campbell had an 80-horsepower Darracq *Red Flyer*. Ford was driving a newly constructed 60-horsepower *Beach Skimmer*, Chevrolet a black 120-horsepower *Fiat*.

According to the research of Henry E. Edmunds, director of the Ford Archives in Dearborn, Michigan, Campbell was first to finish the race, at 38 seconds; Chevrolet was second at 39.4 seconds; Christie third at 39.8 seconds; and Ford fourth at 40 seconds.

There are several area versions of the race and its aftermath. I knew two men directly connected with the Ford story, J. E. Mecray and A. C. Lyle, both of Cape May City, and had long talks with both on the subject. Here is Lyle's version of the story as he told it to me one evening in the spring of 1965 at Fishermen's Wharf in Cold Spring harbor.

I saw the race. I was nearly eleven years of age at the time. On that day it was drizzling rain, and my father paid twenty-five cents for a newspaper to put over me, half down the front and half down the back.

We were on the boardwalk in front of where the Golden Eagle Hotel was located. Abreast of the Admiral Hotel, Henry Ford was on the outside of the racers in the lead. Next came Christy. Somewhere between the Admiral and where I was standing, a wave rolled in, knocking Ford out of the race. Chevrolet looked back to see what happened to Ford, hit a soft spot, and lost his place.

This was a disappointment to both men, especially Ford, who had depended upon the race money to pay his hotel bill at the Stockton. He offered stock in a new company he was forming to a hotel clerk, who refused it. Ford then went around the town trying to sell a touring car which he used to tow his racing machine.

Someone suggested that Dan Focer, a Reading Railroad engineer, might be interested. Ford caught Focer in the cab of his locomotive just as it was about to pull out of the station. He offered his car and as the train started down the tracks, Ford ran alongside, trying to complete a deal.

Focer agreed to buy the car but, having no cash on him, told Ford to see his brother-in-law, Delaware Bay pilot Benjamin Johnson, and tell Johnson to give him a check for $400.

Ford secured the check and hurried to the bank to cash it, only to be told: "You will have to get someone to identify you." Ford returned to the Stockton Hotel, where the manager agreed to vouch for him.

Ford paid his hotel bill, put his racing car on a flatcar, and had it shipped to Detroit. In handing over the touring car to Focer, Ford said "I will make you the first Ford Dealer in America." He did.

I was connected with the firm, which was known as Focer and Mecray. (Focer took J. E. Mecray as a partner from October 1921 until October 1927.) Focer told me many of the details I have been telling you as he liked to sit and spin stories about Ford, whom he referred to as "Hank." When the firm was dissolved in 1937, the famous touring car went to Gideon Stull, distributor of Ford products in Chester, Pennsylvania. (Several attempts to trace the whereabouts of the car, including one of my own, have failed.)

Mecray, who later lived in Ocean City, told me that car selling in the early days was not so much convincing a customer that you had the best bargain and style as that what you were selling would outlast the horse and buggy. Sitting on the steps of his son's home in Cape May, Mecray also recalled another amusing story of Ford.

The future auto giant envisaged a whole country moving on wheels and said that he was the one to put a car in the hands of the average man instead of just the wealthy few.

One of the starters at the beach to whom Ford confided his ideas replied, "That's plumb crazy. This [beach racing] is a good sport. Let's keep it that way."

Ford answered, "Wait and see."

In one of fate's ironies, Mecray was killed in an Ocean City street accident. He was hit by a Ford car.

Additional details of Henry Ford's racing activities in Cape May can be found in Leo Levine's *Ford—The Dust and the Glory* (Macmillan, 1968).

MONUMENT TO A FAILURE

Cape May County harbors the only South Jersey monument to a failure.

In the final months of World War I, lumber and steel were in short supply, and the federal government decided to experiment with low-cost concrete supply ships and troop transports. On April 20, 1918, the government ordered four of these concrete ships from the Liberty Shipbuilding Company of Brunswick, Georgia. The *Atlantus* plunged down the ways on December 4, 1918, a month too late for active wartime duty. It was used, however, on a couple of troop ferry runs.

When the *Atlantus* and its sister ships proved too costly and slow they were ordered scrapped. The *Atlantus* was taken to Norfolk, Virginia, stripped of gear and fittings. Before it could be broken up Colonel Desse Rosenfeld of Baltimore, Maryland, who had long envisioned a ferry service across Delaware Bay, formed the National Navigation Company, secured substantial sums from Cape May County residents, and bought the hulk of the *Atlantus*.

His plan was to tow the vessel to within a hundred feet of Sunset Drive, Cape May Point, couple it with two wooden ships, and pump out enough sand to allow all three to ride free in the water. These ships were to form a terminal slip or dock for a car ferry.

But Rosenfeld reckoned without the tides and storms of the Jersey Cape. Shortly after the *Atlantus* was taken to its offshore position, a nor'easter broke it from its moorings, and it sank about a hundred yards from the beach. In 1937 a seam opened in the side of the vessel, and by 1961 it had broken in two, the stern disappearing in the bay.

The broken hull of the *Atlantus* is a favorite visitor attraction at Cape May Point. An iron historic site marker of the state of New Jersey preserves the story should the mass of concrete eventually disappear entirely.

A CHRISTIAN SEASIDE RESORT

When Cape May County was created in 1693, its northern-most boundary was pinpointed as Peck's Beach, the name by which the island now called Ocean City was known until 1879. Old London documents referred to the locale as Pete's Beach and Pet's Beach. A map and description of Peck's Beach published in 1698 by Gabriel Thomas described it as well timbered.

Many believe the first definite reference to the island (1632) was made by David Pieterzen De Vries, the Dutch explorer in his journal, in which he referred to the area as "flat sand beaches with low hills." A central line of sand dunes ran lengthwise of the island and was marked in many old maps as Central Ridge.

The origin of the name Peck's Beach is open to debate, but John Peck, a whaleman, operated on the island about 1700, according to Burlington court records which name him in an action concerning ownership of a stranded whale. From Peck may have stemmed the name.

Grants to Berkeley-Carteret established subsequent Ocean City titles. These finally came to rest with the West Jersey Society. The first recorded real estate transaction for Peck's Beach land as such was in 1726, when Richard Townsend of Cape May County applied to the West Jersey Society for 663 acres on the island. Townsend was a cattleman, and his purchase brings to mind one of the reasons behind early off-shore island acquisitions. On the mainland cattle were not permitted to roam freely, but on the islands they were marked with ear brands and turned loose to graze.

Townsend bequeathed the land to his sons Samuel and Daniel in 1737. In 1755 they sold to James Willets of Beesley's Point for 180 pounds, showing 400 percent rise in values in a twenty-nine-year period.

In 1750 the West Jersey Society, through agent John Morris, conveyed a tract of 500 acres to Richard Somers. First mention of a house on the island is contained in his will, dated February 8, 1752, in which he bequeathed to his son John "half of my right that is in the island, below the house."

Another notation of early settlement is in a diary of William Lake, first surveyor of the island. Dated 1880, the memo stated "John Robinson moved to Peck's Beach from Bargaintown about 1840."

Parker Miller arrived on the island in 1850. Miller was an agent for marine insurance companies, and his residence on the island was to protect insurance interests in wrecks occurring along the beach. Such wrecks were legally claimed by the first one aboard a ship after it was officially abandoned.

During the summer of 1879 two clergymen, William B. Wood of Philadelphia and S. Wesley Lake of Pleasantville, New Jersey, were attending a camp meeting at Ocean Grove, New Jersey, a favorite revival town for Methodists. Wood and Lake discussed the idea of founding a resort based on Christian principles that would provide special religious privileges while at the same time affording healthful recreation.

Upon returning to Pleasantville, S. Wesley Lake outlined the plan to his brothers Ezra B. and James E., also Methodist clergymen. They consulted their father Simon Lake, farmer, fruit grower, and inventor, who felt that, aside from the religious aspect, there was also a sound financial side of the plan.

On September 10, 1879, Ezra, Wesley, and James Lake and Rev. William H. Burrell rowed over the waterways from Pleasantville to the island, landing on the bay side. They followed a cow path to a high spot on the northern end. Kneeling beneath a cedar tree, they asked for guidance. The old tree still stands, gnarled and stark, on the Ocean City Tabernacle Grounds, as a memorial to this event in Ocean City history. On a bronze tablet by the tree are engraved the names of the four clergymen and the date of their visit, plus the inscription: "Honorable Simon Lake and Reverend William B. Wood joined them in incorporating the Ocean City Association October 20, 1879."

On October 20, 1879, a formal meeting was held during which it was agreed that Simon Lake should be president of the corporation and the name of the island should be New Brighton. It was decided affairs of the Association should be handled by a board of nine stockholders, three of whom must be ministers of the Methodist church. Capital stock of $100,000 was authorized.

At a third meeting in November, it was decided to again change the name of the island from New Brighton to Ocean City.

The Lakes first considered modeling their community along the lines of Ocean Grove, where all land within the limits of the community is owned by the Grove Association. They rejected this idea and substituted a plan of private ownership of land, but under a strict code of conduct. Into every deed went a clause prohibiting the sale or manufacture of intoxicants. The deeds had teeth inasmuch as they provided that land would revert to the Association should the restrictions be violated by owners. To date the deeds have never been successfully challenged.

In the spring of 1880 Isaac Smith of Philadelphia, one of the original stockholders in the Association, began erection of the Ocean House, later known as the Hotel Brighton, the island's first hotel. The structure of 95 rooms was brought to Ocean City by boat. It was precut and assembled on the site.

At the end of the first year of operation, there were thirty-five dwellings on the island. In the fall of 1880 a railroad line known as the Pleasantville and Ocean City Railroad was built from Pleasantville to Somers Point. It made connections with the island by means of a ferry called the Atlantic Coast Steamship Company. The island was connected to the mainland by a turnpike to Beesley's Point in 1881.

Religious gatherings were originally held in tents. The Ocean City Tabernacle was built in 1881 as an open pavilion, later enclosed.

On April 30, 1884, Ocean City became a borough. By this act approved by the voters, local government jurisdiction passed from the Ocean City Association to that of the new municipality. Gainer P. Moore was elected mayor.

In 1890 Ocean City was reincorporated as a borough. It became a city in 1897, with Harry Headley as mayor.

The Ocean City boardwalk, one of the city's most famous and popular features, was built in 1883 on the ground level and extended from the wharf on the bay at Fourth Street across the meadows to Asbury Avenue. It was extended in 1887. In November of the next year the walk was destroyed in a northeast storm. It was rebuilt and extended to Thirteenth Street. In all there have been four Ocean City boardwalks.

Ocean City received severe setbacks in storms of September

A parade of early model automobiles is a yearly event on Ocean City's boardwalk. (Senior Studio Photo)

14, 1944, and in the high tides and 60-mile-per-hour winds of March 5–7, 1962, which tore hundreds of homes from their foundations. However, the city and its people rallied and rebuilt.

The original tabernacle building was replaced by a modern structure in the summer of 1957. Baby parades have been big summer attractions in South Jersey coastal resorts since 1901, when Ocean City staged the first one, called a "Baby Show."

Today the resort continues its original restrictions: no liquor, and no motion picture theatres or businesses operating on Sunday. It is a popular family resort with many new motels and hotels. During the spring and fall it is the scene of national and state religious gatherings.

SAGA OF THE *SINDIA*

There were numerous wrecks on Peck's Beach (Ocean City) during the 1800s and early 1900s, but none gained the area renown of the four-masted British bark *Sindia*, which came ashore in a raging blizzard on December 15, 1901.

The *Sindia*, said to have been named for a red-turbaned Arabian warlord, was built in Belfast, Ireland, in 1887 and first sailed in the British coastal trade. There being more money in the China runs, her owners switched to oriental cargoes. The *Sindia* had been at sea 168 days in 1901 when she anchored at Shanghai, took on rare silks and fine porcelain, then sailed for Kobe, Japan. From there she set sail across the Pacific, around Cape Horn, and was headed for New York with a cargo reportedly worth $2 million when tragedy struck.

On December 16, 1964, at a luncheon given by Friends of the Sindia at Plymouth Inn in Ocean City the guest of honor was an eighty-six-year-old retired seaman, David Jackson, who was twenty-three when the *Sindia* beached on the sands. He told the following story of the incident:

The *Sindia* ran into a storm as she approached the Jersey coast in December 1901. However, Captain [Alan] McKenzie did not consider

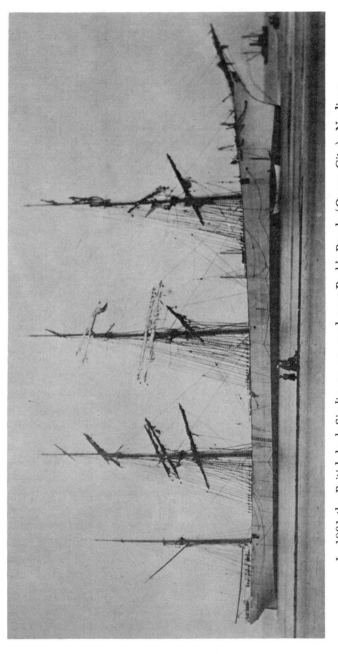

In 1901 the British bark *Sindia* ran aground near Peck's Beach (Ocean City). No lives were lost, but the *Sindia* began to break up. One of its masts could be seen until a few years ago. (Senior Studio Photo)

it too bad and ordered a round of drinks for all hands to mark the successful ending of a long cruise.

We mistook the lighthouse at Cape May for Highland Light near Sandy Hook and thought we were sailing into New York harbor. At midnight I went off watch and to my bunk below. The captain was asleep in his cabin on the poop deck.

Then we struck, and the *Sindia* was trapped between the beach and the offshore sandbars. The helmsman attempted to turn the ship south toward deeper water, but the keel dug in. We hung on until morning, when the Coast Guard [Life Saving Service] threw us a line. The seas were still very heavy. Finally the Coast Guard got a boat through the waves and we were taken off about twelve hours after hitting.

The crew were taken to the 34th Street [Ocean City] lifesaving station and fed hot soup. Captain McKenzie was the last to leave.

The Standard Oil Company, which leased the *Sindia*, dispatched tugs to try to free it; they proved ineffectual. Barges were then brought alongside and part of the cargo salvaged. The ship had about all the battering it could take and began to break up. At the same time parts of its cargo began to appear about town, and the U.S. Customs Service put a watch on the wreck. Several attempts to refloat the ship failed. Some young men of the resort swam out one night and cut off the ship's massive red-turbaned figurehead. Through the efforts of Mrs. Richard Van Gilder, a Cape May County historian, it was recovered, and it now rests in the Ocean City Historical Museum.

At a British Admiralty court of inquiry in Philadelphia in 1902, Captain McKenzie was found guilty of neglect and his license suspended for six months. It was never explained how an experienced captain was so wrong in his calculations.

On December 16, 1967, a marker was placed at 16th Street and the boardwalk in Ocean City by the State Department of Historical Sites. Until a few years ago the tall mast and part of the aft riggings of the *Sindia* were to be seen beyond the breaker line on the beach. Now nothing is left; salvage experts believe the ship will never be uncovered. A great part of the cargo is still in the hold according to authorities in such matters.

The *Sindia* may be gone but as far as Ocean City is concerned the event will be remembered through the Sindia Restaurant, the Sindia Cottage, small Sindia novelties, and an entire room in the historical museum devoted to the artifacts connected with the vessel.

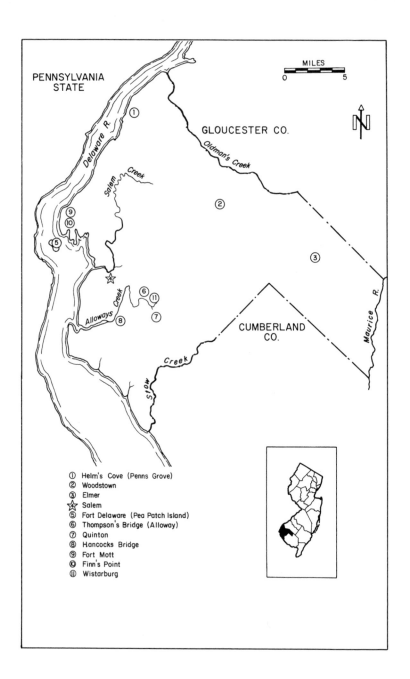

PENNSYLVANIA
STATE

GLOUCESTER CO.

Delaware R.

Salem Creek

Oldman's Creek

CUMBERLAND
CO.

Alloway Creek

Stow Creek

Maurice R.

MILES
0 — 5

N

① Helm's Cove (Penns Grove)
② Woodstown
③ Elmer
☆ Salem
⑤ Fort Delaware (Pea Patch Island)
⑥ Thompson's Bridge (Alloway)
⑦ Quinton
⑧ Hancocks Bridge
⑨ Fort Mott
⑩ Finn's Point
⑪ Wistarburg

SALEM COUNTY

SALEM COUNTY

The first division of East and West Jersey into counties by the General Free Assembly was made on May 2–6, 1682. At that time the counties of Burlington and Salem were created.

Originally Salem County also included all of Gloucester, Cape May, and Cumberland counties. In 1686 Gloucester was formed to include what is now Atlantic County. Cape May County was established in 1692, Cumberland in 1748.

While Salem County was primarily a Quaker settlement, the Swedes were there before the Friends and met in log cabins for divine services. They were attached to the Lutheran congregation of New Castle, Delaware, and made frequent trips across the river to transact important church matters.

According to documents in the possession of the Salem County Historical Society, the first place of Quaker worship was at the home of Christopher White, on the north side of Alloways Creek near Hancock's Bridge, where meetings were held from 1685 to 1718. A deed dated 1681 shows that Samuel Nicholson and his wife Ann gave their home near the Salem Oak for the first meeting house in Salem. A building of logs at Churchtown erected on the site of the present Saint George Church is said to have been the first house of worship in the county other than Quaker meeting houses. Land for the church was given by John Jaquette in 1714; first services were in Swedish. A later church built at the same spot dates from 1811.

An example of early church architecture in Salem County is the United Methodist Church of Alloway, constructed in 1821 and remodeled in 1866. Church and grounds take in an entire block, and there is a beautiful memorial to the war dead of Salem.

The initial highways in Salem County were oystershell roads, the shells collected from the oyster industry piles in nearby waters and crushed to a fine gravellike substance. Aid from the state helped build a road from Pointers toward Woodstown. On June 14, 1899, the Board of Freeholders ordered construction of an oystershell road from Salem to Hancock's Bridge. The last of these roads was approved as late as 1901, from Hogbin's in Elsinboro to Salem. The development of the automobile doomed the oystershell road as the shells cut rubber tires.

In July of 1863 the railroad first made its way into the county, inaugurating service between Salem and Camden. From the Civil War to World War I the railroads added to the prosperity of the area. The advent of automobiles, trucks, and buses sent the railroads into decline so that Salem's rail service today is primarily freight.

The county's industrial trend was changed in July 1891 by the establishment of a manufacturing plant by the E. I. du Pont de Nemours and Company on a 200-acre farm at Carney's Point. Once the site of Thomas Carney's plantation, the Delaware-based company used the land to build a plant and laboratory which had a major impact upon the county's growth. The first product manufactured there was guncotton for the U.S. Navy. During the Spanish-American War the plant was expanded to include 1,500 acres. World War I saw further expansion; it is estimated that in 1917 more than 25,000 people were employed at the plant.

Following World War I the Du Pont Company turned its attention from explosives to dyes. The plant played an important part in supplying the Allies with war products during World War II as the result of which Salem County patriotism ran high. Today Du Pont owns the entire waterfront from Penns Grove to Salem Canal and develops many of its experimental projects in Salem County.

Adding to the industrial picture of Salem County was the construction of the Richman Ice Cream Company plant at Sharptown in 1904, the outcome of young William Richman's general ice cream business begun in 1894.

In 1905 the H. J. Heinz Company opened a large plant at

Salem. Mannington Mills purchased the American Oilcloth factory in 1914 and began making floor coverings.

The founding of Atlantic City as a seashore resort and the need for expanded electrical power not only there but elsewhere in South Jersey led to the building of the Deepwater Generating Plant of the Atlantic City Electric Company on a 365-acre site in Lower Penns Neck Township.

The opening of the Delaware Memorial Bridge linking Salem County and Delaware brought another change in the industrial life of the area. Delaware and the South became as important to its future development as Philadelphia and the North.

LAND OF FENWICK

The story of John Fenwick and the Salem colony harks back to the seventeenth-century New Jersey held by John Lord Berkeley and Sir George Carteret on a grant from the Duke of York. On March 18, 1664, the joint ownership of Berkeley and Carteret ended when Berkeley sold his half interest to John Fenwick of Binfield, County of Berks, England, who was representing Edward Byllynge, a brewmaster who was faced with financial difficulties and unable to negotiate his own purchase.

Quakers William Penn, Gawen Lawrie, and Nicholas Lucas served as trustees to handle Byllynge's tangled financial affairs until all his debts were paid, acting on the Quaker belief that they should settle their own affairs without the help of civil courts.

The trustees divided the Byllynge holdings into quarters, sixteenths and so forth. Fenwick received one tenth (ten) of the original shares for his services in the transaction. Being an enthusiastic individual, Fenwick wanted to launch immediate plans for colonization; the other proprietors advised against it and wanted him to go along with their long-range planning.

Fenwick rebelled and organized his own expedition to the New World. In the summer of 1675 Fenwick and his party, in-

cluding daughters Anna, Elizabeth, and Priscilla, and two sons-
in-law, sailed from England in a craft named the *Griffin*. They
reached the Delaware River on November 23, 1675, landing on
the site of the town he was later to call Salem after what he
believed to be the Hebrew word for peace. (Hebrew scholars
point out that the word for peace is *shalom,* which they believe
Fenwick anglicized to Salem.)

One of the first moves made by Fenwick toward creating a
permanent settlement was working out treaties with the Indians. Today in Salem there is a gigantic oak tree known as the
Salem Oak which, according to tradition, provided shade while
Fenwick completed his first deal with the Lenni-Lenape in
1675. The tree has a spread of 130 feet, is 27 feet, 9 inches in
circumference, and is under the care of the Salem Monthly
Meeting. Beneath its branches lie buried in unmarked graves
many of the Quaker pioneers of the colony.

Disputes arose because of the Dutch rule of the land of West
Jersey before the English conquest of 1664. After a year of
English control, the Dutch reconquered the area (New York and
New Jersey being considered as one colony by the Dutch), and
the original grants to Berkeley and Careret were invalidated.
The English regained control, and the Dutch dropped all claims.
Jersey grants made by the Duke of York were reissued.

In 1676 the trustees and the Duke signed the Quintipartite
Deed, so called because it was signed by five men. This deed
created a dividing line between the Carteret interests in East
Jersey and the Penn, Lawrie, Lucas, and Byllynge interests in
West Jersey. It also mapped a basic plan for rule of the pos-
sessions.

Meanwhile Fenwick mortgaged his tenth of the area to John
Eldridge and Edmund Warner to raise money to finance his
colony. Eldridge and Warner considered this a transfer of all
rights to them. The trustees, including Penn, concurred. At that
point Fenwick declared that Penn had cheated him, to which
Penn replied, "Fall closely to thy business," which has been
translated to mean "You tend to your business and we will tend
to ours."

It is said that John Fenwick made his first lasting peace treaty with the Indians beneath the Salem Oak in 1675. Located in what is now the old Quaker cemetery in the heart of Salem, the tree has a crown spread of 130 feet and is 27 feet 9 inches in circumference. Its age is uncertain. (McMahon Collection)

The trustees felt that Fenwick had already broken faith because of his unwillingness to delay his plans until all could participate in the establishment of a Quaker colony in the New World. Fenwick, angered, went to civil court to regain control of his lands, but the court upheld Eldridge and Warner.

On August 18, 1676, the trustees appointed James Wasse, Richard Hartshorne, and Richard Guy as their commissioners and representatives in West Jersey. The commissioners were instructed to tell Fenwick that he could sell land only with the approval of the trustees. If Fenwick would share with them, they offered to put his ten shares on equal basis with the other ninety.

Fenwick faced troubles on another front. Sir Edmund Andros, governor of New York, claimed jurisdiction over Fenwick's Salem. Fenwick defied the governor and was jailed. He was released but rearrested the following year because of continued defiance of Andros.

When the government of West Jersey was established by the Proprietors in 1681, Fenwick offered no opposition. The constant pressures had weakened him and in 1682, weary of the battle, he turned all his rights to William Penn. In a final emotional meeting in which both admitted hasty judgments, the two Quakers settled differences.

The founder of Salem died in 1683 and is buried in an unmarked grave somewhere in a 6,000 acre plot he called Fenwick Grove. A monument to Fenwick is to be seen along the present Salem-Woodstown road near a spot thought to be his grave. It was erected in 1925 during the 250th anniversary of the founding of Salem.

A bronze tablet on the walls of the Salem County courthouse, erected by the Society of Colonial Wars in 1925, is also a tribute to Fenwick:

> That my said colony and all the planters within
> the same may be settled in the love of God.

In 1695 the town of Salem was incorporated, and the Salem Oak appeared on its seal.

On May 12, 1696, an act was passed to qualify public officials who were not free to take an oath. This was a concession to the

Quakers of the settlement. Such officers, however, had to promise allegiance to William, king of England, and the government of the province of West Jersey.

Officers chosen under the initial act of incorporation were: John Worledge, burgess; Benjamin Acton, recorder; John Jeffrey, bailiff; Richard Johnson, surveyor of streets.

The Salem Fair was established in 1697 and is still held yearly. In 1717 the first courthouse was erected and a whipping post ordered for the jail compound. Whipping was not then an unusual punishment. The court record of February 1733 reported the following action: "Ordered by the court that Mary Kelly, for abusing the judge, Mr. Acton, in her misbehavior to him in the execution of his office, do receive ten lashes on her bare back, for her contempt at the public whipping post."

In the Revolutionary War the inhabitants of Salem took their stand in favor of the American cause. The greater part of the inhabitants were Quakers opposed to war in any form, but they proved they could support a cause in more ways than taking up arms. After the war Salem Town settled down to building an economy based on agriculture.

Colonel Robert Gibbon Johnson, who was to become the first mayor of the city of Salem when it was incorporated in 1858, has his place in history due to his dramatic introduction of the first tomatoes into Salem County in 1820. Most settlers believed love apples, as they were then called, were poisonous. To prove they were not, Johnson announced that he would stand on the courthouse steps and eat one. It is recorded that there was a big turnout. First-aid equipment was rushed to the spot; doctors stood by. Johnson bit into the tomato with gusto and had no ill effects. A cheer went up from the crowd, and Johnson invited his audience to sample the love apples for themselves; many did. Johnson is credited with the start of the million-dollar tomato industry of Salem County.

Mayor Johnson contributed another of his talents to Salem by writing a comprehensive history of the area. His home in the center of today's Salem, across from the Historical Society headquarters, is approached through a landscaped garden and bears a historic marker. Johnson Hall, as he called his home, was built in 1806.

In 1863 the railroad came to Salem. The Salem Glass Works was founded in the same year by H. D. Hall, Jr., D. Pancoast, and J. V. Craven. Within a ten-year period it was to become one of the largest hollow glassware manufacturing plants in the world. In 1874 John Gayner founded a glassworks specializing in the hand blowing and pressing of glass. This plant remained in the Gayner family until 1955. It is now a unit of the Star Glass Company. Other industries making an appearance at about 1874 were two canning companies and a cloth factory. In 1906 the H. J. Heinz canning house was opened.

Salem today maintains its colonial look in midtown. Down the side streets are to be seen some of the prettiest examples of mid-Victorian architecture in the county.

SALEM'S HISTORIC TAVERNS

There were perhaps more taverns per square foot in Salem County than in any other part of South Jersey, despite the fact the county was settled and controlled during most of its early existence by Quakers, who frowned upon public houses. Salem County was on the crossroads of many trails between West and East Jersey and the Delaware shore, and the need for overnight accommodations for travelers of the various stagecoach lines may account for the preponderance of taverns in the area.

John Fenwick's Salem was laid out with two streets, one called Wharf Street (changed to Bradway Street and finally Broadway) and the other known as Bridge Street (now Market Street). There were five taverns on these two streets.

One of the prominent early innkeepers was William Hall. According to the Salem County Historical Society, Hall's inn was located at the foot of Broadway and was built in 1691.

James Ridley was perhaps the second innkeeper of Salem. He went into business in 1704 at Broadway and Walnut Street. The freeholders and even the chief justices and officers of the supreme court found this tavern favorable for meetings. A session of the justices there was reported in the city records of 1740. By that time the tavern had changed hands and was operated by the widow of John Jones, who called it Jones Tavern.

Another old Salem tavern, the Sherron, stood at the head of Market Street in 1693. William Nelson bought the property in 1848, tore down the original building, and built one which he named the Nelson House.

The John Burroughs Tavern, near the corner of Market Street and Broadway, served as a starting point of Samuel Breck's stageline in 1772. The building dates from 1758. Burroughs took part in county politics, serving as sheriff from 1761 to 1764; he was later reelected and served from 1769 to 1770. There were apparently no laws about a sheriff being a tavernkeeper, because he kept his inn until 1774.

Other early tavernmen of Salem were William Harker (1746–53), Robert Johnson (1755–57), Andrew Murdock (1770), Samuel McGregar (1772–74), Samuel Stockton, and John Bilderback.

Among inns outside Salem was one at Pittsgrove called Pole Tavern because of the Liberty Pole which stood in its front yard, marking it as the headquarters for the Liberty Boys, a pre-Revolutionary War group. The first license of record to Pole Tavern was a grant to Joseph Champneys, Jr., in 1770. In 1783 when news of Lord Cornwallis's surrender reached Salem County, the tavern was the center of a countywide celebration during which the 13-star flag was raised and the Liberty Boys fired a 13-gun salute.

Most prominent of the early county taverns still standing and still conducted as a tavern is the Centerton Inn, located at a prominent road junction at a spot once called Centerville, now Centerton. Specializing in South Jersey-style cooking, with special sauces from old area recipes, as well as vegetables grown nearby, the inn retains its colonial flavor. It maintains a large collection of South Jersey farm wagons and stagecoaches in barns adjoining the inn. The place has an authentic date of 1763, when a license was granted to Charles Dayton for a house in which "he now Dwelleth Situated and being in the Township of Piles Grove upon Road Leading from Cumberland County to Grate Eggharbor." The next owner of record, according to Jack Stevenson, who has spent some time assembling its history, was Rosana Erwin. She was followed by Jonathan Woodruff (1816), Cornelius Johnson, Reuben Shull, and Isaac Green. Al Southard took over Centerton Inn in 1968.

The Seven Stars Tavern on the old Kings Highway between Swedesboro and Sharptown just south of Oldman's Creek, is said to have started life in 1741 as a log cabin bar. Abraham Nelson was the first proprietor. By 1762 the log house had disappeared, and a more substantial inn took its place.

The name Seven Stars first appeared when the license was under the name of Joseph Wood. Some of Salem County's best ghost stories, including the one about the man whose head was twisted by the devil, are centered around the old inn, which is now the private home of Dr. Robert A. Brooks, who has done considerable restoration work.

Another old Salem County tavern still standing is the Helm's Tavern of Penns Grove, once known as Helm's Cove, which bears the date of 1732, when it was built of brick by Andrew Helm, who also operated a ferry across the Delaware River. While not used as a public house since 1878, the place has been carefully restored and is now the home of James and Katherine Madole.

The Hancock House at Hancock's Bridge may be classified as an early tavern although the structure, built in 1734, was not used as an inn until about 1761, when it was known as Baker's Tavern and kept by Samuel Baker, who later sold to William Hancock, owner at the time of the 1778 massacre. There is no record of a Hancock license. In the latter part of 1778 David Briggs was listed as innkeeper. The last recorded tavernman to occupy the place was Richard Mulford about 1870. Hancock House is now a state historic shrine and museum.

Wistarburg, the glass-making center about a mile above Alloway, was the site of an inn licensed to Lodowick Hall in 1741. Most likely Hall's best customers were the glassworkers.

Other taverns in the pre-Revolutionary period were located at Sculltown, Quinton, Pittstown, Maul's Bridge, Pedricktown, Pennsville, Remsterville, Sharptown, Stone Island, Friesburg, Daretown, Woodstown, and Wrightstown.

Most of these long ago gave way to fire or the wrecker's ax. A young member of Salem's present police force, in commenting upon the number of taverns in old Salem, remarked, "Our ancestors must have been powerfully thirsty people."

THE BIG CATTLE DRIVE

The first big cattle drive in this nation was not over the trail from Abilene to Kansas City but from Salem, New Jersey, to Valley Forge, Pennsylvania, in the days of the Revolution.

The plight of the colonies never looked more ominous than during the severe winter of 1777–78. General George Washington and the remnants of his army were bottled up at Valley Forge. Tories were openly urging reconciliation with the mother country, and an uncertain Congress was losing valuable time in personal wrangles. Food was scarce at Valley Forge, and desertions were numerous. In desperation Washington summoned Pennsylvania's young General Anthony Wayne and outlined a foraging expedition into the Quaker lands of southern Jersey, especially Salem and Cumberland counties.

On February 16, 1778, Major General Nathanael Greene informed Washington that Wayne had gone to Wilmington to cross the Delaware River to Jersey if the ice would permit; otherwise he would try to go by way of Goshen in Cape May County.

Wayne reached Salem County on February 19 and proceeded to Salem City, where he arrived the same evening. On the following morning, according to a letter Wayne sent Washington from Haddonfield on February 25, Wayne sent several detachments into the countryside. They succeeded in collecting about 150 head of cattle. Wayne spent two days in Salem County and would have tarried, but spies brought news that the British were assembling a force to intercept him at Burlington.

Wayne attempted to get his cattle on their way over the bay at New Castle, Delaware, on boats commanded by Captain John Barry of Salem (who later became the first commodore of the U.S. Navy), but the effort failed. It has never been clearly established whether the failure resulted from the presence of the enemy, ice on the river, inadequacy of boats, or all three.

Wayne decided to drive the cattle along the Delaware River to Trenton and then to Valley Forge. The cattle moved along Kings Highway from Salem to Blessington (now Sharptown) and past the Moravian church at Oldman's Creek to Swedesboro. Captain Barry was ordered to take his boats and make a feint at the mouth of Raccoon Creek to attract the attention of the British. The trick was successful. Wayne slipped past, continuing his drive to the southern end of Woodbury, to Clements Bridge road to Haddonfield. On February 25 the cattle were at Mount Holly.

General Wayne dispatched two letters to General Washington. One was a report of the mission to date, the other reporting that he believed more cattle were available between Cooper's and Dunk's ferries and he was attempting an additional roundup.

A third letter went to Governor William Livingston informing him that an enemy force of approximately 2,000 men had been split at Billingsport, that 1,500 of them had proceeded toward Salem and about 500 had gone to Haddonfield, where they were to be joined by a force of more than 1,300 for the purpose of capturing Wayne and his cattle.

Count Pulaski, who had been at Trenton with about 18 horsemen, was notified of events at Haddonfield and hurried to Burlington, gathering about 50 light horse on the way. At this point both Wayne and Pulaski decided they needed some action and went seeking out the enemy.

Washington, impatient in the face of serious food shortages, was not too pleased at this excursion and informed Wayne to "get those cattle up here without delay."

Meanwhile, a British force under Lieutenant Commander Abercrombie also had gone to Salem County for the purpose of collecting food supplies. He found that Wayne had stripped the place. Still hoping to accomplish his mission, the British commander, acting on inaccurate intelligence reports, attempted to trap both Wayne and his cattle. As he embarked on this mission he received a report that Wayne had suddenly left Mount Holly for Salem with a large force. Abercrombie beat a hasty retreat from Salem, crossed the Delaware River, and sought the safety of Pennsylvania. It has always been suspected that General Wayne somehow was responsible for the false message, as Wayne had never left the Mount Holly-Haddonfield area.

On March 4 after his short but unsuccessful sortie with Pulaski, Wayne dispatched a fast messenger to General Washington stating that he was beginning the last part of his march to Valley Forge the next day. He blamed the delays of which Washington had complained, on the necessity of obtaining shoes for his men, neglecting to mention the activities he and Pulaski had found exciting.

Whether the cattle were driven across the river at Burlington or Trent Town (Trenton) has never been clear in records of the event. They arrived at Washington's camp shortly after the March 4 date.

Wayne himself did not go to Valley Forge at that time as he was still in New Jersey at Bordentown as late as March 14.

Some writers with tongue in cheek suggest that maybe Wayne found more Redcoats to chase.

DEFENDERS OF THE BRIDGE

Quinton is another of those Salem County towns today presenting little evidence of its colorful past. Tobias Quinton was the first English colonist to settle there along Alloways Creek. Others, spreading out from Salem Town, built a drawbridge over the creek and formed a community soon known as Quinton's Bridge.

In 1778 a small company of militia was stationed at the bridge for the protection of the village. British foraging parties had been making life miserable for nearby farmers and had been driven off on several occasions by the militia. To give the foraging groups protection, a force mostly Scots, selected from the 17th and 144th regiments in Philadelphia commanded by Colonel Charles Mawhood, was dispatched to the area on March 17, 1778. Major John Simcoe, who four days later would lead the raid on Hancock House, was second in command.

The two officers executed a deception to draw the militia from the bridge and positions behind breastworks to the south. They sent a small unit into full view. The militia began firing, and the invaders withdrew. Believing the enemy was in full retreat, Lieutenant Duclos, a French officer attached to the American forces, urged Captain William Smith to go after the fast-disappearing British.

The American forces streamed across the bridge only to be cut down from all sides. They beat a hasty retreat, leaving between 30 and 40 dead.

Colonel Elijah Hand of the militia unit in Cumberland, being informed by runners from Colonel Holme of the presence of the enemy, arrived in time to keep the British from crossing the creek. During the bridge encounter Captain Smith received two bullet wounds and had his horse shot out from under him.

A monument marks the site of the encounter. Erected by the Oak Tree Chapter, Daughters of the American Revolution, Salem, New Jersey, on October 17, 1908, it has a plaque that reads:

In memory of Colonel Benjamin Holme, Colonel Elijah Hand, Captain William Smith, Andrew Bacon and those other patriots who defended the bridge at Quinton, March 17, 1778.

Andrew Bacon was cited on the plaque because of his act of heroism in cutting down the draw of the bridge while under fire. He made the span impassable but received a wound that crippled him for life.

Following the war Quinton returned to the role of a quiet country village. In 1815 Benjamin Allen opened a store. Broadstreet's shipyards were in full operation in the 1840s, and Jeremiah Davis's tavern was a popular gathering place. Quinton was the location of a glassworks in the 1860s. It is now mainly a residential and agricultural area.

THE AFFAIR AT HANCOCK HOUSE

The sign on the road read simply: HANCOCK'S BRIDGE SEVEN MILES. It gave no indication of a bitter chapter of Salem County history related to me by Joseph Hancock, current member of the Salem family predating the Revolution, who had invited me to his marina for a cup of coffee and some ancestral background.

At 5 A.M. on March 21, 1778, the hamlet of Hancock's Bridge was sleeping peacefully, so much so that the approach of a force of three hundred men from the direction of Alloways Creek went undetected even by the guards who had been posted against such an occurrence. The objective of the group was the house of William Hancock nearby, where a home guard of thirty volunteers, mostly old men and young boys, were sleeping.

The invaders overpowered the sleepy lookouts, rushed into the building, and bayoneted everyone within. Not a shot was fired.

The raid was a well-planned and cooly executed maneuver accomplished by Major John Simcoe, a youth of twenty and a British regular. He led his men, mostly Loyalists, from Philadelphia to Salem via Billingsport, and by flatboat down Alloways Creek to Hancock's Bridge. Simcoe had the help of those who knew the territory well, and it is an accepted story in Salem that the victims recognized some of the invaders as former neighbors.

The raid was a retaliatory action against the Quakers of Salem County because of the support they gave General Anthony Wayne in his trip to the county to secure cattle for General Washington's troops in Pennsylvania.

Mrs. Mary Hewitt, caretaker of Hancock House, which dates to 1734, showed me bloodstains still visible under the eaves and against the chimneys of the building. She filled in additional details, including one of a terrified youngster who crawled up the chimney to escape the raiders, only to be dragged back to the attic and bayoneted. William Hancock, elderly son of the first William to own the house and grandson of the builder, was among those killed in the raid.

For a long time after the massacre the house remained vacant, there being a story that the grisly scene was reenacted by ghostly forces at the full moon. Eventually the house was used for a tavern. In 1932 it was turned into a state shrine and museum.

Today life moves at a leisurely pace at Hancock's Bridge. The bridge is still there, although it has been modernized. Roads, now paved, are still winding and take the visitor past many old historic homes of the area.

WISTARBURG GLASS

Wistarburg in Salem County, New Jersey, was the first successful glass-factory town in America. But don't go looking for it. Not

In 1778 after the Quakers of Salem County supplied General Anthony Wayne with cattle for General Washington's troops, British and Loyalists massacred a home guard at the William Hancock house in Hancock's Bridge in retaliation. (Courtesy of Mary T. Hewitt)

a trace remains save a highway marker which designates the spot where the town and glassworks once existed.

Glass was important to the early colonists after they had advanced from the log cabin stage, and England could not supply all they wanted. This led to pioneer attempts at glassmaking in America: at Jamestown, Virginia, in 1608; at Salem, Massachusetts, in 1639; at New Amsterdam in 1664; and at Philadelphia in 1683. None of these projects lasted.

Caspar Wistar, of Wald-Hispach in the Electorate of Heidelberg, a twenty-one-year-old buttonmaker who arrived in Philadelphia on September 16, 1717, was the first glassmaker of the New World to establish a permanent operation.*

Although lacking knowledge of glassmaking, Wistar decided that glass, not buttons, represented his future. He secured land in Salem County, which seemed to him able to supply good white sand and plenty of wood for his fires.

Then he sent to Germany, as evidenced in an agreement of December 7, 1738, for four experts who would "teach the art of glassmaking to me and my son (Richard)." Wistar paid sea captain James Marshall to bring these men to America. They were Caspar Halter, John Martin Halter, Johannis Wentzel, and Simeon Kreismayer of the Palantine Region of Germany, known for its fine glassmaking. The four men were offered shares in the Wistar enterprise as an added incentive to make the trip, which leads historians to conclude they were top craftsmen. They left Rotterdam on December 7, 1738. By this time Wistar had acquired about two thousand acres of land on Alloways Creek about seven miles from Salem.

The first Wistar furnace was built in the summer of 1739 and put in operation that autumn. An oddity is that company books contained the name of the United Glass Company rather than the Wistar Works. It is believed this was done to confuse the royal tax collectors.

---

* The original family name was spelled Wurster but, once in this country, Caspar accepted the spelling of both Wistar and Wister. On available records it is spelled both ways.

Many accept Wistarberg as the spelling of the glassworks site. However, a historic marker on the spot spells it Wistarburg. Some historic sources also use the extra *h* on the end.

Once the furnaces were in operation, the Wistars seemed to have changed their minds about learning the actual art of glass-blowing and confined themselves to the business end. Caspar Wistar was considered a wealthy man at the time of his death on February 13, 1752, at the age of fifty-six. Richard took charge of the works.

The glass factory flourished for forty-one years, and the small village of worker homes which grew up around it became known as Wistarburg. It consisted of factory buildings, a general store, homes for workmen, a manager's mansion, barns, a granary, and a wagon house.

Products of the Wistarburg plant were mainly bottles and window glass. After working hours the glassblowers turned their hand to artistic endeavors and competition among themselves. These items—glass canes, pitchers, bowls, and witch balls—are now collector's items of great value. Many examples of the work of Wistarburg glassblowers are to be found in the Salem and Cumberland County Historical Society museums.

When Richard took over, he established himself in Philadelphia and operated the business through a plant manager. Sometime during the Revolution the plant closed, never to be reopened. Many reasons have been advanced for this closing, including the fact that the war disrupted transportation, the Delaware River originally used for this purpose by the Wistars was under constant patrol by both American and British gunboats, Continental money was a shaky affair, acceptable at some places, unacceptable at others. However, one of the most plausible explanations is that Richard Wistar considered his allegiance as belonging to the British, while the countryside in which he was located in Salem County was a hotbed of American patriots.

His son Richard II did not follow his father's choice, sided with and aided the Americans, for which he was read out of Quaker meeting.

On October 11, 1780, Richard Wistar advertised the works for sale; he died in Rahway, New Jersey, in 1781 before the plant was sold. Time and weather soon took their toll of the buildings as workmen drifted away and the operation became a page of history. Many workers found their way to the new glassmaking village of Glassboro.

FERRY VILLAGE

When Peter Minuit arrived in the New World in 1638, one of his group was Anders Seneca, whose son Anders, Jr., bought land from the Indians at a spot the Indians called Obisquahassit, located on the Delaware River about fifteen miles from present-day Salem.

Other Swedes followed Anders, Jr., and they established a small community. John Fenwick's arrival in Salem did not upset the Swedes, who made land rental deals with him and were welcomed into his colony.

One of the early English settlers of Obisquahassit was John Kinsey, who became prominent in the affairs of the village and gave it the English name of Kinseyville.

In the early 1800s Kinseyville became Craven's Ferry, named for a boat operating across the Delaware River to New Castle, Delaware. By 1820 a stage from Philadelphia was meeting all boats, and soon Craven's Ferry became a transportation center connecting New Castle, Salem, the resorts of Cape May County, and Camden and Philadelphia. The village received its present name of Pennsville in 1826, when the first post office was established there.

The ferry service continued until the early 1920s, when it became apparent that the ferry could not handle increasing traffic across the river. A steel span was discussed and in 1951 became a reality with the formal opening of the Delaware Memorial Bridge. In 1968 a second span was opened connecting the Jersey shore with the Delaware Expressway and the New Jersey Turnpike.

Many of the workers and officials of the Du Pont plant in nearby Carney's Point have their homes in Pennsville, which is also a main shopping center for the area.

THE PATTERNED BRICK HOUSES

One of the unusual sights of Salem County is its patterned houses, dwellings with patterns worked into a windowless brick wall, a custom dating to the Flemish-Norman artisans of France. For the most part the patterns contain the date of erection of the building and the original owner's initials; others are more elaborate. A recent survey revealed that thirty-seven of these houses are still in use.

The Bradway house near the wharf at the foot of Broadway in Salem is perhaps the oldest brick house in the state. The date 1691 is worked in glazed brick, numerals being about a foot and a half high. Edward, Lord Cornbury, governor of New Jersey (1703–1708), had headquarters there at various times. The council of West Jersey also met at the house.

Most ornate of the brick dwellings is the Dickinson house (1754), about a mile and a half from the site of the Wistarburg glassworks near Alloway. Designs on this wall consist of the date, initials, diamonds, triangles, and other geometric figures in red and blue brick.

The William Hancock house at Hancock's Bridge contains the very readable date of 1734 plus zigzag designs said to have been patterned after Leigh's Priory, built about 1536 in Essex, England.

Among other patterned brick houses of the area is the Abel Nicholson house in Elsinboro, which bears the date of 1722. For anyone seeking this picturesque structure it is at the lower end of the hamlet of Elsinboro near the north bank of Alloways Creek. In addition to the date this fine old building also has a crisscross pattern from roof peak to cellar.

The John Maddox Denn house just outside Hancock's Bridge is another good example of the work of colonial bricklayers. Bricked into the side wall is the date 1725.

The Padgett house near Harmersville contains a design in red and blue bricks. Although the date is missing, it is said to have been erected in 1735 by James Evans. Outlined on the wall is a design that shows the house was changed at one time from a hip-roofed building to a peaked-roof one.

One mile east of Alloway stands the hip-roofed William Oakford house with its large initials and the date of 1736. It has been slightly changed in design through the years.

On the Harding highway east of Woodstown is the Bassett house with its big *B*, the date 1757, and a scroll design near the point of the roof. Recently a window has been cut into the solid wall.

The John and Hannah Oakford house south of Hancock's Bridge (1764) contains the initials *J. H.* It is another hip-roofed structure.

The majority of these homes were built by local brick artisans who used raw materials at hand in temporary kilns.

The Salem County Historical Society has a copy of a "brick law," passed in 1683, which regulated the size of bricks: $2\frac{3}{4}$ inches thick, $4\frac{1}{2}$ inches broad, and $9\frac{1}{2}$ inches long.

FORT MOTT

Fort Mott, on the Delaware River six miles from Salem, is today a park and picnic grounds operated by the state of New Jersey. Only the hulk of the old fort remains, its guns and other equipment having long since been removed. Although there was never a shot fired from the fort in combat, its position commanding the river was believed important to the defense of Philadelphia in the event of attack by water.

The federal government purchased the 146-acre site in 1837 and established a small fort that was christened Finn's Point Battery, the land being a part of the site known both as Finn's Point and Fischer's Point.

The Finns and Swedes had a settlement and built a fort at Finn's Point in 1643–44 to control Dutch shipping on the Delaware River. Construction was ordered by Swedish Governor John Printz. By 1654 the fort was abandoned. A marker in nearby Churchtown, erected on June 30, 1938, by the New Sweden Tercentenary Commission of New Jersey, reads:

Finn's Point 1638–1938. Near here 300 years ago and later lived the first colony of settlers of Finnish blood upon this continent. . . .

Work on the present fortifications did not begin until 1896, at which time the name Finn's Point Battery was changed to Fort Mott in honor of Gersham Mott, a native of Burlington who had commanded the New Jersey Volunteers in the Civil War and retired with the rank of major general.

The armament consisted of one battery of three 12-inch disappearing rifles, two batteries of two 5-inch rifles, two 5-inch rapid-fire guns, and five Gatling guns.

The New Jersey battery, together with the 10-gun battery at Fort Delaware on Pea Patch Island in the middle of the river, gave the U.S. Army control of this waterway. Any unfriendly craft caught in the crossfire possible from the two batteries would be dispatched to the bottom.

Fort Mott was first garrisoned by Battery 1, 4th Artillery, which arrived from Washington Barracks on December 14, 1897. During the Spanish-American War (April 25 to December 10, 1898) the fort was garrisoned by the 14th Pennsylvania Volunteer Infantry, Colonel J. T. Glenn, commanding. Battery L, 4th Artillery, was also stationed there until September 3, 1898. On June 28, 1899, Battery H arrived from Fort Monroe, Virginia, commanded by Captain Gilbert Cummings.

Although the uselessness of the fort must have been apparent, the army kept it garrisoned until 1922, after which a caretaking detachment remained in charge. Some troop training was carried out. In October 1943 Fort Mott was formally abandoned by the military. In 1947 the installation was acquired by the New Jersey State Department of Conservation and Economic Development. The job of turning the site into a state park was started in the summer of 1949. In June 1951 the area was formally dedicated.

HERE LIE THE DEAD

According to legend Pea Patch Island received its name in colonial days when a boatload of peas was beached on a sandbar in the Delaware River. The cargo spilled over, took root, and the vegetation caused the land mass to grow.

Fort Mott, six miles from Salem, was built in 1896 to help defend Philadelphia in case of attack by water, but it never fired a shot in combat. The area is now a state park. (New Jersey Department of Historical Sites)

Pea Patch Island, almost directly across from Fort Mott, is the site of Fort Delaware.

Designed to help Fort Mott protect Wilmington and Philadelphia from attack by water, Fort Delaware was started in 1848. Due to lack of finances and overspending on pilings, it was not completed until 1859. It covers 6 of the island's 178 acres and was built of brick.

The fort was first occupied in 1861 by the Commonwealth Artillery of Pennsylvania. When it became apparent that the feared assault upon Philadelphia by way of the Delaware River was not in the plans of the Confederates, Fort Delaware was turned into a war prison for Southern soldiers. In 1862, following the battle of Kernstown, Virginia, the fort received its first prisoners, some 250 of Stonewall Jackson's men. By the summer of 1863 this number had swelled to 12,500, housed in facilities intended for not more than 3,100. The overcrowded conditions, inadequate health facilities, lack of medical units, and brutal treatment soon resulted in disease of epidemic proportions, and the dead began to pile up. Each day new corpses were dragged to the parade grounds. Burials were first made in a trench on the island. Later the dead were rowed across the river in open boats and dumped in common graves on the New Jersey site known as Finn's Point. In a short space of time 2,700 Confederate soldiers died amid filth and neglect on Pea Patch Island.

The shocking story of Fort Delaware did not become known until after the war, when pleas of Southern families for news of sons taken prisoner during the conflict were investigated by the government.

In 1875, after receiving a strong letter from the Governor of Virginia protesting the neglect of Confederate graves in New Jersey, the Department of the Army designated Finn's Point as a national cemetery.

Frederick Schmidt, a discharged Union soldier who had lost an arm in the war, was made the first superintendent of grounds. He found the place in an unkempt state and devoted his life to making it a proper memorial to the dead of both sides, some Union soldiers also having been buried there. Schmidt planted the Norway and silver maples we see today; he also laid out a series of walkways.

In 1879 the government erected a marble monument to the Union soldiers buried at Finn's Point. Not until 1910 was a memorial authorized to the Confederate dead. It is an 85-foot high monument of Pennsylvania white granite.

Fort Delaware was considered important to defense even after the Civil War. In 1896 the fort was garrisoned for the Spanish-American War and equipped with disappearing guns. It was reactivated again in 1917 for a short time and closed down at the Armistice.

A small garrison was moved to the fort again in the first days of World War II. It did not stay long, and in 1943 the big guns were removed and melted into scrap iron. In 1944 the fort was closed permanently. Later it was turned over to the state of Delaware. The Fort Delaware Society was organized in 1949 to help preserve the structure; it is now maintained as a museum by the society.

Finn's Point is still maintained as a national cemetery and contains graves other than Civil War dead. Also to be seen are markers of those who served in the Spanish-American War and World War I. In one section there are thirteen white marble headstones marking the graves of German war prisoners of World War II who died at Fort Dix.

A walk through the quiet and dignified surroundings of the 4.5 acre cemetery is an emotional experience as is the reading of the lines from Theodore O'Hara's "The Bivouac of the Dead" on a series of plaques:

> The Neighing Troop, the Flashing Blade
> The Bugle's Stirring Blast
> The Charge, the Dreadful Cannonade
> The Din and Shout are Past.

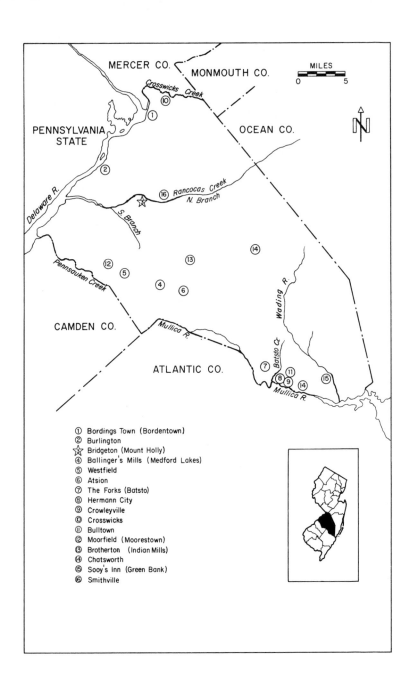

MILES
0   5

MERCER CO.

MONMOUTH CO.

Crosswicks Creek

⑩

①

PENNSYLVANIA
STATE

OCEAN CO.

②

Delaware R.

⑯ Rancocas Creek
N. Branch

☆

S. Branch

⑭

⑬

⑫ ⑤

Pennsauken Creek

④ ⑥

Wading R.

CAMDEN CO.

Mullica R.

Batsto Cr.

ATLANTIC CO.

⑦

⑧ ⑪
⑨ ⑭ ⑮

Mullica R.

N

①   Bordings Town (Bordentown)
②   Burlington
☆   Bridgeton (Mount Holly)
④   Ballinger's Mills (Medford Lakes)
⑤   Westfield
⑥   Atsion
⑦   The Forks (Batsto)
⑧   Hermann City
⑨   Crowleyville
⑩   Crosswicks
⑪   Bulltown
⑫   Moorfield (Moorestown)
⑬   Brotherton   (Indian Mills)
⑭   Chatsworth
⑮   Sooy's Inn (Green Bank)
⑯   Smithville

BURLINGTON COUNTY

BURLINGTON COUNTY

Burlington County is the largest county in New Jersey and one of the most historic. Extending from the Delaware River on the west across the state to the Atlantic Ocean, Burlington County has an area of 827.75 square miles, 40 subdivisions, but only three major cities. On the Delaware River side, it is a busy group of ever-expanding communities closely tied to the economics of Pennsylvania. On the ocean side, it consists of ghost towns, half-ruined ironworks, and the vast Pine Barrens, traditional home of the Pineys.

Before the settlement of Burlington by the English Quakers, who arrived aboard the ship *Kent* in 1677, the only Europeans in the area were three Dutch families at Leasy Point at the mouth of Assiscunk Creek and some Swedes along Swedes Run above Riverton. Leasy Point was also called Lassa Point. On a Dutch map of 1679, it was designated as Luye Hock. In Burlington County court records of 1693, some deeds give it the name of Wingerworth Point. It has also been known as Lazy Point.

A Dutchman, Peter Yegou, settled at Leasy Point in 1668 and opened "a house of entertainment for travelers" known as Point House or Yegou's Tavern. The license to conduct the tavern granted by Governor George Carteret is said to have been the first in that vicinity.

Two parties of Quakers came ashore from the *Kent* on August 16, 1677, one from Yorkshire, the other from London. The Yorkshires bought a tract of land running from Assiscunk Creek to Rancocas Creek; the London party from Rancocas to Timber Creek. For their mutual protection the town of New Beverly (Burlington City) was built. The ship *Martha* out of Burlington, England, arrived later in 1677 and landed another party of Quakers near Burlington.

The county was established by act of the West Jersey Assembly on March 25, 1681. Burlington City was designated the capital of West Jersey, coming into existence before William Penn got around to planning the city of Philadelphia. Original townships of Burlington County were Nottingham (now in Mercer County), Mansfield, Springfield, Wellingborrow, Northampton, Chester, Chesterfield, and Eversham. The act of 1694 setting the county's boundaries as "by the River Derwent on the North and River Crapwell on the South . . ." stood until January 21, 1710, when the limits were more clearly defined. The county area was reduced when Hunterdon County was created by the act of March 11, 1714, which set the northern boundary of Burlington County at Assiscunk Creek. Mercer County was carved from Burlington territory on February 22, 1838. In 1891 Burlington lost land to Ocean County and as late as 1902 gained from Atlantic and Camden counties.

In 1682 Thomas Farnsworth bought property on the Delaware River which is now the town of Bordentown. Mount Holly, Moorestown, and Pemberton were settled before 1700.

The first attorney of record in Burlington County was George Deacon, who was selected by the legislature as King's Attorney (Prosecutor of the Pleas) in May of 1696. A year later Benjamin West served in the same capacity. The bar of New Jersey was organized in 1702. The supreme court of the state was established in 1704, with two sessions yearly, one at Burlington, the other at Perth Amboy. The initial Burlington session of the court began on November 6, 1704.

In 1758 New Jersey's first Indian reservation was established at Brotherton in Burlington County for the Lenni-Lenape.

Loyalties in the county were strongly divided during the Revolution. While most of the county's citizens, including the ironmasters, were allied with the Continental forces, others were Royalists, a condition that led to many bloody incidents.

William Franklin, Tory son of Benjamin Franklin and the last royal governor of New Jersey, was forced from his large estate at Green Bank because of his activities against the patriots. He fled to safety in New York, then held by the British, and lived his last days abroad.

Burlington County's population in 1790 was 18,085. In 1795 the county seat was moved from its original site in Burlington to Mount Holly.

Cranberries and blueberries were early agricultural crops of Burlington County's southern area. Cranberries were known to the Lenni-Lenape Indians before the coming of the white man. The New Jersey Indians bestowed a significant role upon cranberries, making them a symbol of peace. In some tribal ceremonies cranberries were passed around and eaten much in the same way as the peace pipe was used by other tribes. The great sachem of the Delawares was called Pakimintzen, meaning cranberry eater. Cranberry cultivation began in Burlington County in 1840 according to the State Board of Agriculture. Soon after that cranberries were thriving in the pines at such places as Hog Wallow, Double Trouble, Ongs Hat, Penny Pot, and Mount Misery. Today Burlington County is the leading cranberry producer of the state.

There are approximately 524,160 acres of land in Burlington County, of which 184,727 acres are devoted to agriculture, mostly berry farming. Blueberries have been an increasingly important crop since about 1911 when Elizabeth White, daughter of an early New Lisbon cranberry-growing family, showed the potential of cultivating swamp huckleberries, granddaddies of the present cultivated blueberries.

The vast Fort Dix military reservation and McGuire Air Force Base are located in Burlington County. So are Atsion, Bulltown, Batsto, Hermann City, Crowleytown, and Quaker Bridge, all part of a long-forgotten bog-iron era of South Jersey.

OLDEST COMMUNITY

Burlington, sixteen miles below Trenton, was the provincial capital of West Jersey and challenged Philadelphia as the principal port on the Delaware River. It was the center of water traffic for many years. Later, when shipmasters began to prefer the busy young city of Philadelphia because it was nearer the sea, Burlington lost its hold on the shipping trade and turned to other forms of commerce.

The city has a unique distinction. It is one of the first if not *the* first planned town in the nation. Most early settlements were built around wagon trails; layout of streets followed these winding trails, accounting for today's confusion of traffic arteries in downtown sections of cities dating from the first days of the new nation.

Not so Burlington. The first colonists, about 250 Quakers who arrived near Raccoon Creek in August of 1677, planned the town of Burlington in a most orderly fashion. Streets and home plots were laid out according to carefully studied plans.

Richard Noble, a surveyor who had also arrived in the *Kent,* mapped the town around a principal thoroughfare, High Street. Land on each side was laid out in lots. The *Kent* Quakers were of two groups, known as the London sect and the Yorkshires. Each had its own side of High Street in accordance with the Noble plan.

The original map of the area is still in existence and shows the names of the first settlers: Thomas Olive, Daniel Wills, William Peachy, William Clayton, John Crips, Thomas Eves, Thomas Harding, Thomas Mositer, Thomas Farnsworth, Morgan Drewet, William Pennton, Henry Jennings, William Hibes, Samuel Lovett, John Woolston, William Woodmacy, Christopher Saunders, and Robert Powell.

The settlement was initially called New Beverly, later Bridlington, and finally Burlington, after towns in England with which the colonists had ties. Each owner of a share in the enterprise was given a home lot of ten acres and a farm of about sixty-four acres adjoining the town. The colony appears to have been a success from the start. This news reached England, and more settlers arrived.

The "Concessions and Agreements of the Proprietors, Freeholders, and Inhabitants of the Province of West Jersey in America" was drafted by the colonists in March 1677. This model constitution, however, was in for a delay in the hands of the Duke of York, who did not get around to confirming the sale of lands to the Quakers of Burlington until 1680. He named Edward

Byllynge governor without consulting the Burlington settlers. The proprietors felt they had been betrayed but were in no position to argue. Byllynge never came to America; instead he sent as his deputy Samuel Jennings of Buckinghamshire, who arrived in Burlington late in 1680. Jennings found favor with the colonists and when a crisis arose over Byllynge's authority a few years later the Assembly, chosen by the shareholders, ousted Byllynge and installed Jennings as governor. The office occupied by Jennings was on High Street. It is no longer in existence, but the spot is designated by a marker. Jennings and Thomas Budd, owner of considerable land in the West Jersey area, went to London to present the case of the Burlington colony but were given a cold reception; the crown upheld the authority of Byllynge.

Things were futher complicated by the death of Byllynge and the shift of governing powers to Dr. Daniel Coxe in 1687. Coxe was an Anglican, a member of the Church of England. He seemed to get along well with the Burlington Quakers, and friction was kept at a minimum. Coxe also controlled all of Cape May County. He never came to America, appointing deputies to guard his land interests.

Meanwhile Burlington progressed as a town. A highway was mapped between Burlington and the settlement of Salem. In May 1682 the Assembly, with the consent of the governor, made Burlington the official seat of the province of West Jersey.

The first Burlington market, usually the center of all business transactions, was built on High Street near the boat landing; a second existed at High and Broad streets. Later the city provided a long narrow market in the center of Union Street, with a second story for town meetings. In 1852 this building was replaced by a brick one on Union Street.

The Quakers built their first meeting house in 1683 on the west side of High Street. Behind the house still stands the King's Tree, a huge sycamore which shades the burial spot of Ockanickon, an Indian chief and friend of the first settlers. In 1784 it was decided that the first wooden building was too cold and drafty for Burlington winters, and a brick one was erected. A year later the first road was laid out from Burlington to Perth Amboy to connect with a ferry to New York. Another post road extended to New Brunswick, and a third connected Burlington and Bordentown.

In October 1693 Burlington was incorporated. The first town meeting was held on April 5, 1694, with Richard Basnet sitting as chief magistrate. James Hill was named clerk. Constables Jonathan West and Josiah Prickett were appointed in 1695.

On March 25, 1703, the cornerstone of the first Episcopal church in the state of New Jersey was laid. It was named Saint Anne's in honor of the queen who granted its charter on October 4, 1704. A more ample charter was granted the church in 1709, when the name was changed to Saint Mary's by vote of the congregation. This church served worshipers until 1854, when another structure was erected several hundred yards down Broad Street. The 1703 building is kept in fine condition as a tribute to the early Episcopalians of the state.

On May 7, 1734, Burlington was reincorporated by letters patent from George II. One of its oldest organizations is the fire company authorized on March 8, 1742. In 1758 the Burlington library was founded.

During the Revolution troops of both British and Continental forces occupied the town at various times. In December 1776 Count Donop, commanding a detachment of four hundred Hessians, entered Burlington and encamped on the premises of Thomas Wetherill below York bridge.

Many men famous in American history worked or lived in Burlington City. Benjamin Franklin conducted a print shop on High Street in 1728 at a site that has been authenticated and marked. Burlington was also the residence of Governor Joseph Bloomfield, soldier of the Revolution, Attorney General of the United States, governor of New Jersey, mayor of the city, and Grand Master of Masons.

Elias Boudinot, president of the Continental Congress and director of the United States Mint, maintained his residence at 135 West Broad Street. The residence of William Franklin, Tory governor of New Jersey, was located at Green Bank. General U. S. Grant lived at 309 Wood Street at the time of President Lincoln's assassination.

The town's two most famous sons were James Fenimore

Cooper, author of the *Leatherstocking Tales,* who was born at 457 High Street, on September 15, 1789, and Captain James Lawrence, American naval hero, who was born in the house next door on October 1, 1781. His dying words, "Don't give up the ship," became the motto of the United States Navy.

The Cooper family moved to Cooperstown, New York, on October 10, 1790, so James Fenimore spent only his boyhood years in Burlington. Legend has it that Mrs. Cooper opposed the move, plumped down in a chair, and refused to budge, whereupon husband William, a determined person, moved both chair and occupant onto the family wagon. A complete account of this incident is found in Henry Boynton's *Life of Fenimore Cooper.* It is possible the Coopers returned to Burlington for a short time in 1794.

Captain Lawrence also spent very little time in Burlington. While the two men never knew each other as youngsters, their paths crossed later when Cooper, who had enlisted in the navy, was assigned to a vessel commanded by Captain Lawrence.

According to Burlington County archives, the Lawrence house was built in 1742, an additional unit added in 1767. It was re-modeled in 1820 and stuccoed in 1844. Its last restoration was a WPA project of the 1940s. The house was never owned by any of the Lawrence family; it was rented. It is now maintained by the Historic Sites Department of the New Jersey State Department of Environmental Protection.

The Cooper house also was rented. It is now the headquarters of the Burlington County Historical Society.

Isaac Collins, founder of the state's first newspaper, the *New-Jersey Gazette,* operated a print shop on High Street in the same location used by Franklin. A plaque at the site dates his activities as 1770 to 1778. Prior to the advent of the Collins publication on December 5, 1777, colonists read newspapers from Pennsylvania and New York. One of Collins's great achievements as printer and publisher was his 1791 edition of the King James Bible. In 1776 Collins was printing money for the colonies at the command of King George III. However, his feelings soon turned to the cause of the new nation, and he became one of the most ardent advocates of revolution. For this he was read out of Quaker meeting. Collins was an important figure in the establish-

Paddle-wheel excursion boats were popular on the Delaware River at the turn of the century. The *Columbia* is shown at the wharf in Burlington. (McMahon Collection)

ment of the free press of America. He coined a phrase which has become a part of the heritage of American journalism: "My ear is open to every man's instruction but to no man's influences."

Burlington is a town of many historic sites the majority of which have been carefully restored; others which have disappeared in the passing years are identified by historic markers erected by the state of New Jersey and historical societies. Among the structures preserved is the Shippen house at Talbot Street and Riverbank. Built in 1756, it was the summer home of the Shippen family of Philadelphia. Peggy Shippen married Benedict Arnold. Burlington wharf at the foot of High Street was the site of a ferry which operated from 1675 until the building of the Burlington-Bristol bridge. The Revel house on East Pearl Street, built in 1685, is probably the oldest house in the county; it was mentioned by Benjamin Franklin in his memoirs.

Anderson's drugstore at the corner of High and Union streets, built in 1731, was a station of the Civil War underground railroad. The Metropolitan Inn, High and Broad streets, was once the Blue Anchor Tavern, built before 1761. Other historic spots include the Governor Bloomfield house, High and Liberty streets; Friends Meeting House; and Saint Mary's Hall, which was founded in 1837 by Bishop Doane as an Episcopal school for girls.

Through the years Burlington, while maintaining a steady growth, has also had periods of excitement, such as when the silkworm industry started there in 1838, giving promise of overnight fortunes before the bubble burst, causing many investment losses. James H. Birch established an international carriage industry there during the Civil War period.

Today's Burlington is the setting for a score of successful industries. The population is estimated at 13,200.

RIVER TOWN

The city of Bordentown is an old river town preserving its eighteenth-century atmosphere to a remarkable degree, with many fine sturdy houses built flush with the red brick sidewalks, pastel-shaded buildings and winding streets which take one past formal gardens. It was settled in 1682 by English Quaker Thomas Farnsworth. Bordentown derives its name from Joseph Borden, an early settler. It was popular at various times as a river port, a terminal of the Delaware-Raritan Canal, and later a station on the Camden and Amboy Railroad.

The intersection of Park Street and Farnsworth Avenue, Bordentown, is perhaps one of the most interesting four corners in the nation. On the southeast side is the Francis Hopkinson house, home of a signer of the Declaration of Independence; directly opposite on Farnsworth Avenue is the Patience Lovell Wright house, once the home of America's first internationally recognized sculptress. On the northwest corner of Farnsworth Avenue and Park Street is the Borden house, the original of which was burned by the British in retaliation for Colonel Joseph Borden's efforts in behalf of the American forces. The Hoagland Tavern, operated during colonial times by Colonel Oakly Hoagland of the Continental Army, is on the northeast corner.

Bordentown won a niche in history as the place from which gunpowder kegs were launched in an attempt to destroy British shipping off Philadelphia during the Revolution. It was in January of 1778 that submarine-experimenter David Bushnell embarked upon his project. Kegs were floated down the river but failed to sink any ships. However, the kegs made the British troops so jittery that the soldiers began firing at any piece of wood floating in the Delaware. As we would say today, the British "lost face" in these actions and became the further object of ridicule when Francis Hopkinson of Bordentown wrote and distributed his mocking poem of twenty-two verses, "The Battle of the Kegs," which was sung in colonial taverns from Massachusetts to Virginia. One stanza read:

> The cannons roar from shore to shore,
>   The small-arms loud did rattle.
> Since wars began, I'm sure no man,
>   E'er saw so strange a battle.

Hopkinson, born in Philadelphia on September 21, 1737, was an ardent supporter of the American cause. Living in Bordentown in 1776, having married Ann Borden, daughter of Colonel Borden, in 1768, Hopkinson was made a delegate to the Continental Congress from New Jersey. He took part in drafting the Declaration of Independence. A man of many talents he also designed the great seal of the state of New Jersey, the seal of the University of Pennsylvania. According to tradition, he made the original drawing for the Stars and Stripes.

In 1788 Hopkinson published a book of *Seven Songs*, said to have been the first published by a native American. Hopkinson's son Joseph followed in his father's footsteps in that he wrote the words to the stirring "Presidents' March," now known as "Hail, Columbia." Francis Hopkinson's literary output was considerable, but he never topped his funny "Battle of the Kegs." He died on May 9, 1791.

During the Revolutionary period, Bordentown was several times in British hands. Early in 1778 the British forces in possession of Philadelphia sent an expedition up the Delaware River to destroy ships anchored in Barnes and Crosswicks creeks. The invading force consisted of about 800 men, 2 row-galleys, 3 armed craft, and 24 flat-bottomed boats. It anchored opposite the city and succeeded in destroying two frigates. Then landing at Bordentown the British burned the home of Joseph Borden and vandalized the home of Mr. Emley, an influential Whig. British officers dined at the home of Hopkinson, the statesman and his family being absent; a housekeeper was forced to provide food.

In 1816 Joseph Bonaparte, former King of Naples (1806) and Spain (1808) and eldest brother of Napoleon I, arrived to take up residence on an 1,800-acre tract he had purchased in the northern part of the city along Crosswicks Creek.

The exiled monarch, whose power had depended entirely upon the successes of his brother and the French Army, fled uprisings in his kingdoms following the battle of Waterloo in June 1815. He lived for the better part of a year in Philadelphia before settling in Bordentown, where he lived for nineteen years in the grand style of the French court, surrounded by priceless art treasures.

Joseph Bonaparte named his estate Point Breeze (a current housing development perpetuates the name). The former king, using the title Count de Survilliers, cleared the wild acres and built a beautiful mansion which was destroyed by fire in 1820. Many of the great masters' works of art were lost in the blaze. Joseph built a second and even more elaborate dwelling upon the ashes of the old.

A delegation from Mexico waited upon him in 1820, offering him the Mexican throne. He refused the offer much to the displeasure of his brother, who was at that time in exile on St. Helena.

Joseph made his first trip back to Europe in 1832. In 1837 he returned to Bordentown and stayed for two years before returning permanently to Europe, where he died in 1844 at the age of seventy-six. His estate passed into the hands of Henry Beckett, once a British consul in Philadelphia. Joseph's wife never joined him in America, where he was known to local residents as "the good Bonaparte."

Beckett promptly demolished the royal mansion, much to the disgust of the townspeople, who had come to relish Bordentown's new title of "New Spain." Talking to Bordentown residents today one receives the impression that "Becker the Destroyer," as they dubbed him, has never been forgiven. In 1912 Harris Hammond, a Philadelphia millionaire, took over the property and attempted to revive its original splendor. Many of his efforts can still be seen, including attractive grottoes and piles of gray-white rock which once lined an ornate swimming pool. The original Bonaparte gatehouse still stands. The center building of the estate, as remodeled by Hammond, is now the administration office of the Divine Word Seminary, which has taken possession of the sprawling acreage.

Secret tunnels lead from the house to the river. Originally they were used as a means of bringing goods from river boats to the house and also as escape passages. Bonaparte constantly feared political assassins.

The white-calcimined Hoagland Tavern is still intact, although looking strangely out of place with its Spanish design and iron balconies reminiscent of New Orleans. Today it is a private residence.

Looking down Park Street, the eye meets an attractive block of row houses. Bordentown residents refer to the structures as Murat Row, the houses being what is left of Linden Hall, a boarding school for girls opened and operated by Caroline Fraser, a Bordentown belle who had married Napoleon François Lucien Charles Murat, nephew of Joseph and Napoleon Bonaparte. The young prince was a playboy and squandered both his own and his wife's fortunes. Caroline opened the school to recoup her finances.

On November 12, 1831, when Bordentown turned out to see the arrival of the first Camden and Amboy Railroad locomotive, Princess Caroline led the crowd. As the smoke-bellowing engine came into view, many ran for cover, fearing it would explode. Not so Princess Caroline; she stepped forward for a better view. The townspeople followed. Caroline boarded the train and, after a short ride, presided at a luncheon in Arnell's Hotel. A marker at the north end of Bordentown commemorates the event.

After the French Revolution of 1848, Napoleon III recalled Murat to France. Bordentown friends of Princess Caroline were reported to have paid her way to join him.

Clara Barton, founder of the American Red Cross, was a famed daughter of Bordentown. She established one of the first successful free schools in the state in 1852. The school building, said to have been constructed in 1739, is now owned by the New Jersey State Board of Education. It contains Miss Barton's original chair and desk. Miss Barton was thirty-one years of age when she persuaded the city fathers of Bordentown to open the school, donating her services as teacher. The contention that this was New Jersey's first free school is contested by Allaire Village, which had a free school dating to 1834.

Patience Lovell Wright gained recognition for her sculpturing abilities at the age of forty-seven, when she was the mother of four sons. A full-length statue of William Pitt the Elder, executed by her, was placed in Westminster Abbey. Her son Joseph designed some of the first United States coins.

Today Bordentown is a quiet, residential town of 5,400 in-

habitants, steeped in its historic past. It is also the home of the
Edward Johnstone Training and Research Center.

MILITARY "CONVERSATION"

Did you ever attend a "conversation party" or partake of "conversation cards"? Perhaps not, as they seem to have been unique
with the Bordentown Military Institute, founded in 1885 by the
Rev. Thompson H. Landon, D.D., who remained its director
for thirty-two years.

A Methodist clergyman of the old school, the Rev. Mr. Landon
followed a stern "no compromise on liquor, tobacco, or hazing,"
a line which once appeared in the school catalogue. The cadet
of 1885 who violated this canon speedily found himself at the
railroad station with a ticket for home.

Under this strict regime dancing also was taboo. When members of the literary societies desired to entertain their girl friends,
whom they were permitted to invite to the school on a Friday
evening (not more often than once a month from 8 to 10 P.M.),
finding something to do in the way of entertainment called for
a high degree of ingenuity. Thus was the "conversation party"
invented. The girls on arrival were handed "conversation cards"
containing ten subjects, each good for five minutes of conversation with a partner. Subjects included such ideas as "Skating
on the Canal," "Sodas at Carslake's," and "Sleigh Rides to
Columbus."

F. Granville Munson of the class of 1900, writing in a sixtieth
anniversary book of the school, recalled: "There was no checkup
to see the subject was closely followed. I do not recall out of
town guests at these hilarious functions." The word *hilarious* was
used, I am inclined to believe, rather loosely.

The girls involved in these parties were usually from private
schools of the vicinity, the Bordentown Female College on the
hilltop at Farnsworth Avenue (long since replaced by private
dwellings), the Priscilla Braislin School on Prince Street overlooking the Delaware, and the Convent at Crosswicks Street.

A color guard at the gate of Bordentown Military Institute, which was founded in 1885. B.M.I. discontinued its operation in Bordentown in 1972, merging with Lenox School in Lenox, Massachusetts. (Courtesy of Bordentown Military Institute)

The cadets were allowed to escort the girls back to their schools but in a specified time which allowed for no detours or delays.

For at least fifty years prior to 1885, the main building of B.M.I. housed a series of schools. In 1881 William C. Bowen, then president of the Bordentown Female College, purchased the property and named the school Bordentown Military Institute. In 1885 Dr. Landon and his wife and family came to Bordentown and leased the institute from Dr. Bowen. The founding of B.M.I. is officially dated from that time. In 1887 Dr. Landon purchased the property; he served as principal until his death in 1919.

The first faculty consisted of four teachers in addition to the two Landons. A student body numbered twenty-nine. The main building housed all students, the full-time faculty, and the Landon family.

By 1892 the cadet company had increased to sixty-eight and the faculty to twelve. Additions were made to the main building and a drill hall was built which was later converted to a gymnasium.

The Spanish-American War of 1898 interrupted the smooth flow of events at the academy when Dr. Landon's son Thomas D., then commandant, was promoted to the rank of major of the 3d New Jersey Infantry and went off to Cuba. The major gave the academy its note of discipline. To him all students were cadets. He was affectionately known as "Blackbeard" because of the tradition that a razor never touched his face. It took World War I to remove the beard and earn him a promotion to colonel.

The school has provided officers for every war this nation has fought, starting with the Spanish-American. On Arbor Day 1920 twenty-three memorial trees were planted on the school property to honor B.M.I. men who had given their lives in the service of their country in World War I. In the Second World War 1,044 B.M.I. men served their country; 39 were killed in action.

The first faculty of four teachers had grown to 25 by 1970; an original student body of 29 had increased to 300. B.M.I. then had dormitory buildings, 20 classrooms plus a library, administration offices, gymnasium, and several lounges.

In June of 1972 Bordentown was shocked by Headmaster John

B. Huett's announcement that the tight economy and antimilitary feeling had combined to reduce enrollment to the point that the military academy was discontinuing its operation in Bordentown.

The staff was merged with that of Lenox School of Lenox, Massachusetts, under the name of Bordentown-Lenox School. Many cadets transferred to the Massachusetts institution, which offers military training under the auspices of the ROTC on a voluntary basis.

By the end of June 1972, the Bordentown Military Academy was closed, the furnishings removed, and FOR SALE signs were posted on the premises, ending a ninety-one-year tradition.

TAVERNS AND BRIDGES

Remove automobiles from the winding Indian-path streets of Crosswicks, and you might be back in the period when homes were built close together for mutual protection against both foreign invaders and roaming outlaw bands. Stop in at the Hilltop Inn, and you will find an institution that has existed since before the Revolution. The present innkeeper will be happy to show you the sign of the original inn, a treasured possession. Walk across the street to the Crosswicks Meeting House and gaze on the great oak which was there before William Penn founded Philadelphia.

Crosswicks—or Crosswicke, as it is sometimes spelled on old maps—is on a creek of the same name about four miles from Bordentown. It derives its name from the Indian word *Crossweeksung,* meaning a separation. Some people maintain that the separation referred to was the creek. Indian authorities say it was customary for Indian maidens to leave the village at certain times of the year and live in a hut for a fixed number of days before returning to the tribe; therefore the "separation" of Crosswicks.

Crosswicks was first settled by members of the Society of Friends in 1681 and grew to a place of importance in the days just prior and during the Revolution. The General Assembly of the state met there in October of 1716 and continued the sessions until January of 1717. Tradition says the meetings were held in the open under the trees; historians favor the old meeting house.

The town gained its page in American history in June of 1778, when the British troops, who had already passed through Bordentown scattering destruction as they marched to Monmouth, attempted to cross the drawbridge at Crosswicks. To prevent the crossing, local patriots had disabled the bridge. The troops attempted to repair it, but were attacked by the patriots on the Crosswicks side and forced to retreat, carrying with them four dead and several wounded. The British regrouped, made another attack, and in a skirmish a British officer and several men were wounded and one Continental soldier was killed—Job Clevenger, who had been shot as he attempted to cut the last underpinning of the bridge. In their second attempt the British succeeded in passing over the span, which was the one link between the village of Crosswicks and Woodwardville.

During this action colonial troops entrenched on the Woodwardville side fired their small cannon at the invaders. One of the cannon balls lodged in the Crosswicks Meeting House. This ball can be seen today in its original niche, although for a time it was missing. An ardent villager had taken it as a memento of the occasion. Upon his death, trustees of the Crosswicks Meeting regained possession of the cannon ball and returned it to its spot in the walls.

The meeting house at Crosswicks, known officially as the Chesterfield Meeting, is perhaps one of the largest in the southern Jersey area. The original house of worship dates to 1693; the present two-story building of brick with its white shutters was built in 1773.

On the spacious grounds stands the Crosswicks Oak, estimated to be about three hundred years old. It is 17½ feet in girth and more than 80 feet high. In the center of the meeting house is an iron stove with the inscription ATSION, indicating that it came from the Atsion furnace. After the battle of Trenton, Crosswicks was occupied by Continental troops, who, according to village historians, always made sure pews were back in place and the main rooms in perfect condition for First Day meeting.

The first tavern at Crosswicks was set up shortly after the founding of the village in 1681 by John Bainbridge, who in 1689, according to available records, lost the license for selling "firewater" to the Indians. There is a 1743 record of Joseph Borden offering a house for sale "near the meeting house," which according to the advertisement had "been a Publick House for many Years past." It is possible that this house was the one originally operated by John Bainbridge, although actual proof is hard to come by, according to Charles Boyer.

Thomas Douglass, son-in-law of Joseph Borden, Sr., secured a tavern license for Crosswicks in 1744 and kept it until his death in 1768. Joseph Douglass, son of Thomas, operated the tavern during the Revolutionary period. He was also township clerk from 1790 to 1796. His son Benjamin conducted the business for a couple of years before turning it over to William McKnight. In 1812 John Horsfall ran the McKnight tavern; he was the first of a succession of operators, mostly renters. In 1845 Job Silver applied for a license for the Crosswicks Hotel or Douglass House. The place was known as Stead's Hotel following the appearance of Joseph Stead as owner in 1852. A map of Crosswicks in the Scott Atlas of 1876 shows the present Hilltop Tavern as the Crosswicks Hotel and next to it the home of J. Stead.

There were two other taverns in Crosswicks. The Bird in Hand was located on the north side of the Old York Road, now Main Street. Benjamin Davis was the original owner (1762–67). Sometime after 1826 the tavern was turned into a private dwelling. (It does not appear as a tavern on the Scott map of 1876.) The Red House was established in 1789 by James Davison, who kept it until 1817.

The oldest house in Crosswicks is said to be that belonging to Joseph Hendrickson on Buttonwood Street. It dates back to 1750.

At the Union Fire Company hall, built in 1882, there is an old hand-pump engine dated 1774 once owned by the Union Fire Company of Philadelphia, which was founded by Benjamin Franklin.

Before enactment of the law creating public schools, Crosswicks had three sectarian schools, one Methodist and two Quaker; the latter were conducted by the Orthodox group until 1901.

An 1876 map shows a harness and carriagemaker—Hartman Brothers—on Main Street, a Methodist and a Presbyterian church as well as I. and J. Woolman's store, also on Main Street.

Crosswicks had its place in the Civil War as the setting of an underground railroad depot conducted by Enoch Middleton in and around his fine mansion on the north bank of Crosswicks Creek. Middleton was a retired Philadelphia merchant. He had twelve children all of whom seemed to have been engaged in the runaway slave enterprise. The railroad had a number of routes, including one from the Delaware Breakwater along the river to Bordentown, then across the state to New York by way of New Brunswick.

Middleton had many narrow escapes with the law but always seemed able to outwit the constables and sheriffs, who knew of his activities but could never prove them.

Crosswicks today is a charming blend of present and past. Through good planning the village has been able to outlaw the unsightly signs and neon lights that would otherwise detract from its quiet charm. Walking down Main Street is like stepping into an elaborate movie set of colonial America.

A MOUNT OF HOLLY

Mount Holly was one of the first towns settled by the Quakers south of Burlington. Today the township contains some 1,500 acres, three quarters of which are within the town itself. Under a deed conveyed by Edward Byllynge and trustees on March 2, 1676, Thomas Rudyard and John Ridges ran out lines of 871 acres of land which constitute the present site of the town. In 1681 a parcel of land on Rancocas Creek was surveyed. It contained a hill of holly trees. From this comes the earliest reference to the area as Mounthalli or Mount Holly.

On July 15, 1685, Ridges authorized Samuel Jennings to sell

his land. Sixteen years later, on March 14, 1701, Jennings sold the entire 871 acres to Edward Gaskill and Josiah Southwick. On March 19, 1720, they divided the property. Gaskill and James Lippincott dammed Rancocas Creek and erected a sawmill on Mill Street in 1723; a year later a gristmill was added. Samuel Brian purchased land adjacent to the gristmill and erected a bolting mill. All the early mills were destroyed by fires.

Josiah White, a native of Salem County, appeared on the scene about 1730 and bought land south of the millrace known as Gaskill's Neck. The seller was Samuel Gaskill. White built a fulling mill on Pine Street which was destroyed by fire in 1881.

Isaac Pearson, Mahlon Stacy, and John Burr started an ironworks in 1730 on land south of Rancocas Creek near the old Pine Street sawmill site. When the British invaded Mount Holly in 1778 this mill was the first building they destroyed; it was never rebuilt. A house occupied by Carr at 21 Garden Street is among the oldest identified houses in the community.

In the late 1700s the Rancocas was navigable as far as Mount Holly. As a result the town had a boat landing and considerable water trade. Timber was floated downstream and cut at Mount Holly. The last merchant boat known to have made the trip to Mount Holly was the *Fleetwing,* owned by William B. Wills. By 1888 the creek began to shallow, and all boat commerce stopped.

Mount Holly boasts the oldest organized fire company in the United States, Relief Fire Company No. 1, formed in 1752 as the Britannia Fire Company, which name appears on several of the old leather buckets preserved in the original building located on the premises of the current company on Pine Street. The city also has the fifth oldest library in the state, chartered by George III on June 11, 1764, through William Franklin, governor general of New Jersey. A photostat of the charter and 150 books of the original collection are on display at the present library building.

Another Mount Holly institution received its charter from King George III—Saint Andrew's Episcopal Church in 1765. The present building dates to 1844.

Mount Holly was originally known as Bridgeton because of

the many bridges over the creek. It was under the name of Bridgeton that the original library was chartered. The town was a hotbed of patriots in the Revolution, with the townspeople determined to hold the place against the invading British with whatever means they could muster. These means were inadequate to stem the tide of the better-equipped British troops who overran the town and made the residents pay for their resistance by many humiliations.

Troops were quartered with people who were forced to feed them under threat of destruction of their homes. A fine old Quaker meeting house in the center of the town, dating from 1775, was turned into a butchershop and stable by the invaders. Cuts made by the meat cleavers can still be seen on some of the benches of the old building.

The British also took possession of a church and school on what is now Brainerd Street. So deep was the feeling of the British against patriot-preacher John Brainerd that they burned his church before the troops left town in 1778. The school, constructed in 1759 by a group of Mount Holly citizens, escaped destruction. It is the oldest school building in the state still on its original site. A restoration was accomplished by the National Society of Colonial Dames in the State of New Jersey in 1959.

The old meeting house was the site of two joint sessions of the state legislature while Mount Holly was the temporary capital of New Jersey when the British descended upon Trenton in 1779.

Among Mount Holly's famed citizens of the colonial period was Stephen Girard, founder of Girard College, who moved there in 1777 after the British occupation of Philadelphia. He operated a small candy and rum store on Mill Street. The house, said to have been occupied by Girard from July 1777 to July 1778, is still standing at 211 Mill Street.

Another well-known citizen of the community in those days was John Woolman, who won fame as the "Quaker preacher." He built a house at 99 Branch Street in 1783 which is still in existence. The Thomas Budd house at 20 White Street is the oldest identified and authenticated house in Mount Holly; it bears the date 1744.

Burlington City was the original county seat of Burlington County. In an election on February 18, 1795, Mount Holly was chosen as the new county seat. The vote was Mount Holly 1,675, Burlington 1,432, and Black Horse (Columbus) 142. A courthouse, still in use, was built in 1796 on land purchased from John Powell for the reported sum of 210 pounds. It is considered one of the finest examples of colonial architecture in the nation. Samuel Lewis, who also drew the plans for Congress Hall in Philadelphia, designed the courthouse building.

The first court session in Mount Holly was held in 1796. Sitting were Judges John Lacey, Isaac Cowgill, Josiah Foster, and Ebenezer Tucker. A bell cast in England in 1755 which had hung in the old Burlington County courthouse was moved to the new court building. Here it announced the opening of sessions until 1959, when major courts were transferred to a new county structure on Rancocas Road. Two small buildings flanking the courthouse were added in 1805.

During its infancy Mount Holly had a public market place located at the intersection of Main and Mill streets, Dobbins Avenue, and Washington Street. The last market was built on the site in 1799; it was torn down in 1838. A whipping post and stocks stood at the eastern end of the market house.

BICYCLES, BANDS, AND A MOOSE

There are two Smithvilles in South Jersey. The one in Burlington County is usually referred to as the "bicycle town" to distinguish it from the Atlantic County complex of restored stores and inns. Smithville acquired its unique title because of the bicycle railway which existed between the H. B. Smith Machine Company plant in Smithville and Mount Holly, where most of the plant's workers had their homes. It operated from the late 1880s to 1894, and its prime purpose was to afford quick and cheap transportation for the Smith company workers.

The railway was constructed by William H. Hotchkiss of Vermont from plans developed by Hezekiah Bradley Smith, founder

The American Star bicycle, with its seat over the high rear wheel, was invented by George Washington Pressey of Hammonton in 1888. Manufacturer Hezekiah Smith publicized it by developing a grooved iron track, which he called "The Bicycle Railway," on which employees could ride the American Star from the plant in Smithville to their homes in Mount Holly. (Courtesy of the Smithsonian Institution)

of Smithville. He was assisted by Thomas Shinn and Ivins Russell. The bicycles used were the famous American Star brand invented by George Washington Pressey of Hammonton, New Jersey, who revolutionized the wheel industry with his high-wheel vehicle. These cycles were manufactured at the Smith plant; the ones used on the railway were both single and tandem.

Hezekiah Smith was a unique combination of businessman and publicist. Born in Bridgewater, Vermont, in 1816, Smith—

like many a New Englander before him—saw a promising future in South Jersey. He found a spot he liked near Mount Holly. Two brothers by the name of Shreve operated a waterpower mill there and called the place Shreveport.

Smith envisioned a guild village of master craftsmen, like those popular in Europe. He bought the Shreve plant and about two thousand acres of land and began modernizing the operation. One of Smith's first acts was to change the name of the community from Shreveport to Smithville, with the Post Office Department concurring. Smithville it has since remained.

The new owner constructed his town around the plant. He built a hall for theatricals and meetings, encouraged founding of a library, and laid out small farms on the outskirts of his holdings. The machine shop was incorporated as the H. B. Smith Machine Company.

Workmen found it difficult to get from Mount Holly to Smithville as there was no public transportation available. Some walked; some rode horseback. The cycle railway was Smith's solution to the situation. Big things were predicted for this transportation facility, but it fell into disuse when Smith died.

In a bid for publicity Smith organized his own band and campaigned for public office—he was never bashful. Smith was elected to Congress and served from 1879 to 1881. He was elected to the state senate, serving from 1883 to 1885. Smith always took his musicians with him on public appearances and was an expert at the grand entrance style. The band even played a concert at the Academy of Music in Philadelphia.

Another of Smith's publicity projects was a moose broken to harness. Smith would drive about the countryside in this odd setup. According to tradition, many a tippler coming unexpectedly across Smith and his moose took a dive in the nearest stream to sober up. The moose apparently was popular with Smith but with no one else as it frightened horses and caused many a rig to be wrecked. Rare flower cultivation was another of Smith's hobbies.

With the death of Smith in 1877 his town and business went to pieces, the band played its last note and disbanded, the moose found a new home in a zoo, and Smith's greenhouses were soon victims of neglect. While still a community today, Smithville never recovered its colorful past when Hezekiah dominated the scene and brought his town fame as the home of the nation's only bicycle railway.

BLACK HEALER OF THE PINES

The pines of South Jersey spawned many interesting characters. One of the most beloved was James Still, known to history as the "black doctor of the pines." You will not find his name in the proceedings of the New Jersey Medical Society or in state license records, for as far as can be ascertained Still never possessed a license to practice. Yet in the deep pines, where he served as a healing physician, there were those who swore by him. Still gave generously of his natural talents, and his patients had utmost faith in his simple remedies.

James Still was born April 9, 1812, in a log cabin at Indian Mills, the offspring of freed slaves Levin and Charity Still. The family had the bare necessities of life and little hope of improving their lot. Levin Still, who had bought their freedom, worked hard and long at woodcutting and land clearing. Things were not easy for a freed slave in the North in those days. There was always suspicion and fear of being picked up and returned to bondage in the South. That is why the Stills, although supposedly protected by law, chose the deep woods in preference to the white man's world of uncertainty. Most of their friends were either fellow blacks or Indians who had preferred to stay at Indian Mills after most of the red men of the area moved to New York state.

James Still might have lived out his life in the drudgery of a farmhand had it not been for the chance visit by city physician Dr. Fort to vaccinate children of the area. The boy watched in wide-eyed wonder what to him was a miracle man, almost a reincarnation of the Jesus he had been told about from the Bible, the only book in the Still household. James became fired with an ambition that was to dominate his life—to become a doctor. His

Unable to afford formal medical training, James Still learned how to use herbs from his Indian neighbors, read medical books, and cared for the sick in the Pine Barrens in the mid-1800s. (Rutgers University Library Special Collections)

mother, knowing the great odds against this uneducated black youth in a hostile environment, did not encourage him, saying, "You just tend to your chores and keep out of trouble."

In 1877, writing in autobiographical fashion as he reviewed his years, Still stated: "My parents were poor and unable to school their children. Their main object was to provide bread for us." Still's formal education, as he recalled, was: "Three months' instruction in reading, writing, and numbering."

As soon as the boy was able to work he was bound out to farmer Amos Wilkins, who had cleared land for the raising of vegetables. An older brother had already been bound to another farmer of the vicinity. According to common custom in those days, James was to do whatever jobs Wilkins demanded, in return for which he was provided with room and board and one month's schooling each year. On his twenty-first birthday he was free of the contract, given a new suit and $10 in cash. During his indenture James Still spent all his spare hours reading, especially books he could find on botany.

Out of bondage at age twenty-one, James decided to seek work in Philadelphia. After a tearful farewell, he set out by back roads, in fear of being picked up as a runaway slave, and made his way to the Delaware River, crossing in a horseboat, a flat craft used to transport animals.

James Still found his race and his lack of education severe handicaps. The only jobs open to him were menial ones. Instead of bitterness, these conditions spurred his determination to achieve his one ambition. He secured a job at a glue factory. This did not suit his sensitive nature, but he persevered until he was promoted to a better position. Meanwhile the young black boy met and married a girl named Angelina Willow. There was one child. Angelina contracted tuberculosis and died a few years after this marriage. Their baby, given to Still's mother, also failed to survive.

Still was once more alone. He left the glue factory and spent more and more time with books, teaching himself the meaning of Latin medical terms and increasing his knowledge of basic medicines. During his years in the pines he had become friendly with Indian neighbors, going with them on excursions to pick herbs which they taught him to use. The combination of book knowledge plus Indian know-how served him as a base of his future work.

He married again, an orphan girl who worked on one of the pineland farms. They returned to the vicinity of Indian Mills, and Still began clearing a farm of his own. Believing that he had sufficient knowledge to produce medicines, Still bought distilling equipment. His mixtures were those of herbs furnished by the pines, such as sassafras root, skunk cabbage, and snakeroot.

One of his first cases, as recorded by Still in his writings, was a neighbor's child who had contracted scrofula, a condition of tuberculous nature manifesting itself in the swelling of glands, especially of the neck, with a tendency of chronic inflammation of the skin and tuberculosis of the bones. It occurred mostly among the children of the Pineys.

Still explained this case: "To this time I had made tinctures for my own family. One of the neighbors brought his daughter to me. She had developed scrofula, and he asked me to help. I gave her medicine which soon cured her. I thought it no great thing, for it always seemed to me that all diseases were curable and I wondered why doctors did not cure them."

Word spread along the pines that "we have a doctor among us." Others began coming to Still for help, and he ministered to them.

Charles and William Ellis, Philadelphia pharmacists, also heard of the doctor and offered to buy all the mixtures he could give them. With this extra money, Still bought a small house at a place known as Cross-Roads. He constructed a wagon and began traveling the dusty roads of the pines, his medical kit a box under the seat of his wagon. He was known to spend long hours at the bedside of a patient in a cabin, nursing a fever until it broke, and then, after a cup of strong coffee, continuing his way in the early dawn.

As his "practice" increased, doctors of nearby Medford filed a protest against Still for practicing without a license. Still refuted the charges on the grounds that he never asked fees, nor did he ever actually claim to be a doctor. Friends advised him to consult the law. He talked to attorney John C. Ten Eyck of Mount Holly who, according to Still, advised: "You can sell medicine and charge for delivering. . . . There is a fine for giving prescriptions but you don't give them. You sell medicine and nothing can stop you."

With this assurance Still returned to a growing list of patients. Everyone referred to him as Dr. Still. His greatest successes were with scrofula although he treated some cancer cases and claimed to have effected cures when other physicians pronounced them hopeless. There is no real evidence to this effect.

Still paid off the mortgage on his property and traded his

rickety wagon for a better carriage. In 1849 he moved into a larger house next to a tavern. Eventually he bought the tavern near the crossroads at Mount Holly Road and Church Road for his headquarters. Finding himself too busy for root digging, he hired Abraham Corson to do it for him.

Through hard work and long hours Still acquired much land in the vicinity of Medford and Indian Mills, but tireless devotion to medical duties brought on a slight stroke. This necessitated an end to his wagon trips. Thereafter he confined his activities to treating patients at his home. According to the people of the region, long lines of horses and carriages clogged the road to the Still house. These people came from such towns as Medford, Red Lion, Beaverville, Friendship, Hampton Gate, Buddtown, Oriental, and Indian Mills.

Still might have been another lost tale of the pinelands were it not for the discovery of his autobiography and the early writings of Henry C. Beck concerning him. Interest in the man was revived in 1966, when the New Jersey Bell Telephone Company commissioned a portrait of the "black doctor" for a folder. This painting by Charles Waterhouse later hung in the Burlington County National Bank and was shown in offices of the phone company throughout the state. The Medford Historical Society arranged a permanent home for it in a museum at Kirby's Mill.

THE DREAM THAT FAILED

The crossroads in Indian Mills, Burlington County, was the site of the final New Jersey campfire of the Lenni-Lenape Indians.

As early as 1758 members of the Lenape tribe living in southern Jersey felt crowded by the white men who continued to arrive and settle on Lenape land. The Lenapes moved back into the forests as the seashore areas became more densely populated.

In the northern part of the state, especially in Sussex County, things were not as peaceful as in the pines of southern Jersey. The French were still using Indians to fight the British and had brought a number from Canada, turning them loose on the settlers. Twenty-seven persons were murdered by those Indians between May 1757 and June 1758.

This prompted newly arrived Governor Francis Bernard to call a meeting of the Provincial Assembly at Burlington on August 9, 1758, to deal with the situation. To this conference were invited tribal leaders of the Lenni-Lenape, especially Chief Teedyuskung of the Delawares and Chief Benjamin of the Munsees. At that time the Lenape presented a written request for a permanent home. They asked for the region of Shamong in Eversham Township, Burlington County (Indian Mills).

As a result of this meeting another session of the Assembly was called by the governor for August 12, at which time 1,600 pounds were appropriated to buy approximately 3,000 acres for use of the Lenape tax-free. The purchase—3,284 acres—was made from Benjamin Springer and Richard Smith at a location known as Edgepillock, which became the first Indian reservation in the state. Governor Bernard suggested that it be called "Brotherton," where all men could live as brothers—all red men, that is. Privileges of the reservation were later extended to the Narragansetts, the Mohicans, Mohawks, Pequots, and Nanticokes, although there is scant evidence that members of any of those tribes ever occupied the reservation for any length of time.

About two hundred red men settled in Brotherton, and no white man was allowed to fish or hunt there.

In 1746 missionary David Brainerd had set up a mission at Cranbury, Middlesex County. He died on October 9, 1747, but his younger brother John continued the work, laboring and preaching at Crosswicks, Vincentown, and Cranbury. John Brainerd settled in Brotherton in 1758. In 1958 the Archeological Society of New Jersey erected an iron marker bearing the dates 1758–1801 which depicts the Rev. John Brainerd preaching to the Lenape at that spot.

Brainerd was appointed superintendent of the reservation in 1762. He worked under many handicaps, especially lack of funds. Small amounts of money came from the Presbyterian Synod and a few dollars from the College of New Jersey at Princeton, but there was never enough. Brainerd advanced $200 of his own money to build a log church. He taught the Indians agriculture as practiced by the white man so their garden plots would yield a variety of food. For fifteen years he toiled at the reservation. Then the rigorous demands of the Indian life he led, suffering from poor food, many times the lack of it, took its toll of him as it had his brother. John Brainerd died in March of 1781.

In the next twenty years, during which the Lenapes were more or less left to shift for themselves, various persons stopped at the reservation, preached, and drifted on. By 1800 there were only one hundred of the original two hundred Indians at Brotherton.

Many of the younger Lenape who had been taught trades by Brainerd found work in the iron forges and glass factories. Others helped in the damming of Edgepillock stream and set up a saw-mill and a gristmill. Brotherton eventually took the name of Indian Mills, by which it is known today.

However, the older tribal members were unhappy. When the Oneida Indians of New York state issued an invitation to the Brothertons, to "pack your mat and come eat out of our dish," they accepted. They petitioned the state of New Jersey to allow sale of the reservation to raise money to pay for the transportation of those who wanted to move. The legislature acted favorably on this petition in 1801.

In May of 1802 a wagon train of twelve rented vehicles started to New Stockbridge, New York. Leading the train was Elisha Ashataina, also called Lashar Tamar, last chief of the Brotherton Indians. The few who stayed behind soon became integrated into the white communities of South Jersey and lost their tribal identity.

Chief Tamar stayed with his people for a time in New York and then returned to New Jersey, settling on the Woolman farm near the town of Rancocas.

After sharing the hospitality of the Oneidas for several years the surviving Brotherton Indians, now numbering only about forty, decided to move west and purchase lands from Indians living near Green Bay, Wisconsin. The New Jersey legislature appropriated $3,551.23 out of money which had been held in trust for the Lenape after sale of the Brotherton reservation; this provided for the resettlement in Wisconsin in 1832 which they called Statesburg.

Bartholomew S. Calvin, known also by his Indian name of Wilted Grass, carried on much of the negotiation between the tribe and the state of New Jersey. It was he who penned the letter of thanks to the lawmakers in which he stated: "Not a drop of our blood have you spilled in battle; not an acre of our land have you taken but by our consent. These facts speak for themselves and need no comment. They place the character of New Jersey in bold relief, a bright example to those States within whose territorial limits our brothers still remain."

Small groups of the Indians from New Jersey settled in lands west of the Mississippi River with the Cherokees and Osages. Some later went to Indian Territory, now Oklahoma. In 1964 the New Jersey Tercentenary Committee brought back, as guests of the state, representatives of the former Lenapes—who had left Indian Mills in 1802.

There was a postscript to this story in the legal wrangling resulting from the clause of the original act involving the Brotherton Indians which exempted their lands from taxation "for all times." The act of 1801 authorizing sale of the lands was silent on this matter—a legal oversight. In 1803, with the Lenape gone from the area and the land in private hands, the township assessor declared the land taxable and proceeded to assess.

The new owners took the case to court in September of 1804, and the assessments were set aside. In December 1804 the state repealed the act of 1758 creating the reservation. In 1805 the tax collector again ordered the lands assessed. In another court action the assessment was held legal by the State Supreme Court in November 1807. Owners carried their case to the United States Supreme Court, which in 1812 ruled the act of 1804 unconstitutional.

In 1814 the local assessor ignored the Supreme Court ruling and again assessed the lands. Owners decided to pay without protest, and such payment continued until 1877. In that year the assessment was again challenged. The State Supreme Court affirmed the validity of the assessment on the grounds the owners had acknowledged the right of the township to assess by paying taxes between the years 1814 and 1877 and thus had surrendered the right of exemption. This seemed to settle the matter.

INDIAN ANN

Indian Ann was a basket weaver in the Indian Mills, Tabernacle Township, farmlands of Burlington County. Descendants of old area families recall tales of Indian Ann told by their parents. I believe the facts have been extended to the point of becoming legend rather than history.

According to most of these tales, Indian Ann was of average height and build and wore her long black hair in braids. Her usual costume was the typical shirtwaist housedress of the day. Ann was a pipe smoker and usually had a clay one in her mouth.

One of the last known survivors of the Brotherton Indians, Ann made straw baskets for a livelihood. They were of varied sizes and shapes, and it was Ann's habit to wander about with a basket under her arm. If a housewife had just baked she might put a loaf of fresh bread into the basket. If a farmer had a hog killing he might put in a piece of pork. It is the legend of Indian Mills that Indian Ann never went home empty-handed.

She was the possessor of a clock that had to be wound each week with an iron key. Afraid to undertake that task herself, she usually had someone do it for her. Howard Weeks of Indian Mills noted that he served as clock winder on many occasions.

It is not known where Indian Ann was born. Her father was Chief Lasha Tamar.

Ann was twice married. Her first husband was Peter Green, said to have been a former slave. Her second husband was John Roberts, a Negro who settled with Ann in a small frame house on the Dingletown Road, not far from Indian Mills. Ann reared seven children, Peter, John, Samuel, Richard, Hester, Ann, and Lydia.

John Roberts served in the Civil War as a member of Company A, 22d Regiment of Colored Troops, having enlisted in this all-volunteer company in December 1863. He died in an army hospital, at Yorktown, Virginia, on February 17, 1864. In 1880 Indian Ann applied for and received a pension of $8 a month; it was increased to $12 in 1886. Her age on the pension application was given as seventy-five, which suggests that she may have been born on the Woolman farm near Rancocas in 1805 when her father returned from New York.

Indian Ann lived on this small pension supplemented by what she earned from her basket sales and in picking wild berries. She became a familar figure, traveling to Vincentown and Mount Holly to sell her baskets.

Ann died in December of 1894 and is buried in the Methodist cemetery in Tabernacle. A stone marker was put on her grave through the efforts of N. R. Ewan, an authority on New Jersey Indians, and the Burlington County Historical Society.

The old house in which Indian Ann lived was destroyed by fire shortly after her death.

THE PINE BARRENS

The vast Pine Barrens, stretching through most of the lower part of Burlington County and on into Ocean County, have been many things to many people. This still-undeveloped region was a haven for the Tories of Philadelphia and upper Jersey fleeing the wrath of the Continentals following the Revolution. It was also the jungle into which roving bandit bands such as the Mulliners and the Gibersons could disappear when law forces were too close on their trail. Early iron empire builders found that the Pine Barrens were lands of plenty with unlimited resources for their enterprises. Wandering preachers found the Barrens a place where their gospels of hellfire and brimstone were easily accepted. To Joseph Wharton, Philadelphia industrialist, the Barrens represented a vast watershed whose underground rivers would assure Philadelphia a pure water supply for generations.

Others found the Barrens offered a way of life where few questions were asked and the pace was easy.

For many years residents of the Pine Barrens have been called

Pineys and likened to the Hatfield and McCoy clans of the Kentucky mountains. They eke out what some might term a miserable existence, but they are quick to point out that they do not consider themselves the comic characters they have sometimes been painted. Their principal complaint these days is that so many writers and newspaper feature specialists have invaded their domain that they have no privacy left; every time an article appears a fresh load of tourists follows. Contrary to popular opinion, most of the Pineys are hardworking at tasks often considered mean, such as gathering moss, picking cranberry and blueberry crops.

The Pine Barrens, named for the stunted growth found there, contain nearly two million acres of timberland. They are the home of most of the remaining wildlife of South Jersey—deer, fox, rabbits, quail, beavers, raccoons, and skunks. Actual boundary lines are a matter of guesswork. Ownership of much of the land cannot be traced, and taxes in many parts of the Barrens are nonexistent.

The Wharton Tract occupies the greater part of the pinelands and barrens in Cumberland County. This great tract was assembled by Joseph Wharton in his plan for a Philadelphia watershed. When this fell through, he sold it to the state of New Jersey. The state now owns nearly 150,000 acres, which are designated a green-acre area. Cranberry bogs around Hog Wallow and Chatsworth are highly productive.

An old map of 1889 shows names of many towns in the Pine Barrens which today are practically impossible to locate. Among these are Herrmann City, Quaker Bridge, Washington, Crowleyville, Speedwell, Friendship, Bulltown, Calico, Martha, Mount Washington, Jones Mill, Long Causeway, Duke's Bridge, Eagle, Hampton, Delletts, Pestletown, Hedger House, Butler Place, Lebanon, Four Mile, Munton Field, Upper Mill, Ong's Hat, Union Clay, Howardville, Mount Misery, Double Trouble, Friendship Bogs, Boar Stag, Ceder Grove, Mary Ann Furnace, Lower Mill, and Harrisville.

Among the better-known places, because of either state restoration projects or current boating prominence, are Atsion, Batsto, Lower Bank, Green Bank, and New Gretna.

On a recent visit to the ruins of Harrisville I passed a place called Leektown which contains a half dozen houses and two hunting lodges. According to the villager who gave me directions to Harrisville—"You just passed it"—most of the inhabitants are named Leek, hence Leektown. Then there is Friendship, a crumbling gathering of old houses. Jenkins Neck does a bit better with about fourteen houses and two hunting shacks.

Chatsworth is the city of the pines. Only three miles off State Route 72, it has a population of about three hundred and a general store, a gas station, and a post office.

Despite what some people want to believe, the present-day Pineys are a friendly lot once they are convinced you don't have hidden motives in prying about their diggings. There is some moonshining going on in the pines, but not as much as one might think. The Pineys are too busy with other activities. One old fellow told me that if the visitors keep coming he might even set up a motel, "with outside plumbing, of course."

According to local lore, pirates once buried their treasure along the Jersey coast. More practical historians feel that this was not true as the treasure would have been dug up by other pirates. They point out that the Barrens offered a natural hiding place. Although there have been many attempts to find this treasure, searchers have received only muddy boots for their efforts.

It was noticed at one time that a number of the old Pineys spoke with a German accent. This may have been the result of the many Hessian mercenaries of the Revolution who, after the first battle of Trenton, disappeared into the pines, deserting their regiments and setting up a new life. There are believed to be many descendants of these men.

The Pineys claim the "Jersey Devil" as their own, stating that the legendary monster still roams the swamps near the Mullica River. There are plenty of other folklore characters in the pine belt such as Fiddler Sammy Buck, who according to legend once outfiddled the Devil himself in a contest. The Barrens also have a version of Paul Bunyan in Jesse Johnson, who is said to have been capable of carrying a whole wagonload of stone on his shoulders. Henry Bisbee tells me that there are many versions of this story and the one about Jerry Munyhon, the wizard, who is said to have caused trees to chop themselves down. Hunting season is the best time to get a line on these tall stories, a warm fire and a few bolts of "Jersey lightnin'" being an ideal combination to garnish the telling.

Many signs point to the ghost towns of the pines, some so faded as to be barely readable. It is foolhardy to take some of the sand roads to which they point, unless you are on foot. A car is sure to get stuck.

The younger generation of the Pineys are gradually leaving the wilderness as schooling takes them farther afield than their kinfolk. Many have gone to college and said goodbye to the pines forever. Migrant workers come in to help with the cranberry harvest. They usually prove clannish and leave when the picking season is over. Some of the pickers are employed by William Haines, who owns the big Hog Wallow cranberry operation. Haines is a Piney in reverse—he was not born in the pines, but arrived there from Vincentown to take over the bogs started by his grandfather. Haines is a scientific farmer, and his farm is a favorite place of experimental crews from Rutgers Agricultural College. Haines has 575 acres of his 3,000-acre holdings in cranberry bogs. His equipment is mechanized; he lives in a ranch-type house.

It is interesting to note that the geographical center of the East Coast megalopolis lies in Washington Township near Hog Wallow. Civilization has made many inroads of the vast pinelands of Burlington County and will no doubt make more; meanwhile the Pine Barrens is a still picturesque, distinctive part of the Garden State.

ATSION, AN IRON GHOST

Atsion, in Shamong Township near the Burlington-Atlantic county line on Route 206, was rescued from the wilderness by historians.* Hewed from thick forests in 1765 by Colonel Charles Read, Atsion flourished as an ironmaking town until 1846, when, with the collapse of the iron industry in South Jersey, the town was partially abandoned. It revived as a papermill operation until the depression of 1854. Cottonmaking was tried but also failed, and the community was finally left to nature. Its disappearance would have been complete had it not been for a successful campaign by historic groups of the area, including the Batsto Citizens Committee, to have it declared a historic site and restored by the state of New Jersey. The state acquired Atsion as part of the Wharton Tract purchase.

Charles Read, builder of the Atsion furnace, was the third of that family by the name of Charles. His grandfather Charles, a Quaker, came from England about 1669 and settled in Burlington, later in Philadelphia. The second Charles was a Philadelphia merchant and mayor of that city in 1726–27. Charles of Atsion was born in Philadelphia on February 1, 1715, and spent much of his life working for his father. He was fifty-one years old when he began his ironmaking career. Earlier he had been a midshipman in the British Navy, assigned to Antigua, where he met and married Alice Thibou, daughter of a rich plantation owner. The couple returned to Philadelphia. Finding society there cold to his new bride, Read moved to Burlington, where he planned his iron empire.

Read also dabbled in state politics and held numerous offices. He was collector of customs at Burlington during the height of the hijacking of British ships by the privateers of Chestnut Neck, Tuckerton, and Toms River. He was commissioned a justice of the State Supreme Court on August 17, 1753, although there is no evidence that he had studied law.

Read operated Atsion until 1773, when a series of financial

---

* The name Atsion, also used for the portion of the Mullica River above the village of Atsion, was Indian in origin. A small group of Lenni-Lenapes calling themselves Axions referred to the area as Atsyunk and Atsiung. On Thomas Budd's survey of 1838 the name appears as Atsyunk. A map by Van der Donck used the spelling Atsayonck. The first post office used Atsion on August 18, 1797. All iron and cotton operations used the name Atsion Works.

failures forced him to sell. He departed suddenly for the West Indies without bothering to resign from his many state jobs. Later he returned to the United States and settled in the backwoods of North Carolina, where he died in obscurity.

In 1774 Atsion had new owners in Henry Drinker, Abel Jones, and Lawrence Salter, who continued the iron operations. Atsion next changed owners in 1805, when the land and buildings passed into the hands of Jacob Downing.

In 1823 Samuel Richards, whose father William operated Batsto, a few miles from Atsion, became owner. The restored ironmaster's house on the site today is considered one of the finest examples of Greek Revival architecture in South Jersey. It was built in 1826 by Samuel Richards.

Thirteen iron columns cast at Weymouth support the porch roof. Window sills are of iron. A north veranda was later added. This was removed in the restoration to give the place its original lines. There are thirteen rooms in the mansion; cooking was done in a basement room. Richards spent the spring and summer months at Atsion, returning to his Philadelphia home for the winter.

Samuel Richards had learned the ironmaking business from his father at Batsto. By 1808 he had made his first personal iron acquisitions, Martha Furnace and Weymouth Furnace. It was during his occupancy that Atsion reached its peak. When Richards died on January 4, 1842, Atsion consisted of some 24 dwellings and a church besides the factory buildings. The working force numbered more than 120 men. Richards left the Atsion estate to his daughter Maria and son William Henry.

Maria married William Walton Fleming of Charleston, South Carolina, who took over the operation of Atsion. The couple lived in the mansion. Fleming is important to the Atsion story as he carried on the work there until the time of the bog iron collapse and then built a paper factory on the site between the years 1851 and 1854. His operation lost heavily in the depression of 1854. With liabilities of more than a half million dollars, Fleming signed over his properties. Here history repeats itself— Fleming left the country hurriedly as had his predecessor. Unlike Read, he never returned, settling in Brussels, Belgium.

The home of ironmaster Samuel Richards at Atsion before restoration by the New Jersey State Department of Conservation and Economic Development. Built in 1826, the house had iron window sills, and the porch roof was supported by thirteen columns of iron cast at the Weymouth works. (William McMahon Collection)

After several transactions Atsion came into the hands of Colonel William C. Patterson of Philadelphia in 1862. He renamed the place Fruitland and offered the estate in lots for farming. Patterson soon was in financial difficulties and took the usual procedure of assigning the property to creditors. In 1871 the estate passed to Maurice Raleigh of Philadelphia, who rebuilt the mill and fitted it out as a cotton factory. This is the building that stands today, a giant ghost partly hidden by large trees and underbrush. In 1882, the year of Raleigh's death, the mill was employing about 150 hands and turning out 5,000 pounds of cotton per week.

Raleigh was responsible for having the name changed back from Fruitland to Atsion. His heirs attempted to rename the place Raleigh. They planned a home community there, but the project failed. Like many other parts of the pines, Atsion soon found itself in the Joseph Wharton acquisitions in 1892 and became a ward of the state when New Jersey took over the Wharton holdings.

Atsion Lake is one of the prettiest settings in the South Jersey woodlands, a favorite of artists. The state has allowed a few cabins along its sides, but commercialism has been kept at a minimum to preserve its natural beauty.

HARRISVILLE

Amid the tumbling ruins of Harrisville, once a prosperous paper manufacturing town of Burlington County, you cannot fail to sense the contempt of nature for man's efforts to conquer it. Here on the west border of Bass River Township on the east branch of Wading River can be traced outlines of a village that at one time was the shopping center of the area.

As early as 1795 Isaac Potts of Philadelphia built a slitting mill at Harrisville. While early historians placed the mill in the "vicinity" of the later community of Harrisville, Arthur Pierce pinpointed the operation as having been located at the same site as the paper town. The slitting mill changed hands several times.

The real history of Harrisville began when William McCarty arrived on the scene in 1832 and established a papermaking industry. Until about 1880 the place was known as McCartyville. The name Harrisville was born with the arrival of the four Harris brothers, William, Benjamin, Richard, and Howard. The last two lived in Harrisville, while the other brothers cared for the business interests of the mill in Philadelphia and New York.

Richard was director of the enterprise and built an imposing house at the entrance of the town, which was painstakingly laid out with a main street illuminated by gas lamps. Ornamental standards were imported from Philadelphia, and the gas for them was manufactured on the spot. These standards were still to be seen as late as 1914.

Waterpower to run the mill was supplied by a canal from a lake created by the mill operators through a dam on the Wading River. Besides the houses of workers, owned by the company and rented to employees, there was a store, a school, a church, and a gristmill.

The Harrisville mill produced a thick, tough brown paper referred to in some circles as "butcher's paper," which was usually used for wrapping packages. Working hours were typical of the times, 6 A.M. to 6 P.M. Wages were standard at $1.25 per day. A seven-day week was worked.

Instead of using wood pulp as basis for its operation, the Harrisville plant utilized such materials as salt hay, rags, rope, and waste paper shipped in by barge from New York. Harris Station, of the old Raritan and Delaware Bay Railroad located eight miles to the west of the town, was its shipping point. The finished products of the mill were hauled along sandy roads to the station by mule cart. Two attempts to have a railroad into the town failed.

In its heyday the mill operation was valued at $700,000, sizable for the times. For more than forty years the Harris brothers continued to build and expand the town, which became a gathering place and supply center for the area.

Eventually other papermaking methods were developed, and the Harrisville mill business declined. By 1877 it had lost many

A paper-manufacturing town from 1832 to about 1877, McCartyville became Harrisville, then a ghost town. This photograph, believed to have been taken about 1914, shows at left one of the ornamental lamp standards imported from Philadelphia, which burned gas manufactured locally. (Mathis Collection)

workers. The Harris brothers found themselves in financial difficulties. After two reorganizations, neither of which helped the situation, the property went to other owners.

At a sheriff's sale in 1891 the land and buildings passed to Maria Robbins, who later sold it to Alexander W. Harrington. On July 16, 1896, it was added to the ever-growing landholdings of Joseph Wharton.

As all mill activity had long since ceased and workers had moved to other places, Wharton left the village to the ever-creeping vegetation of the Pine Barrens. Richard Harris lived for some years amid the tumbling buildings, finally going to the Philadelphia home of relatives, where he died.

A fire in 1914 completed the destruction of Harrisville. Junkmen came and carted away the ornamental standards. Vandals wrecked whatever remained of the buildings. Today Harrisville is just a name on old maps, a few jutting walls reminders of more happy days. It is a part of the Wharton Tract now owned by the state of New Jersey. Artists and nature lovers find its sandy trails inviting.

OTHER GHOST TOWNS

There are perhaps more ghost towns in the pines of Burlington and Atlantic counties than in the entire so-called wild West. They differ from the western towns in that the latter were generally the outcome of one wild plunge after gold and consisted mainly of loosely put together wooden buildings along a muddy main street. The ghost towns of the Burlington pines were no overnight sensations. They were carefully planned at their conception and many times resembled the spokes of a wheel around a central industrial hub which was the reason for their existence. They consisted of substantial buildings, churches, company stores, hotels, and homes in addition to the main industrial structures.

These towns are ghosts because progress passed them by. Great dreams tumbled in the pines when the railroads drew a straight line through the South Jersey wilderness from Camden to Absecon Island ignoring old stage trails and leaving former industrial towns isolated. Stage lines went out of business overnight, water transportation became obsolete on the Mullica and Great Egg Harbor rivers, bog iron production was killed by discovery of coal in Pennsylvania, and the glass industry faded with the emergence of the first giant companies locating their works in more centralized spots. Workers drifted away, furnaces were extinguished, stores were boarded up. The rats took over the inns and hotels, churches fell in ruins, deer roamed former streets. Vandals, time, and the elements did the rest.

Towns such as Batsto and Atsion became state-protected sites. Others simply vanished.

The Mullica River, rising back of Long-a-Coming (Berlin) and tumbling past Pleasant Mills, Lower Bank, Green Bank, and Clark's Landing into Swan Bay and thence to Chestnut Neck and the open waters of the Atlantic Ocean, was the road of commerce to the South Jersey settlers in the 1700s and 1800s. It carried their iron, glass, and wood to New York and other metropolitan centers. On old maps you will find the river designated as both Little Egg Harbor and Amintonck. Captain Eric Mullica explored the river in 1645 and gave it his name. Prior to 1860 many maps designated the part above Atsion as Goshen Creek. An 1875 map shows the name Atsion for the middle section of the river.

Crowleytown

On the bend of the river just below Batsto is a picturesque picnic area now maintained by the state of New Jersey as part of its supervision of the Wharton Tract. If you look closely you will find a sign reading CROWLEY'S POINT. This is the site of the once-thriving village of Crowleytown, where the famous Mason jar was blown in the glassworks.

Samuel Crowley operated two glassworks there, the first in 1851. Although accounts are a bit confused between a Samuel Crowley and a Samuel Crowley, Jr., on old records, both names are believed to refer to the same man. Crowley also dabbled in politics and at one time laid out ambitious plans for Crowley-town, trying to sell the idea to New York and Philadelphia investors. Crowley had four hundred acres of land and erected two glass factories, stores, a hotel, and houses for employees. Plans were drawn for a canal to the Delaware. A fleet of boats lay off-shore to take his goods to metropolitan centers. Twelve blowers were employed in one plant. The principal products were glass bottles and druggists' glass.

Crowley failed to interest investors with his town ideas and finally sold the glassworks to a New York group who renamed it Atlantic Glass Works. The operation was beset by fires. After the one in 1866 the plant was abandoned. The glass factory was blown down in 1874. The *Wharton Title* (Vol. 38) shows a lease, April 1, 1862, to Isaiah Weeks and Samuel Crowley, Jr., to Crowleyville Glass Company, two lots, fourteen houses at $400 an acre; another, January 26, 1866, Isaiah Weeks to Burlington, Atlantic, Cape May, and Philadelphia Glass Company for $10,000 (a notation on the book says, "description looks like a swindle"); also a lease, November 24, 1869, from John Dougherty, president of the company, to George Langdon, director and "practical glass maker." He took over operation for $16,500 in stock for land. Crowley remained a director. The operation failed, some say, for lack of proper finance; others, for lack of attention. Crowley-town became a ghost of the past and has so remained.

Hermann City

On the Mullica River, not far from Crowleytown, there is a point designated as Herman or Hermann City. Financed by New York capitalists, Hermann City was expected to become a permanent community of impressive proportions. The original village was built in 1870 by Joseph Wippler and Company. At one time it was a community of seventy houses, a store, and a hotel clustered about a glassmaking plant. Today, there is not even a beaten path back to the jungle which hides what remains of the glassworks—a walled hole in the ground.

From the river there is evidence of an old landing, with the hulks of three ships rotting on shore visible when the tide is low.

Two of these craft were the *Frances* and the *Argo,* tied up awaiting cargoes of New Jersey glass for shipment to New York. When the town went to pieces the ships were left to the elements. The old Hermann City Hotel still stands in a sad state of disrepair. Beside it is the ruin of an old springhouse constructed of Jersey stone. The tavern was once known as Koster's Inn.

The glassworks at Hermann produced luxury items, such as Christmas decorations and "shades." In the terminology of the times, a shade was a glass enclosure to cover stuffed owls and wax flowers, once popular as parlor ornaments. One of the principal streets of Hermann City was Skin Row. A railroad was once pledged to come through from Tuckerton, but it never materialized.

Hermann City came to a standstill in the panic of 1873, the year of its heyday. It was sold to Joseph Wharton for $1,500 at the time he was amassing his gigantic estate. The inn property is not state-owned, although the rest of Hermann City property is part of the Wharton Tract.

Bulltown

Most historians are vague as to the exact location of Bulltown. However, it can be found not far from the ruins of Hermann City, if one were to look close enough, dig in the ground, and use plenty of imagination. Bulltown, built by Samuel Crowley as his second glass empire adventure, is two miles inland from the Mullica River, in a straight line from Hermann City, on Bull Creek, hence the name "Bulltown." This second glass house was built by Crowley after he sold the one at Crowleytown. The new factory was the smallest in New Jersey, having but one furnace of five pots. This was operated from 1858 to 1870. Bottle glass was blown. The operation failed and was abandoned in 1870.

Quaker Bridge

Between Atsion and Batsto on the upper branches of the Batsto River there was a meeting place of early Quaker settlers called Quaker Bridge, where the Quakers of Atlantic County crossed over on their way to meeting at Tuckerton before the establishment of the meeting at Smithville. The hamlet of Quaker Bridge received its name officially from a meeting held in 1772 when the Quakers, some from Tuckerton and others from Burlington, Medford, and Mount Holly, met at the lower side of the river to discuss community problems. The preceding year several of their number drowned in crossing the river, and it was decided to build a bridge. Cutting down cedars, they constructed a substantial crossing, which lasted for many years.

Quaker Bridge's second bid for fame came thirty-six years later when the curly fern, *Schizaea pusilla,* was discovered there by Edward C. W. Eddy, a naturalist. This rare plant has since been found in other scattered spots of South Jersey.

At one time Quaker Bridge boasted a hotel which was destroyed by fire some time after 1849. Available records of the spot are vague. Quaker Bridge is accessible today by foot only. A small footbridge still spans the river. Digging in the ground might reveal the foundations of the tavern. Everything else has returned to its primitive state.

Washington

Washington is the center of Washington Township and can well be classified as a pineland ghost. As early as 1795 a tavern was located there, and it was the favorite stopping place of stage drivers. In 1859 a hotel and several private dwellings occupied the spot. These have disappeared. I had a hard time locating the place myself. Persistence, however, uncovered the remains of what was a building about 150 feet long. There is evidence that horse breeding was conducted at Washington in its early days and that this building was the stable.

In recent years the remains of a tavern cellar have been located about three tenths of a mile from the ruins of the stable. This was without doubt the original Washington Tavern, which was conducted by Nicholas Sooy from 1795 to 1820. It was said to have been the headquarters for army recruiters up to the War of 1812. On old maps of the district, the Washington Tavern is located at the same spot as the wine cellar ruins, an intersection of the old Tuckerton State Road and the road to

Speedwell from Green Bank. Another road, which once ran from the tavern to Batsto, is now but a trail, fit for hiking only.

Nicholas Sooy was prominent in the affairs of the county, being a member of the Board of Freeholders and the Township Committee. During his stay the tavern was mostly known as "Sooy's."

This is borne out by the very informative Martha Furnace papers in which we find: "October 10, 1809. Election at Sooy's," also "March 13, 1810, Town Meeting at Sooy's." At the death of Nicholas Sooy, Samuel Bodine became innkeeper. Licenses allow us to trace the tavern to 1845, after which the trail becomes vague. Today Washington is among our interesting ghost towns.

A number of Washington Taverns existed in the Jerseys. Naming inns after the first President was a common practice. Many inn signs were dominated by a stern likeness of Washington. A rather famous Washington Inn at Woodbury was kept by Abraham Chattin, who was licensed in 1748. Originally called Middle Tavern—there was an inn on each side about one block apart—it was later named Washington House and Washington Tavern. In more recent times it was known as Newton's Hotel.

There was a Washington Tavern at Bordentown at the intersection of Farnsworth Avenue and Crosswicks Street. Benjamin Franklin frequently stopped there in 1723, when it was known as the Brown Tavern. Princeton had its Washington Inn on Nassau Street. Burlington's Washington Tavern was located at the corner of High and Broad streets.

Hampton Furnace

Hampton Furnace, Hampton Gate, and Hampton Forge are ghosts within the sprawling Wharton Tract in Burlington County. The furnace site is located on a path that branches off U.S. Route 206 just a few miles above Atsion. This is now cranberry country. There is practically no evidence of the former furnace, the Gate is gone, and the Forge is rubble. The site, however, is pinpointed on the Wharton Tract map.

Hampton Furnace was built in 1795 by Clayton Earl and Richard Stockton, who had purchased the land thereabouts on April 10, 1795, from Restore and Mary Shinn. A sawmill was on the property at the time. Deeds describe Earl as an ironmaster; he had built the Hanover Furnace near Browns Mills in 1793. Earl did not seem to hold property for any great length of time, which leads one to believe his role was that of speculator and banker rather than actual operator. He kept his interest in Hampton for only one month, selling in May of 1795 to William Lane and John Godfrey, merchants of Philadelphia who were also speculators.

Richard Stockton died on January 2, 1797, and his heirs sold their half of the Hampton Furnace to George and William Ashbridge, who had secured the Clayton Earl interests, thus making them sole owners. About 1810 a forge was built nearby. Samuel Richards of Atsion secured the property at a public sale on February 3, 1825. There is indication that a fire destroyed the buildings about that time and that Richards reconstructed them. Atsion records note a rebuilding job in 1829.

Richards kept the works in connection with the Atsion operation until his death in 1842, after which successors operated until 1850. About this time Hampton, along with other iron spots in South Jersey feeling the effects of the new competition from Pennsylvania, shut down.

Martha Furnace

Martha Furnace, located within the state-owned Wharton Tract, on a sandy road just off New Jersey Route 563, is a ghost which now echoes to the din of campers and, in deer season, a few hunters. Isaac Potts, member of a Philadelphia firm of iron merchants, purchased the place on October 1, 1793, from Samuel Hough, who had operated the sawmill there. According to an entry in the Martha Furnace records, the furnace was built in September 1793 and "Made First Casting 30th at 3 o'clock in the morning 1793." It was named for Potts's wife, a custom of the times. Workers lived at a nearby settlement called Calico. The old Tuckerton stage route passed the furnace.

In its day the village had about 400 people, 50 houses, a store, school, sawmill, and gristmill. Two years later Potts offered it for sale. It was 1800 before he finally found buyers, a group which included Samuel Richards and Joseph Ball, two names closely connected with iron in the South Jersey woodlands.

Martha Furnace prospered until the 1840s, when it too felt the Pennsylvania boom. Richards sold to his veteran manager Jesse Evans in 1841. Midcentury saw the fires of Martha go out, after which the place was used for the production of charcoal. This continued until 1848 according to Charles Boyer in his *Early Forges and Furnaces in New Jersey.*

When Joseph Wharton started assembling his vast holdings in southern Jersey he took the Martha Tract, which by that time had returned to a wilderness. It is now state owned.

Also among the ghosts of the pines could be numbered The Forks junction of the Batsto and Mullica rivers, at one time a thriving boating center fed by the iron and glass works of the area.

BATSTO, THE IRON TOWN

On the upper reaches of the Mullica River in Burlington County stands Batsto, one of the early successful iron villages of the South Jersey pines. Climaxing a career dating from pre-Revolutionary times, the place is now under supervision of the Historic Sites section of the New Jersey State Department of Environmental Protection.

The place-name Batsto is one of many reflecting the early activity of the Swedes as traders and settlers in South Jersey. In Swedish the word meant "bathing place." The form Batsto was used for the name of the iron village, but over the years it appeared in the following variations as the name of rivers and streams: Batso, Batstowe, Battstoe, Barthstow, Batstoo, and Badstove.

The land on which the original Batsto furnace was built was acquired from the Council of Proprietors in 1758 by John Munrow, an early land speculator. Another who bought considerable Batsto land was Israel Pemberton, who erected a home there which he called Whitcomb Manor. In 1765 Munrow sold his holdings to Charles Read of Burlington, who erected the iron-works the following year. The furnace consisted of a 30-foot cupola built into the side of a hill to make it possible to charge it from the top.

In 1765 Read further increased his holdings by purchase of several thousand acres from Richard Wescott (spelled Westcoat in some deeds), who later became his associate in the iron business. The price was 200 pounds sterling. Within a month of this purchase Read bought from John Estell the rights to a vast tract stretching almost to Atsion. Records show that Estell worked closely with Read as the latter secured permission from the state to dam the Batsto River, a branch of the Mullica. The dam was needed to provide waterpower for the new industry. Read eventually extended his holdings into four furnaces. He became a Supreme Court justice and an assemblyman.

Read got into deep financial difficulties and very suddenly in 1767 unloaded his holdings on his partners, John Cooper, "a gentleman"; Reuben Haines, a Philadelphia brewer; Walter Franklin, a New York merchant; and John Wilson, of Burlington. Wescott retained a half interest in his former holdings. There were several subsales of the property which, according to record, were managed by William Doughten for the former partners.

The next outstanding figure to appear on the scene was Philadelphia merchant and trader John Cox, a zealous patriot of the Revolution, a member of the Committee of Safety, and later a colonel. Together with a partner, Charles Thompson, Cox first bought out Haines on October 12, 1770, for 1,000 pounds sterling; next the former Wilson interest for 250 pounds; and on October 24 of the same year Cooper's share for 750 pounds. They paid 350 pounds to the Franklin family for the remaining shares, acquiring the whole for 2,350 pounds.

Under Cox, Batsto became a principal arsenal for Washington and the Continental Army. When the British occupied Philadelphia, Cox moved to Batsto and gave full time to supplying cannon shot and other iron to Washington. With Elijah Clark of Pleasant Mills and Wescott, he organized blockade runners, built the defenses of the Mullica River, and laid out a smuggling route direct to the Continental Army. So important had Batsto become to Washington that on June 5, 1777, Cox was given a military exemption for all his workers and authorized to set up a company of "minutemen" in case of sudden invasion. Cox rose fast in the colonial ranks and society and was named Assistant Quartermaster General of the army.

In 1778 he decided to sell Batsto. There was a fast transaction to Thomas Mayberry of Mount Holly on October 5, 1778, at a price of 40,000 pounds and an equally fast transaction to Joseph Ball, the "fighting Quaker," on April 8, 1779, for 55,000 pounds.

Ball was thirty-two years old when he acquired Batsto. Being a practical man, he went about building the business and the town. He built the first part of the mansion. His patriotism overcoming his Quaker beliefs, Ball also joined forces with Washington and kept the forges going night and day to supply the army.

Colonel Thomas Proctor's Pennsylvania State Regiment of artillery and a battalion of New Jersey militia were stationed there in 1778. In October of that year, the activities of the patriots and the South Jersey ironworks became so bothersome to the British that the high command sent an expedition from New York under Captain Patrick Ferguson with orders to destroy the fleet of privateers at Chestnut Neck and the warehouse and ironworks at Batsto and Pleasant Mills. Captain Ferguson burned Chestnut Neck and much of its shipping, but a spy succeeded in getting the news to Washington, who dispatched General Casimir Pulaski to the scene. On forced march Pulaski did not make Chestnut Neck in time, but did arrive at Batsto and set up a defense. A Tory carried this news to the British, who were halfway to Batsto. Captain Ferguson called a hasty retreat. As the flames of Chestnut Neck lit the background, the expedition sailed out of the harbor, its task only half accomplished, and Batsto continued its service to the Continentals.

After the surrender of General Cornwallis to Washington at Yorktown, October 19, 1781 Colonel William Richards, a friend of Washington and an uncle of Ball, became manager of Batsto and in 1784 acquired full control. He had learned the iron business in Pennsylvania and for a time worked for Colonel Cox at Batsto before joining the Revolutionary forces. It was under Richards and his son Jesse that Batsto reached its peak. Colonel Richards died in 1807, and the property passed to his son and nephew Thomas S. Richards. By 1830 the Richards family owned more than half of what is now Atlantic County—over 150,000 acres of land. When Jesse first came into the picture the bog-iron industry was approaching its height in the boom created by the War of 1812. However, soon the bog-iron deposits started running low. Then came the discovery of anthracite in Pennsylvania—and the crash. The iron industry in South Jersey was doomed. The Batsto furnace fires were extinguished in 1848. Jesse Richards died in 1854 at the age of seventy-two, and with him went the last of the South Jersey iron barons.

His son Thomas H. carried on glass and lumbering operations at Batsto and lived in the great mansion house. In 1858 the old furnace was dismantled.

Most of the buildings at Batsto were destroyed by a fire on February 23, 1874, caused by a spark from the house of Robert Stewart. Within two hours eighteen of the best dwellings had been destroyed. The villagers of Pleasant Mills took in the homeless.

As William Richards had left as a legacy to his sons a love of thrift and power, Jesse left to his sons a love of strong drink. Thomas, Samuel, and Jesse Jr., were executors of the estate. They put the plantation into the hands of manager Robert Stewart and left for Philadelphia. One account says they lavished their wealth in every possible pleasure and demanded all the profits of the factories. Workmen went unpaid. They threw down their tools, and the glass furnaces died out. The once-busy village was idle. Houses began to crumble. The foundry tumbled in, the canal choked up, and the mill stopped. Stewart, heartbroken at the turn of events, gave Batsto everything he had. Eventually he had to secure a judgment of $20,000 against the heirs to pay wages and recoup his own money. Finally, foreclosure proceedings were brought, and Batsto was put up at a master's sale. Joseph Wharton bought it for $14,000 in 1876. Under his supervision major repairs were made, and the 80-foot tower was erected over the mansion. Wharton presided there, also more or less in the lord-of-manor style. He began acquiring much adjacent property and planned to utilize it as a water supply source for the city of Philadelphia. The plan was killed when the New Jersey legislature passed a law forbidding export of water outside the state. Wharton died in 1909, and the estate offered the tract to New

No photograph of the Batsto furnace is known to have survived. This view of the original farm buildings is taken from an early postcard. (McMahon Collection)

Jersey for $1,000,000. The offer was rejected by the voters in 1915.

But on January 17, 1954, the state of New Jersey and the Girard Trust of Philadelphia, trustees for the Joseph Wharton estate, entered into a sales agreement for Batsto and the entire tract assembled by Wharton. As a result the state acquired 53,304 acres by deed dated December 28 of that year for $3 million. On September 28, 1955, the state acquired an additional 38,260 acres. This last deed conveyed lands in the town of Hammonton and Mullica Township, Atlantic County; in Bass River, Medford, Shamong, Tabernacle, Washington, and Woodland townships in Burlington County; and lands in Waterford and Winslow townships in Camden County.

Batsto looks today much as it did of yore, a curious mixture of colonial, early nineteenth-century, and mid-Victorian architecture. Each owner seemed to have left his mark. Formation of the Batsto Citizens Committee brought about pressure for a step-up in restoration. The committee works under the supervision of its own officers in cooperation with the State Environmental Department.

A mansion subcommittee of volunteers has been responsible for the restoration of rooms with the Batsto mansion house and decoration in the proper time period. A post office has been installed in the general store building and an official postmark authorized by the U.S. Post Office Department. Thousands of letters are stamped and mailed from there to collectors in all parts of the world.

A blacksmith shop was completed through the effort of Donald Streeter, an expert on old American iron. On May 15, 1964, in connection with the tercentenary year, the state opened the first part of a three-wing Information Center. A permanent glass exhibit was set up at the general store under direction of early South Jersey glass authority J. E. Pfeiffer. The store building itself will eventually take on its original lines. The gristmill has been restored and was opened with official ceremonies on June 25, 1967.

Homes of former ironworkers along the principal street of the village are being restored and opened to the public as craft shops. An oar boat raised from the Batsto pond is also on display.

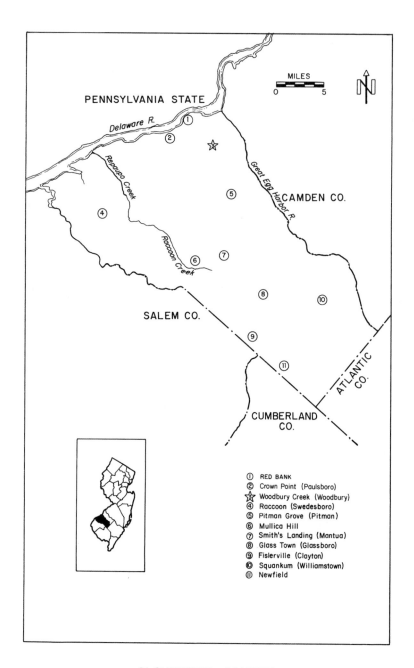

MILES
0   5

PENNSYLVANIA STATE

Delaware R.

Repaupo Creek

Raccoon Creek

Great Egg Harbor R.

CAMDEN CO.

SALEM CO.

ATLANTIC CO.

CUMBERLAND CO.

① RED BANK
② Crown Point (Paulsboro)
☆ Woodbury Creek (Woodbury)
④ Raccoon (Swedesboro)
⑤ Pitman Grove (Pitman)
⑥ Mullica Hill
⑦ Smith's Landing (Mantua)
⑧ Glass Town (Glassboro)
⑨ Fislerville (Clayton)
⑩ Squankum (Williamstown)
⑪ Newfield

GLOUCESTER COUNTY

OLD GLOUCESTER

Gloucester County, directly across the Delaware River from Philadelphia, is affectionately known to most residents of South Jersey as Old Gloucester. It once included all of the present Camden, Atlantic, and Gloucester counties, an area of nearly 1,200 square miles. I have personal fondness for Old Gloucester, having spent some of my youthful years growing up in Woodbury Heights, then a small home community on the outskirts of Woodbury.

A lot of early state history occurred within the bounds of Old Gloucester beginning with the Lenni-Lenape Indians, one group of which had headquarters within the original county at a place called Armewamexes, which the first white settlers shortened to Arwamus. This is now known as Gloucester Point.

In 1609 the Dutch laid claim to the Delaware Valley as the result of chartings by Henry Hudson, an Englishman in the service of the Dutch East India Company. On his second voyage to the Delaware River valley in 1623, Cornelius Jacobsen Mey of Hoorn, Holland, built a trading post he called Fort Nassau at the confluence of the Sassackon (Timber Creek) and the Delaware River. In 1631 Captain Pieterzen De Vries visited Fort Nassau and attempted to revive trade with the Indians.

The original settlers brought to the fort by Captain Mey, mostly Walloon refugees, were recalled to New York by Governor Peter Minuit, and the fort remained deserted until the Dutch became uneasy about English activity in that section of Jersey.

In 1634 English explorer Thomas Young attempted to start a settlement at Pennsauken Creek. In 1636 Wouter Van Twiller, who had replaced Minuit as governor of New Amsterdam, heard of Young's effort and sent troops to again man Fort Nassau.

Two years later the Swedes made their first bid to take over the

Delaware Valley. They established themselves at Fort Christina, now Wilmington, Delaware, and proceeded up the river. When their ships attempted to pass Fort Nassau, they were fired upon and returned to base.

When John Printz became governor of New Sweden, as the colonists called their settlements, he nullified Fort Nassau by building Fort Elfsborg at the mouth of Salem Creek. In 1646 Governor Peter Stuyvesant sent 320 reinforcements to Fort Nassau. Proceeding farther they captured both Fort Elfsborg and Fort Christina, giving the Dutch control of the area.

In 1651 the Dutch built Fort Casimir across the river from Elfsborg and the latter became useless; the garrison from Fort Nassau was moved to Casimir and the Dutch governor ordered Nassau destroyed. The soldiers did a complete job. Even today the exact site of the fort has never been ascertained to the satisfaction of historians, although a monument was erected by the state in 1919 at Broadway and Cumberland Street, Gloucester, calling attention to the fact the fort once existed.

In 1664 England laid claim to the New World, and King Charles II gave New Jersey to his brother James, Duke of York. The Dutch regained control of the Gloucester County area in 1673 but were dispossessed within a year and the Jersey lands divided between Berkeley and Carteret, signaling the start of more solid colonization.

Prosecution of Quakers in England was at its height and, following the lead of John Fenwick, many groups of Quakers settled along the Delaware River from Salem to what is now Camden. By 1678 the Quakers had established themselves at the Old Indian village of Arwamus.

In 1661 a group of colonists from Dublin, Ireland, had arrived under leadership of Robert Zane. Some went as far as Burlington; some stayed in the Gloucester County area. The division of the tenths having been completed under the Concessions and Agreements signed in 1676, this group was allotted the third tenth, which became known as the Irish Tenth of Old Gloucester. Its boundary extended from the south branch of Pennsauken Creek on the north to Big Timber Creek on the south and from the Delaware River to the ocean.

The fourth tenth started at Big Timber Creek, extending south to Oldman's Creek and from the river to the ocean.

On May 26, 1686, residents of the third and fourth tenths met at Arwamus and compiled what became known as a County Constitution. This was the actual beginning of Gloucester County as such, the only county in the state that can trace its existence from a direct compact between the inhabitants, who deemed themselves a body politic with power to legislate.

Gloucester Point was selected as county seat and served the young county for 100 years. County boundary lines were set but were disputed for some years. In 1765 Samuel Clement was appointed by the surveyor general to make a survey and mark lines. By 1843 there was enough dissatisfaction with Clement's work that another survey was ordered. This report filed in 1847 confirmed the 1765 survey, and lines remained unchanged until the creation of Atlantic County in 1837 and Camden County in 1844.

The first Gloucester County courts were held in taverns and in private houses. In 1696 the county governing body issued an order for the building of a prison and courthouse in Gloucester City. In March of 1786 the question of a more centralized county seat was submitted to voters, and as a result Woodbury was chosen. A courthouse was erected there in 1787.

Gloucester County was the scene of an important Revolutionary War battle, that of Red Bank on October 22, 1777. The county was overrun by foraging parties from both sides as they sought food for troops.

Woodbury had to fight to maintain its status as county seat. On February 8, 1925, the question was again on the ballot and the voters showed their preference to retain the town as the county's legislative center.

Although a glass industry was established at Glassboro by the Stanger brothers as early as 1775, Gloucester County's industrial potential began to make itself felt about 1870. George C. Green started his patent medicine plant in Woodbury in 1872. Gibbsboro was the site of a dynamite plant founded in 1879 by Lammot du Pont, who was killed in a blast at the plant in 1884.

Among Gloucester County's industrial plants of today are Columbia Records, Owens-Illinois, Del Monte Foods, Shell Oil, Monsanto, Du Pont, Texaco, and Socony-Mobil. Eighty-three percent of the county area is still in farms and woodlands despite the inroads of sprawling housing developments. Grapes were once a big crop, but in 1849 a disease killed the vines and the farmers turned to potatoes. The sweet potato has become one of the state's largest crops, and Gloucester County contributes a major share of the harvest. It is also the site of Glassboro State College and Gloucester County Community College.

THE SWEDES OF RACCOON

In 1640 Peter Hollander Ridder, a Dutchman in the service of Sweden, arrived at the settlements that comprised New Sweden on the South (Delaware) River and took over as governor succeeding Peter Minuit, who had drowned when his ship was lost in a hurricane near Saint Christopher in the West Indies. The Swedish government had great faith in Minuit; this was not transferred to Ridder, who was given the task of attempting to strengthen the Swedish hold upon the Delaware Valley.

In 1641 Ridder began negotiations with the Indians for the entire side of the Delaware River from Raccoon Creek, site of the present borough of Swedesboro, south to Cape May. Within the next three years Swedish families increased in the area which they referred to as Raccoon. They were for the most part trappers, and raccoon pelts were plentiful (and still are) in this part of South Jersey which would make the name a natural choice. Later the name was changed to Swedesboro, which was considered more appropriate and substantial.

Ridder failed to achieve the progress the crowd desired, and he was soon ordered to give way to a successor, Johan Printz, who was to rule the colony with an iron hand from 1643 to 1653, giving it new drive and spirit. Printz built Fort Elfsborg on the Delaware at the mouth of Salem Creek. The place became better known as "Mosquito Castle" because of hordes of Jersey 'skeeters that made life miserable for its defenders.

Printz believed in absolute rule and left no doubts about his position in the matter. However, the colony needed a strong hand to keep going; Printz supplied it. His original assignment was for three years; when he asked for a successor his request was ignored for another two years, when he was finally told he must stay until an appointment (time unspecified) was made.

In 1647 Governor Peter Stuyvesant arrived in New Amsterdam and built Fort Casimir on the river opposite Fort Elfsborg, threatening Printz. Fort Elfsborg was finally abandoned in 1653, and Printz departed for home, never to return. In 1667 Stuyvesant overpowered the colony, but Swedish culture continued principally through the Swedish church.

The first settlers of New Sweden, as the colony was called, had strong political and religious ties with the Swedish colony of Christina, now Wilmington, Delaware. By 1703, when the Kings Highway from Burlington reached the vicinity of Raccoon Creek, the settlement had taken on some semblance of a village or town.

About 1701 a young preacher, Lars Tollstadius, fresh from Sweden, arrived in the colony. He was not officially designated to the church by the mother church and in fact had some religious views not in keeping with higher church officials, including one of self-government for parishes in the New World.

In one of his first moves Tollstadius advocated the building of a church at Raccoon. Prior to that the Swedes on the Jersey side of the Delaware River paid tithes to the church at Christina and attended services there when they could cross the river. Tollstadius's new church project in Raccoon loomed as a financial as well as political threat to the Delaware authorities, who protested this activity to the mother church in Sweden.

The Rev. Andreas Sandel, who had clashed on church matters with Tollstadius in the Old Country, arrived in the Delaware colony in 1702 and ordered Tollstadius out of the Jersey settlement. This gained additional followers for Tollstadius, who defied the edict and continued building his church at Raccoon.

In 1703 the log structure was completed and given the name of Swedish Evangelical Lutheran Church at Raccoon. It is known as the first Swedish church in New Jersey.

An old South Jersey expression "All talk—no cider" is said to have originated from an incident at the Swedish church of Raccoon. According to the legend, an Indian stopped in for the services, listened to a long-winded sermon, and left after expressing his reactions with the words: "Here is a great deal of prattle and nonsense but neither brandy nor cider!"

Tollstadius was a colorful if controversial figure, and his importance depended upon which side one happened to be associated with. To the Swedes of Raccoon he was a Don Quixote fighting Old World windmills; to the church in Sweden he was an irritating radical.

The settlement grew, and the church prospered under his administration. Raccoon soon became the center of Swedish life on the New Jersey side of the Delaware. In 1765 townspeople decided to change the backwoods name of Raccoon to Swedesboro. The church continued as the center of activities, and in 1784 the original log structure was replaced by a larger building which is still in active service. In 1786, after continued disagreements with the parent Lutheran church, jurisdiction of "Old Swedes" (The Church of Raccoon) passed to the Episcopalians, with whom it has since remained under the name of Trinity Episcopal Church.

One of the outstanding pastors of the church under Episcopal jurisdiction was John Croes of Philadelphia. Although not yet ordained a minister, Croes accepted a call to the Swedesboro church in 1789. According to present pastor Parker F. Auten, who spent an afternoon showing me about the famed structure, Croes walked from Philadelphia to Swedesboro to assume his new charge. The evening before his arrival in Swedesboro he spent at the Death of Fox Inn, in Clarksboro, where he met several men who were to play helpful roles in the church.

According to the Rev. Mr. Auten, Croes was a remarkable young preacher. He was ordained in 1790 and continued his pastorate at the Swedesboro church until 1801. Swedesboro is proud of the fact that in 1815 the Rev. John Croes was consecrated as the first Episcopal Bishop of New Jersey. He served in that capacity until 1832.

Trinity Church itself is one of those beautiful structures that have been fast disappearing. It has a white sacristy, a balcony on either side running the length of the church, pews with individual doors (needed by its first communicants to help keep out the cold), and a large Swedish flag draping the choir loft. It treasures the Swedish Bible presented to it in 1926 as a gift

from Crown Prince Gustaf Adolf of Sweden and Crown Princess
Louise.

The church front is on Kings Highway, but its steeple and bell
tower, added in 1839, are at the back of the structure. At the far
end of the cemetery, on a small hill overlooking the surrounding
area and the church, is a park dedicated in 1964 as New Sweden
Park. A tablet placed in the park the same year by the New Jersey Lodge, Vasa Order of America, reads: "On this site was built
in 1703 the First Swedish Church in New Jersey.

A part of Swedesboro known for a long time as Laddtown, was
owned by John Ladd, Sr., under a warrant dated November 2,
1714. The place was noted for ground rents, which were to be
paid in Spanish milled silver dollars on the 25th of March each
year, and according to original deeds "forever." Ladd died in
1771, and his widow Hannah Ladd inherited the land, which she
left to the diarist Samuel Mickle, who recorded that he found it
impossible to collect the Spanish-dollar ground rents, which it is
believed were so designated because of mistrust of other currency available.

Swedesboro today is a small community in the center of a
large agricultural area in which the principal crops are tomatoes,
pickles, and apples. It was incorporated as a borough in April of
1902 with a mayor and council form of administration. The town
is the home of the eastern division of the Del Monte Corporation.
It is also the site of a large warehouse storage conducted by the
Casella brothers, and two cucumber pickling plants, operated by
the Giorinazzi brothers and Joseph Graffo. The population, according to the latest census figures, is 2,287.

The surrounding countryside is dotted with large trees, shaded
lanes, and flower gardens. A sign on the roadway just outside the
town reads: "This is God's Country, don't drive like hell!"

A HILL CALLED MULLICA

One of the almost legendary figures of South Jersey and
Gloucester County was Eric P. Mullica, who in the middle 1600s
arrived with a group of Swedish settlers bound for the villages

along the Delaware River. After spending some time with his countrymen in and around Raccoon, Mullica decided to move farther inland to the banks of the Little Egg Harbor River, which separated Burlington and Old Gloucester counties. He established a community at a spot on the river now called Lower Bank, said to have been the first white settlement in that part of the Jersey pinelands.

Mullica arrived in America on the man-of-war *Kalmar Nyckel* or the sloop *Grippen*—no two sources agree—when he was about fifteen years old. He laid claim to much land in both Old Gloucester and Burlington counties. Mullica apparently moved around quite a bit, keeping Lower Bank as his home base, until at an advanced age he sold his property to Joseph Pearce and moved to the spot in Gloucester County which bears his name, Mullica Hill. The roaming Swede was also responsible for the present designation of the Little Egg Harbor River as the Mullica, as well as Mullica Township in Atlantic County.

Eric Mullica seems to have baffled not only historians trying to trace his activities but early spellers as well. In some deeds of 1778 the name is spelled Mulicus. A survey of 1726 shows it as Mollicas, while still another source referred to Mullicus.

The community now known as Mullica Hill was originally a thinly settled area boasting a sawmill, a gristmill, a carding mill, two taverns, and a scattering of farmhouses. It was in fact two settlements, one on the north side of Raccoon Creek long known as Blue Bell, and one on the south side of the creek called Spicerville. For many years lack of transportation retarded the growth of both places.

Blue Bell took its name from the Blue Bell Tavern, dating back to August 3, 1724, when a petition to conduct a "publick place" was filed by Robert Gerrard. The Spicerville tavern dated to 1772 and was operated by Captain John Cozens.

According to local tradition, and much of the Mullica story is just that, Eric Mullica lived in Mullica Hill until his death in 1723 at the age of one hundred. He is buried in the graveyard of Trinity Episcopal Church, Swedesboro. An ancient grave map in possession of the present church shows a spot designated for

"Erick Mullica." I viewed the flat sandstone marker at the grave. It has been worn smooth by the elements and therefore is no help in supporting the map notation. Church authorities believe the grave authentic.

The Swedes were not the only early settlers of Mullica Hill. A group of Quakers led by John Fenwick settled the area as early as 1675. The Mullica Hill Friends Meeting was founded in 1797. A brick meetinghouse was built in 1808. In spite of the Quaker feelings concerning participation in war efforts, it is recorded that a complete military unit of Quakers was formed at Mullica Hill and saw action in the Civil War.

Another early religious congregation of Mullica Hill were the Episcopalians, who used the gristmill for their first services. A small frame cabin-type church was built in 1813, with the rector of Trinity Episcopal Church of Swedesboro making visits to conduct services. In 1850 the log cabin church, named for Saint Stephen, was replaced by a stone one. Five years later Saint Stephen's and Saint Barnabas' church of nearby Mantua merged.

Today Mullica Hill is a small rural community of approximately 500 persons on the Bridgeton pike about 19 miles from Camden.

PLACE OF BLACK BURRS

The Indian name for Woodbury, county seat of Gloucester County, was Piscozackasing, which meant the place of black burrs. There are several versions as to how Woodbury got its present name, many having to do with wood and berries. The Indians most likely derived their version from the burrs of the many chestnut trees in the vicinity. In some old legal papers the name is spelled Woodberry.

The most plausible explanation of the name is that Henry Wood and his family moved there from Bury, Lancashire, England, in 1683. As was the custom of many early settlers who were first arrivals at a spot, Wood combined his name with that of his former home, calling the place Woodbury. A record of the Wood family is preserved in a certificate of removal from the Friends

Meeting of Chetheroe, Lancashire, England, to the Friends organization in America, in the name of Henry Wood, Sr., and his son John and their families. It is dated April 2, 1682.

An additional record shows that on April 3, 1683, John Wood bought from Edward Byllynge 100 acres of land in West Jersey. Henry Wood, Sr., bought another 100 acres. Constantine, Jeremiah, and Henry Wood, Jr., three brothers of John and sons of Henry, purchased 100 acres, making the Wood holdings 300 acres of land. These purchases were made in England before the family set sail for America.

The first official record we have of the name Woodbury is a survey of 300 acres on the lower side of Red Bank, secured by John Wood in November of 1683. The survey mentions "Woodbury Creek."

John Wood was active in the political life of Gloucester County. He served as a member of the provincial legislature in 1685 and was a justice of the first court held in the county.

In 1716 the Quakers of Woodbury built their first meeting house. The Presbyterians were not far behind with a church erected in 1721 on ground donated by John Tatem.

During the Revolution the village was occupied at various times by both American and British forces. After the battle of Red Bank, many of the wounded were brought to Woodbury, and the Presbyterian church was turned into a temporary hospital.

Those who died were laid to rest in a place known as Strangers' Burial Ground, originally used for those who died without religious affiliation. The Gloucester Board of Freeholders exercised control over the place for a number of years before abandoning it. Strangers' Burial Ground was condemned in the early 1900s, the bones dug up and disposed of in a spot a mile or so outside the town.

On July 3, 1792, Woodbury Lodge No. 11, F. and A.M., received its charter, the first Masonic lodge of Gloucester County. The following year the Gloucester County Abolition Society was formed in Woodbury, and it played an active part in securing freedom for slaves.

In 1793 Woodbury gained national recognition as the terminus of the first airborne flight in the New World. The trip was made on the morning of January 9 from the old Walnut Street Prison yard on Sixth Street, Philadelphia. President George Washington was on hand when balloonist Jean Pierre Blanchard and his small dog made the ascent in a hydrogen-filled balloon.

Blanchard reached an altitude of about one mile and landed safely forty-six minutes later at Woodbury, a distance of about 15 miles. He returned to Philadelphia by horseback, carriage, and ferry in six hours and presented Washington with a flag he had carried on the flight.

When the War of 1812 began, Woodbury organized the Gloucester Blues, a military company which took part in several engagements.

The first newspaper in Gloucester County, the *Gloucester Farmer,* appeared on January 1, 1817. The *Columbia Herald* commenced publication in 1819; it merged with the *Farmer* the following year. In 1823 there was a change of name to *Herald and Gloucester Farmer and Weekly Advertiser.* The *Constitution and Farmers and Mechanics Advertiser* started publication on August 19, 1834. The name was later shortened to *Constitution;* it has remained in continuous existence. The *Woodbury Times,* for which I sold papers on the corner opposite the courthouse, came into the picture in 1822.

Woodbury was provided with good rail service to Philadelphia early in its life, the Camden and Woodbury Railroad being incorporated on April 5, 1836. The first train ran on January 20, 1838. There were five trains daily between Woodbury and the Quaker City. The fare was 25 cents.

Woodbury became a borough in 1854 with a population of about 1,300. It was incorporated as a city in 1870 with Alexander Wentz as its first mayor under this form of government. The town's first financial institution, the Gloucester County Bank, opened for business in 1855 in the home of James W. Caldwell.

War again touched Woodbury with the bombardment of Fort Sumter in 1861, and its young men rallied to the Northern cause. The Board of Freeholders voted $300 for the support of families of volunteers. A further act provided fixed sums for wives, widows, and children of Woodbury men in the battlefields. The Soldiers' Monument on Broad Street was erected following the war.

With the end of hostilities Woodbury experienced an industrial boom. Many new homes were built, many new establishments located along its main street. The advent of the Woodbury Glass Works, Standard Glass Works, and Green's August Flower Works added to the growing industrial picture. In 1890 the Blasius Piano Works erected a large factory at Woodbury which continued operations until World War I. The Balbar Trunk Company took over the factory building, which in recent years was replaced by garden-type apartments.

Today Woodbury is a busy business center with a population of 12,408 according to census figures.

ENGAGEMENT AT RED BANK

Among the more important Revolutionary War engagements fought in South Jersey was one at Fort Mercer at Red Bank, on the Delaware River below Camden. Fort Mercer was planned December 23, 1776, when Major Thomas Proctor suggested to the Pennsylvania Council of Safety that a works be placed on the New Jersey side of the Delaware for the protection of Philadelphia against an attack via the river.

The fort was named in honor of Brigadier General Hugh Mercer, who was killed at the Battle of Princeton on January 3, 1777. According to records found by the Gloucester County Historical Society, Pennsylvania militia first occupied the site on April 16, 1777, and began construction of fortifications. By the fall of 1777 the fort was supplied with cannon and turned over to the New Jersey militia. On October 18 the command changed to the continental forces by order of General Washington.

Following the battle of the Brandywine on September 11, 1777, and the occupation of Philadelphia, it became necessary for the British to keep the Delaware River open for passage of both warships and supply craft. Fort Mercer, along with Fort Mifflin on

Mud Island, almost opposite on the Pennsylvania side of the Delaware River, proved troublesome, and General William Howe, in command in Philadelphia, decided to eliminate both of these installations.

Capture and destruction of Fort Mercer was assigned to Count Carl Emil Kurt von Donop. Three battalions of Grenadier Guards and a foot regiment were assigned for the task. Donop requested more artillery, but this was denied by Howe after a bitter exchange of words. On October 21, 1777, Count Donop started for Red Bank by way of Haddonfield after landing at Cooper's Ferry.

The defense of Fort Mercer was entrusted to Colonel Christopher Greene, a veteran of the northern campaigns under General Benedict Arnold. His second-in-command was Colonel Israel Angell. They had at their disposal only 400 men to carry out General Washington's orders to hold the fort at all costs. These men were from Rhode Island, mostly Negroes and mulattoes, according to the *Historical Collections of the State of New Jersey* by John W. Barber and Henry Howe (New Haven, Conn., 1844). Although ragged and ill equipped, the men had been molded into good fighting forces by Colonel Greene.

Defense of Fort Mercer was aided by a series of strong wooden frames sunk in the Delaware between the two forts as *cheveaux de frise* to damage the wooden bottoms of any ships venturing that far up the river. Timbers from this *cheveaux de frise* have been preserved and are on display at Red Bank State Park.

Colonel Greene deemed Fort Mercer undefendable. He ordered M. Plessis du Mauduit, a French engineer attached to his command, to redesign the works so that defense of the fort could be conducted from the smallest possible centralized position. M. du Mauduit discarded a large part of the entrenchments to the north, reducing the whole to a pentagonal redoubt. This done, the defenders prepared the attack. On the morning of October 21, Colonel Greene received information that a British and Hessian force had landed at Cooper's Ferry.

The information proved correct. Count Donop decided to spend the night of October 21 in Haddonfield and start for Red Bank at dawn of October 22. His first plan was to go by way of Mount Ephraim, but scouts reported that a bridge at Big Timber

Creek had been destroyed. The advance was then rerouted to Clement's Bridge, passing through the towns now known as Barrington and Runnymede. This detour upset Colonel Greene, and he sent a scout to find out why the enemy he had expected hours sooner had been delayed. Unfortunately for Greene the scout was captured.

On arriving at Fort Mercer, Donop found that he could approach through a thick woods on three sides without exposing his troops. (It is thought by many that Donop had intelligence concerning the positions of sentries which caused him to avoid a direct route to his objective.)

An interesting description of the battle that followed is given by the Marquis de Chastellux in a pamphlet he wrote after he returned to France following the American Revolution entitled *Travels in North America*. He quotes M. du Mauduit, who was present at the battle and with whom he spoke on a visit to the fort some time after the encounter:

The twenty-second of October, in the morning, we received intelligence that 2,500 Hessians were advancing. They were soon after perceived on the edge of the wood to the north of Red Bank, nearly within cannon shot. A Hessian officer advanced preceded by a drummer. He was suffered to approach, but his harangue was so insolent, that it only served to enrage the garrison.

"The King of England," he shouted, "orders his rebellious subjects to lay down their arms; and they are warned, that if they stand the battle, no quarter whatever will be given."

Colonel Greene deputized a man to mount the parapet and give reply: "We'll see King George damned first. We want no quarter!"

This terminated the interview and the Hessian officer returned to his lines.

At four o'clock in the afternoon, the Hessians made a brisk fire from a battery of cannon. Soon after, opened and marched to the first entrenchment, from which they believed they had driven the defenders, as they found it deserted. Waving hats in the air they shouted "victory!" and advanced toward the redoubt. The same drummer who had appeared earlier and his officer led the advance. Both he and the officer were knocked in the heads by the first fire.

The Hessians, however, kept advancing within the initial entrenchment. They had already reached the abattis and were endeavoring to cut away the branches when they were hit by a shower of musket shot, which took them in front and in flank. Officers were seen rallying their men, marching back and falling amid the branches they were endeavoring to cut. Colonel Donop was particularly distinguished by the marks of the order he wore, by his handsome figure, and by his courage. He was also seen to fall like the rest.

The Hessians, repulsed by the fire of the redoubt, attempted to protect themselves from it by attacking on the side of the encampment. Fire from galleys anchored in the river sent them back with great loss of men. [Here the Marquis de Chastellus's account changes to the third person.]

While this was passing to the north side, another column attacked on the south, and, more fortunate than the other, passed the abattis, traversed the fosse and mounted the berm. Here they were stopped. M. du Mauduit ran to this post as soon as he saw the first assailants give way; others followed him. Wishing to replace some palisades which had been torn up, M. du Mauduit sallied out of the fort with a few men and surprised about twenty Hessians standing on the berm. They were taken into the fort.

After fixing the break, M. du Mauduit again sallied out with a detachment. It was then he beheld the deplorable spectacle of the dead and the dying, heaped one upon the other.

A voice arose from amidst these bodies and said, in English, "Whoever you are, draw me hence." It was Colonel Donop. M. du Mauduit made the soldiers lift the fallen Colonel and carry him into the fort. The next day Donop was removed to the home of a Quaker nearby, where he lived three days. He had frequent conversations with the Colonel. One of Donop's last statements was, "I die the victim of my ambition and of the avarice of my sovereign."

Thirty-seven Americans were killed in the engagement, some by the bursting of one of their own cannons. Hessian losses were 36 officers and 600 men, according to most accounts of the battle, including that of M. du Mauduit. A monument erected on the site of Fort Mercer on October 22, 1829, to commemorate the battle cites the number as 400 on its inscription, which reads:

To transmit to posterity a grateful remembrance of the patriotism and gallantry of Colonel Christopher Greene, who with 400 men conquered the Hessian army of 2,000 troops, then in the British service, at the Red Bank, on the 22nd Oct. 1777.

While the Hessians were attacking at Red Bank the British began a second attack upon Fort Mifflin, at the mouth of the Schuylkill River on the Pennsylvania side of the Delaware. They bombarded the fort for about a week, reducing it to rubble.

The garrison at Fort Mercer could see the punishment at Fort Mifflin and, in an attempt to help, mounted an 18-pounder they had captured from a wrecked British ship. This cannon exploded at the first shot, killing one man and injuring eight.

Mifflin commandant Lieutenant Colonel Samuel Smith was severely wounded and carried from the fort. Major Thayer of Rhode Island, who had assumed command, decided the place was no longer defendable. He ordered all stores that could be carried be piled into small boats and with about fifty men, all that was left of the garrison of nearly 400, made his escape to the Jersey shore under fire of the enemy.

Colonel Greene was shortly ordered to evacuate Fort Mercer as the British fleet, with the destruction of Fort Mifflin, had gone by and was in Philadelphia harbor. Just as a troop of British Light Infantry sent by General Cornwallis to take Fort Mercer were approaching, there was a burst of flame and the total destruction of the installation was accomplished by a picked squad according to plan. The Americans made their escape by water.

In recognition of his valor Colonel Greene was given a sword by Congress. He never received it himself, the presentation being made to his son following the war. Colonel Greene was killed in ambush on May 13, 1781, at Croton River, New York.

The site of the battle of Red Bank is now a twenty-acre park administered by the Gloucester County Board of Freeholders. A second monument was unveiled on June 21, 1906, to commemorate the battle. Some of the earthworks of the old fort remain. Nearby, marked by a plain gray stone, is the grave of Count von Donop.

The Whitall house, home of American patriot Ann Cooper Whitall, "The Angel of the Battle of Red Bank," adjoins the battlefield site. According to local tradition, the Gloucester County woman refused to budge from her home when informed the battle was impending and sat spinning wool throughout the engagement, disregarding personal danger because "I will be needed after the battle." She was indeed needed; her home became a hospital for friend and foe alike. Von Donop himself was taken there for treatment before being removed to another residence south of Woodbury Creek, where he died.

HOUSE OF GLASS

Glassboro's early bid for fame resulted from its association with the glass industry of South Jersey and the pious Lutheran family of Jacob and Catherine Stanger of Dornhagen, Germany, and their seven sons.

The Stangers were successful glassmakers in Germany in 1739 when that country was still a group of states. Conditions were unsettled because of the war activities of Frederick the Great and the Stangers decided to seek their fortunes in the New World. When German authorities refused them permission to sell their glass factory in Dornhagen, they abandoned it, fled to Rotterdam, Holland, and sailed to Portsmouth, England. At the latter port they gained passage for America aboard the English ship *Betsy*, whose destination was Philadelphia.

The Stangers did not linger in the Pennsylvania city but made for Alloway, in Salem County, New Jersey, home of the Wistar Glass Factory, whose fame had already spread to Europe. The five older boys obtained jobs at the glassworks while the younger two became apprentices.

In 1770 young Jacob Stanger, one of the apprentices, left the Wistarburg works at Alloway. Evidence that he decided to leave suddenly is found in this advertisement in the *Pennsylvania Chronical and Universal Advertiser* on April 18, 1770: "$20 reward for two German servant lads, Jacob Stenger and John Kendiel . . ." The advertisement gave a description of both. (According to practices of that time, apprentices were required to give so many hours of work in return for room, board, and training. They were not free to leave a place until the agreed-upon apprenticeship time was served.) Also in keeping with the times and carelessness in spelling of names, the name Stanger appears in many places as Stenger, including the above advertisement. Five years later the other brothers left the Wistar plant, having decided to cut out for themselves. They bought land in Gloucester County on a location which appealed because of an abundance of natural glassmaking elements—fine white sand, clay, and wood for the furnaces. In addition the location was close to the Philadelphia market.

The first glasshouse of the Stangers at what is now Glassboro was completed in the fall of 1781. Sharing in the enterprise were the brothers Jacob, Solomon, Daniel, Francis, Peter, and Phillip. Adam and Christian were employed as blowers at the plant, which was named the Olive Glass Works.

The Stangers' enterprise soon became known for its fine product, and success seemed assured. However, revaluation of the U.S. coinage system, with the government setting forty dollars of Continental money to one dollar of gold, dealt the budding firm a financial blow from which it never recovered.

Following a series of negotiations between 1783 and 1786, ownership of the glassworks passed to Thomas Heston and Thomas Carpenter of Salem County. The new owners enlarged the holdings and merged with the Whitney Brothers plant in 1813. By 1880 the combined operation represented the largest glass business in South Jersey, and Glassboro was known far and wide as the Jersey glassmaking town.

While the glass industry declined elsewhere in South Jersey, Glassboro kept good market contacts. It was on a stage line operated between Camden and Cape Island (Cape May City). Heston's Tavern, built in 1790 as a replacement of Solomon Stanger's log-house tavern, was the stage terminal.

Eventually the glassworks passed to Heston's grandsons, the Whitney brothers, who operated it for more than forty years, preserving the original Wistarburg and Stanger art with regard to color, form, and decorations that are associated with what is known among collectors as South Jersey glass.

From 1800 to 1820 the Glassboro community was under the jurisdiction of Greenwich Township although it had acquired status as a town as far back as 1780. In 1820 a new township was cut from Greenwich, Glassboro, Clayton, Malaga, and Franklin-ville. This union continued until 1858, when Glassboro, Clayton, and Elk created a new division called Clayton Township. This was not the final chapter. In March 1878 the New Jersey legislature passed Senate Bill 276, giving Glassboro independent status under the name of Glassboro Township. It became a college town in 1923 with the establishment of the Glassboro Normal School, now known as Glassboro State College.

On the evening of June 22, 1967, the town was anticipating nothing more exciting than an invasion of about 300 high school cheer leaders for a training session. Suddenly it was catapulted into the world spotlight when the TV news broadcasts announced that a long-discussed meeting between President Johnson and Soviet Premier Alexsai Kosygin would be held in the 118-year-old stone mansion known as Hollybush, residence of college president and Mrs. Thomas Robinson. The same broadcast announced the meeting would take place the next day.

Disbelief was the first reaction. This was soon dispelled as special agents and workmen descended upon the quiet town. Telephone linesmen working throughout the night and predawn hours installed 750 phones, most of them in the college gymnasium, where the basketball floor was ruined. The town's 12-man police force was swiftly augmented by State Police and the FBI until there were 450 men on the spot to guard the official parties.

Local area news sources, caught off guard, began frantic preparations for coverage. I remember a phone call: "We need a background story on Glassboro. Deadline is two hours!"

This was the exciting picture the evening before the big event. Glassboro was chosen for the meeting after Washington and New York were ruled out for political reasons. President Johnson wanted sessions in Washington, Premier Kosygin in New York. Glassboro, a halfway point, was a compromise.

Thousands descended upon the town. Traffic was out of hand. There was a lot of pushing around. Police were broadcasting appeals for people to keep out of the area. Glassboro citizens found themselves sleeping on sofas to make room for VIPs.

The two principals appeared and talked in a small library of

Hollybush after a roast beef lunch. Following the session there was an appearance for newsmen and TV on the ruined lawns of Hollybush. It was announced that a second meeting would be held on Sunday. Kosygin drove back to New York. President Johnson flew to Los Angeles for a scheduled speech. The two heads of state returned to Glassboro on schedule. While history now agrees that no earth-shaking decisions were made there, the town of Glassboro was on the map for all time, and Hollybush has since been a favorite attraction. Chances are, if you approach a Glassboroite and mention the occasion, he will answer by saying: "It was just over there beyond that tree. I was standing there myself. . . ."

Although the community has returned to the business of education, it will never forget "the day."

THE BOOZ BOTTLE

When a friend called and asked if I wanted a couple of booze bottles I did not hesitate, on the presumption that at least one would be Scotch. What I received was a matched pair of bottles of a beautiful amber shade, hand blown or razor-thin glass, shaped like a log cabin.

Edmund C. Booz, who was responsible for the creation of the amber bottles, was a prominent Philadelphia wholesaler of hard spirits, with a business at 120 Walnut Street. During the so-called log cabin campaign of William Henry Harrison in 1840, Booz conceived his log-cabin bottle idea.

Booz had his bottle blown at the Whitney Glass Works in Glassboro under the direction of Captain Even Whitney. Soon Booz's Old Cabin Whiskey in the unique bottle became a familiar sight in every bar. The drinking public began referring to the Philadelphia man's product as *booze*, and the word became of common usage.

Booz died suddenly on July 18, 1870, but the bottle he created lived on. Today it is a collectors' item. In recent years there have been reproductions but none duplicating the fine craftsmanship of the original.

THE CAMP MEETING TOWN

The two things that I remember best from my days as a youngster at Pitman are the boardwalk at Alcyon Lake Park and hearing evangelist Billy Sunday calling for sinners to come forward. Alcyon Lake Park was Pitman's one concession to the pleasures of this world. Its boardwalk was a small affair compared to those now famous at Jersey seaside resorts; but to me then it had the combined glory of a circus and traveling carnival show with a merry-go-round which seemed the last word in elegance. I also remember a ring-toss game in which you always won something, if only a colored feather.

The boardwalk and ring-toss concession have been gone many years, and housing developments now surround Alcyon Lake. However, the tabernacle in which Billy Sunday, the Reverend Charles Pitman, and others preached, is still standing. Visiting preachers are still heard throughout the summer months, but they lack the leather-lunged capacities of their predecessors; they use electronic sound equipment. The hell and brimstone sermons of past days have given way to more refined testaments of love. Marshall Joyce, whose hobby is collecting facts and pictures of the old camp meetings, has established the date of Billy Sunday's last sermon at Pitman as August 6, 1928.

The town of Pitman had its beginning in the summer of 1871, when the Pitman Grove Camp Meeting was organized by a small group of ministers from the New Jersey Conference of the Methodist Church. It was named in honor of the Reverend Charles Pitman, D.D., a powerful camp-meeting preacher of his day. Reverend Pitman was the son of Daniel and Hannah Pitman and was born near Cookstown, Burlington County, on January 9, 1796.

During the camp-meeting season, word that Dr. Pitman would speak resulted in an invasion by thousands of people. A writer

Focer and Sickler's general store in Pitman about 1902. Beside
it was the entrance to the Pitman Grove Camp Meeting where,
beginning in 1871, thousands heard such fervent speakers as
Billy Sunday. The meetings are still a yearly event. (Marshall
Joyce Collection)

of the time describing the effect of Dr. Pitman's two and a half
hour sermons reported: "When he had finished it was difficult to
distinguish between the rejoicing of Christians and the weeping
of awakened sinners."

The extent and success of the great revival era is hard to under-
stand today. The formula was simple. Religious buildings were
not then constructed as they are at present. There was no ma-
chine-regulated air conditioning, and many churches stopped
services completely in the summer. The more zealous of the
preaching fraternity felt that this hiatus would give the devil a
foothold and so developed summer camps, which provided the
physical benefit of a country vacation plus the spiritual reward
of daily reminders of Christian doctrine.

There was a close relationship between camp meetings in Pitman Grove and Ocean Grove in Monmouth County through Dr. A. E. Ballard, who was an officer in both associations. Dr. Ballard arranged the meeting dates so that those of Ocean Grove and Pitman did not conflict.

The first purchases of land for the Pitman camp were made from West Jessup, a large landowner of Mantua Township. About 60 acres were assembled at a cost of $6,000. Ten more acres were bought from Joseph Jessup. The Pitman Grove Association eventually came into possession of all land from what was later Summit Avenue, east of the railroad, extending westward through the Grove section to Cedar Avenue, with a strip to Alcyon Lake. Dwellings within this tract were sold to Methodist ministers only. It was thought in this way to keep the original camp meeting intact. But the ministers eventually died and, as there were no clauses preventing the transfer of land titles, heirs sold to the highest bidder, regardless of religious affiliation.

The Grove had trouble involving rights to sell goods to those using the grounds. There was also the problem of trains stopping at Pitman on the Sabbath. Harkening to the wishes of the association, railroad officials banned Sunday stops. As the nearest stations were Glassboro and Sewell and as the means of travel to the Grove from those stops was by uncomfortable open wagons, residents considered the situation unjust. But the Sunday ban was in effect until the early part of the twentieth century, when residents of Pitman not directly connected with the camp meetings were numerous enough to force a change.

The Woodbury newspaper of 1878 gave a picture of the progress of Pitman, noting that the early white tents and straw beds of the campgrounds had given way to "nicely gravelled walks, four restaurants, barber shop, butcher shop, ice cream saloon, a book store and three hundred cottages." The meetings of 1880 attracted 10,000 visitors. In 1882 a new tabernacle, much larger than the original one, was erected.

Throughout the 1890s Pitman Grove resounded to the preachings of the top evangelists of that day. At the 1898 meeting Evangelist Boswell reported sixty-one conversions, thirty-four backsliders reclaimed, and 150 sanctified.

Since the sale of concessions was a primary source of income, there were a few rumbles with neighborhood farmers and traders who tried to sell supplies on the camp ground without permission. In 1880 George Skinner sold hay to those who came by horse and buggy. The management seized his goods which they later disposed of by public sale. There is no further record of the incident. Again in 1893 the association went to court when F. S. Dodd assaulted a camp meeting director in an argument over whether Dodd could sell his goods from a pushcart inside the camp grounds. There seems to be no record of the outcome.

By 1900 trains were unloading fifty cars of camp enthusiasts every weekend of the meetings. Facilities were overburdened, and soon Pitman was growing beyond the bounds of the Grove and a permanent population was becoming evident.

Pitman gradually took on the status of a year-round town, and it soon became apparent to the permanent settlers that home government was indicated. In 1903 a newly established newspaper, the *Pitman Grove Review,* launched a move of divorcement from Mantua Township, the parent governing body. On October 20, 1904, a meeting was held in the Knights of the Golden Eagle Hall, and the vote was 122 for and 35 against incorporation. On May 24 Governor Edward C. Stokes signed the Avis Bill, and Pitman Grove became the municipality of Pitman.

Camp leaders did not view this trend of events with enthusiasm and came into conflict with the new town leaders on several occasions, especially when the Sunday train ban was lifted. On June 27, 1905, the first borough election was held. J. M. McCowan was named first mayor; six councilmen were elected.

The borough of Pitman lost no time offering inducements to new residents. The Pitman Electric Light Company was organized, gas and water mains laid, a board of trade formed, and an advertising campaign launched. A new electric line improved train service between Pitman and Philadelphia so that travel time to the latter city was only twenty-six minutes. Alcyon Park developed as a focal point for farm picnics and the local Grange Fair.

Today Pitman has a well-designed business center but remains primarily a residential community with a population of approximately 10,257. Camp meetings are still held yearly by the Pitman

The Pitman Fire Patrol, founded on September 4, 1905, posed for this picture in front of their headquarters in 1910. (Marshall Joyce Collection)

Grove Camp Meeting Association. Walking about the grounds recently on a late winter's afternoon, I could still imagine the early preachers exhorting sinners to hit the trail to salvation. This seems to be the one unique part of Pitman that modern social practices have been unable to erase. Pitman will always be a camp meeting town.

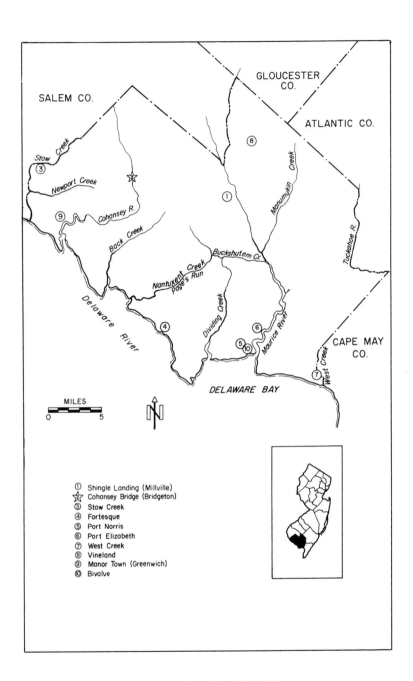

MILES
0 ———— 5

N

① Shingle Landing (Millville)
☆ Cohansey Bridge (Bridgeton)
③ Stow Creek
④ Fortesque
⑤ Port Norris
⑥ Port Elizabeth
⑦ West Creek
⑧ Vineland
⑨ Manor Town (Greenwich)
⑩ Bivalve

CUMBERLAND COUNTY

CUMBERLAND COUNTY

Cumberland County came into being on January 19, 1747/48,* by an act of the legislature cutting it from Salem County. The new county was named by Governor Jonathan Belcher in honor of his patron William Augustus, Duke of Cumberland, brother of King George II and victor over Bonnie Prince Charles, the young pretender to the throne. In July 1748 Cohansey Bridge (present-day Bridgeton) was named county seat.

Cumberland County was originally divided into six townships—Greenwich, Hopewell, Stow Creek, Deerfield, Fairfield, and Maurice River. In 1772 the township of Downe was added by slicing land from one of the original townships, and given the maiden name of Governor William Franklin's wife Elizabeth Downes, whose name was misspelled Downe in the legislation and never corrected.

In the 1800s as populations expanded, there were many subdivisions of the original townships. Bridgeton, also appearing on some documents as Bridgetown, was set off from Deerfield and given individual township status in 1845. Three years later Cohansey Township was created out of Hopewell Township. Vineland made its appearance as a city in 1861. In 1865 after many years of study, the townships of Bridgeton on the east of the Cohansey River and Cohansey Township on the west were merged into the present-day city of Bridgeton. Millville, incorporated as a city in 1866, began life as a township in March of 1801, and continued as originally laid out until the creation of the township of Landis on March 8, 1864. Landis was sliced from Millville. In 1874 Commercial Township was created by taking land from Downe Township. Lawrence was added to Cumberland County in 1885, being cut from Fairfield Township.

*At that time the official legislative year started in March. To try to avoid confusion, official documents contained the two-year designation.

In December of 1774 Cumberland County had its first local newspaper, the *Plain Dealer,* published by posting it on the walls of Potter's Tavern in Cohansey Bridge (which has been restored by the city of Bridgeton and the Bridgeton Historical Commission). The paper demanded separation from English rule, and tavernkeeper Matthew Potter risked a charge of treason in backing the publication. When the first Cumberland County militia marched off to war, the editor and others connected with the enterprise were in the ranks.

On July 7, 1776, Cumberland County's own Liberty Bell summoned the people of Cohansey Bridge to a formal reading of the Declaration of Independence advocated by the colonial representatives in Philadelphia. Dr. Jonathan Elmer, chairman of the Committee for Inspection of the County of Cumberland, was the principal speaker at the gathering, after which the peace officer staves, on which were depicted the coat of arms of George III, were burned in the street.

Cumberland County continued a steady pattern of growth with the glassmen and agriculturists leading the way. As Cohansey River was navigable as far as Bridgeton, Greenwich was the center of trade as a port, and by 1800 Bridgeton had become the business hub of the county.

A MANOR TOWN

The picturesque community of Greenwich, founded in 1675 in the southwestern corner of Cumberland County, still has all its original homes (save one) on Greate Street, its main thoroughfare, and thus retains much of its colonial charm.

John Fenwick planned this, his second settlement, as a manor town with homes located on sixteen-acre lots. Although Fenwick did not live to see his dream come true, his son-in-law Samuel Hedge, together with William Penn, Samuel Smith of Smithfield, and Richard Tindall, who had been Fenwick's principal surveyor, carried out his ideas, mapping a street starting at Cohansey River and extending two and a half miles north toward the town of

Salem. The street is one hundred feet wide to the first bend, ninety feet wide to the second, and eighty feet wide to the Pine Mount Run, where the Presbyterian church is located.

The first manor tract was sold to Mark Reeve, an English Quaker, on February 18, 1684. Fenwick, Penn, and the other Quakers who settled in New Jersey, Delaware, and Pennsylvania had suffered much persecution in England because of their beliefs and their refusal to join the Church of England. As a result, they vowed that the colonies they would found in the New World would be void of religious persecution, places where all faiths would be welcomed. Thus we find Thomas Watson, a Baptist, buying property directly across the street from Mark Reeve, the Quaker. Further up the street Nicholas Gibbon, an Episcopalian, bought land and gave several acres to the Presbyterians for a parsonage. Benjamin Baker, a Quaker, gave an acre of ground on which was erected in 1705 the Presbyterian church, to which were attracted well-known preachers Charles Beatty, Samuel Finley, and Gilbert Tennent.

As early as 1695 cargoes from foreign ports unloaded at the wharf at Greenwich, where merchants came from as far away as Burlington and Philadelphia, then a small village, to buy goods that were transported in flatwagons or floated up the river in small barge-like boats.

In 1701 Greenwich was designated an official port of entry for West Jersey, with customs located there. Market Square was picked as a site for annual fairs authorized by the royal governor from 1695 to 1765.

In 1725 Zachariah Barrows, a Greenwich resident, died and in his will left his estate for the establishment of a school in which children of the poor would be taught to read, write, and figure.* The stone schoolhouse built as the result of Barrows' gift still stands. It is now the home of the Society of New Jersey Artists.

Greenwich had six taverns in its early days. It is believed that Jeremiah Bacon, who bought land from the Fenwick heirs, was

* In those times only the rich were literate as only they could afford private teachers. This is one reason so many old tavern and craft signs consisted of pictures instead of words. Most customers could not read. Such places became known as "At the sign of . . . ."

already dealing in spirits when he received his first recorded license in 1697.

William Watson opened a tavern in 1733, almost directly opposite the Quaker Meeting House, which he conducted until his death in 1743. Watson was a ferryman operating under a patent from the crown issued on July 28, 1733. His boats ran from Greenwich wharf across the Cohansey River.

Most famous of the old inns of Greenwich was the Stone Tavern kept by Jacob Ware from 1728 to 1729 and from 1741 to 1743. Other owners included James Caruthers, Enos Woodruff, and Samuel Woolson. This inn located opposite the Richard Wood mansion has been restored and is the home of Mr. and Mrs. Mark Ewing, descendants of a pioneer Greenwich family.

John Butler operated an inn about 1742 on a lot purchased from Mark Reeve. Another tavern was kept by Seth Bowen between 1763 and 1772 on the south side of the main street. It was the principal stage stop of the town.

Alexander Smith conducted a tavern in North Greenwich nearly opposite the Presbyterian church in what is now known as the Samuel Ewing house. Smith first petitioned for a license in February 1744.

Greenwich was named county seat of Cumberland when the county was divorced from Salem on January 30, 1748. Before the year was out, Cohansey Bridge had won an election and become the county seat. Some Greenwich residents were so incensed over the vote results that they rode their horses into the tavern where the ballots were counted and tossed mugs of beer at the owner.

Greenwich was home to many sea captains through the middle eighties. The house now owned by Mr. and Mrs. James Wasson was built by Captain Charles Miller and his wife Harriet. Captain B. Franklin Maul built a substantial home on the Bridgeton Road.

The Nicholas Gibbon house built in 1730 is now the home of the Cumberland County Historical Society and contains many collections including weapons and Indian relics. A red barn to the rear houses early farm artifacts. The Richard Wood mansion built in 1795, a former home of the Historical Society, is being restored by heirs of Wood.

Other famed buildings on Greate Street still standing (all private homes) are the Anchorage (1850), the Harding house (1734), Ewing house (1834), Reeve house (1797), Allens house (circa 1800), Bay Marsh (date unknown), Pirate house (tradition says it was occupied by a genuine pirate), and the McChristie home (just off Greate Street). Once a year these old houses are open to the public in a tour sponsored by the Cumberland County Historical Society.

Two other places worth seeing are Richard Wood's general store (1795), believed to be the oldest general store in South Jersey still in use, and the Quaker Meeting House with its burial grounds. The latter structure, built in 1771 on grounds bought in 1686, is a Georgian-style brick building, the interior of which has been restored with careful attention to detail. The first session of the Cumberland County court was held at this location May 31, 1748, in a building that later burned.

TEA FOR BURNING

In December of 1774 the brig *Greyhound* sailed up the Delaware River with a cargo of tea from the East India Company in London consigned to merchants in Philadelphia. At Lewes, Delaware, Captain J. Allen took on a river pilot who informed him that there was a good chance he would not find a welcome in Philadelphia because the heavily taxed English tea was decidedly unpopular there. The pilot also told Captain Allen that the ship *Polly* carrying tea to Philadelphia a short time previously had been refused permission to dock and threatened by a group of angry patriots.

Not wanting to endanger his vessel, Captain Allen decided to put into the port of Greenwich. Knowing of a Tory, Daniel Bowen, who lived near the Greenwich wharf, the captain secured permission to store his cargo of tea in Bowen's cellar while awaiting further instructions from his consignees.

Cumberland County was then the home of patriots who were

already talking about separation from England, and on December 13, 1774, when news spread of the tea cargo in Bowen's cellar, indignation ran high.

Philip Vickers Fithian kept a journal in which he noted, "The County met at Cohansie Bridge and Chose a Committee and it was recommended to them to examine into and take Proper care of the aforesaid Goods." This committee, composed of thirty-five citizens of the area, decided to proceed with caution. The more militant and youthful element decided to take matters in their own hands.

On the night of December 22 a group of youths dressed as Indians, smeared paint on their faces, and went on horseback to the home of Fithian. There they met a similar group who had met at the home of the Howell twins, Richard and Lewis, in Shiloh. Together the "Indians" rode to the house of the Tory Bowen, broke open the cellar door, and tossed out boxes of tea to willing hands who carried them to Market Square. Soon a huge bonfire lit up the central part of the village. As the flames leaped higher and the significance of the action became known, others from the town gathered to cheer.

When the fires died, the tea burners mounted their horses and with loud whoops raced down Greate Street and out of the village. There was no attempt to conceal identities, so all the youths who took part were known by name.

As in Boston, the "Indians" were held accountable for the destruction of property. Consignees John Duffield and Stacy Hepburn of Philadelphia, who had paid for the tea, made several attempts to gain restitution, both in civil and criminal courts.

Sheriff Jonathan Elmer was charged with making arrests and getting together a grand jury. The sheriff's two brothers Ebenezer and Timothy were two of the "Indians," and Elmer selected a jury from relatives of the tea burners or known sympathizers. After the presentation of enough evidence to convict anyone, the grand jury voted "no cause for action."

Consignees Duffield and Hepburn took their cause to Governor William Franklin, who was known for his Tory leanings. Franklin removed Elmer as sheriff and appointed the Tory Daniel Bowen in his place with instructions to get a new jury and conduct a second trial. This Bowen did; but again the patriots were in the majority, and the remaining Tories were timid. This jury also brought in "no cause for action." The two merchants finally gave up.

A majority of the tea burners served in the Revolution in both Jersey regiments and in the Continental Army. Two of them, Andrew Hunter, Jr., and Philip Vickers Fithian, were chaplains of the American army, both being ordained ministers of the Presbyterian church. Hunter eventually became a professor at Princeton and an official U.S. Navy chaplain.

Of the others involved in the escapade, Richard Howell became governor of New Jersey. Thomas Ewing became a surgeon. Five served in various positions in the state government. Joseph Bloomfield, who acted as attorney for the tea burners during the two trials, was elected governor of the state; the city of Bloomfield, New Jersey, is named in his honor.

On a September day in 1908 some eight thousand South Jerseyans gathered at Market Square in Greenwich to take part in the unveiling of a monument to the tea-burning heroes of 1774. The monument was provided through the efforts of the Daughters of the American Revolution, Warren W. Sheppard, and the Cumberland County Historical Society. Governor John F. Fort accepted the monument in behalf of the state; former governor Edward C. Stokes spoke.

Inscribed on the monument are the following names: Ebenezer Elmer, Richard Howell, David Pierson, Stephen Pierson, Silas Whitecar, Timothy Elmer, Andrew Hunter, Jr., Philip Vickers Fithian, Alexander Moore, Jr., Clarence Parvin, John Hunt, James Hunt, Lewis Howell, Henry Stacks, James Ewing, Josiah Seeler, and Joel Fithian.

FROM CORDWOOD TO OYSTERS

Port Norris, picturesque home of Delaware bay oyster boats, occupies an advantageous position at the mouth of the Maurice River, which was known to the Indians as Wahatquenack. Ac-

In 1957 the oyster industry centered at Bivalve and Port Norris in Cumberland County was nearly wiped out by MSX disease. This photograph shows a truckload of oyster shells from Chesapeake Bay being dumped onto a barge for distribution among the area's oyster beds, where the oyster ova will attach themselves to the shells and grow. (*Atlantic City Press* photo)

cording to local tradition, half a mile below Mauricetown, New Jersey, a band of roving Indians attacked and sunk the Dutch sailing vessel *Prince Maurice,* after which event early settlers began referring to the stream as Maurice. Eventually Maurice became the river's official name.

In 1691 John Worledge and John Budd, surveyors in the employ of the West Jersey Proprietors, visited the Maurice River area and surveyed ten thousand acres for Dr. James Wasse of London. This covered land between the Maurice River and Dividing Creek.

The Wasse tract was sold in parcels, and in 1738 William Dallas moved to the region, purchased a large slice of the land, and began operating a ferry service across the Maurice River. A settlement springing up around the ferry house took the name Dallas Ferry.

When Dallas sold his holdings in 1810, they were bought by Joseph Jones, son of a wealthy Philadelphia coffee merchant. Jones, better known in the vicinity as "Coffee," became active in village life and changed the name of the settlement to Port Norris for his oldest son.

Jones built a tavern for John Ogden and Norton Harris near the landing, and much of the town's life was centered there. A wide avenue near the dock and tavern was used for racing horses. Jones had a growing wood supply business and maintained several boats to take his cut lumber to Philadelphia, where it was much in demand. He also attempted to operate a large sheep range and bought several thousand animals. About 1812 the sheep were hit by an illness that killed most of the flock. Jones took the remainder of the animals to Hog Island and sold them in a lottery in which he also included his property at Port Norris.

During the time of "Coffee" Jones, the cutting and shipping of cordwood was a principal industry. Shallops would come up Ware Creek to take the wood to the Philadelphia market. Bit by bit the harvesting of oysters began to overshadow the lumber business. By 1955 the oyster industry had reached its peak with twenty-nine shippers giving it their full time. Before train service in the area, oysters were iced and transported to Gloucester by relay teams. They were taken from Gloucester to Philadelphia by boat.

The railroad came to Port Norris in 1860. A station, round-house, and turntable were built, and at times there were four freight trains and two passenger trains per day on the schedule.

In 1872 Steve Mayhew built the first hotel in Port Norris; it replaced an earlier Main Street tavern. This hotel was three stories high, contained about forty rooms and a bar. The bar was a rowdy place, specially on payday along the waterfront. The Anti-Saloon League combined with the Baptist and Methodist congregations to get the hotel's license revoked. On May 1, 1928, the hotel burned to the ground.

Port Norris continues today as one of the centers of the lower Delaware oyster industry.

THE MEDICINE SHOW

For many years in Cumberland County spring was heralded by the arrival of the medicine man and his traveling show. These men were nearly always assured an audience because there wasn't much else to do and the towns visited were lenient in regulations regarding them. Their brightly painted wagons would stop at a community's gathering place, where they would set up a boxlight stage, break out a couple of oil flares, and go into the business of selling cure-alls between acts of low comedy and music.

Most of the tonics sold were about ninety percent alcohol with a little "Indian herb" flavoring. For the moment, the purchaser, urged to take his first dose in front of the wagon, would feel better. By the time he discovered he had been duped, the medicine man and his crew were well on their way to the next stop. They never played the same village twice in the same year—on the assumption that if they did not return too soon, all would be forgotten and forgiven.

In time some of the more intelligent medicine salesman developed root and herb mixtures with merit. These men were welcomed back; the others usually had to work one step ahead of the sheriff.

An early medicine show proprietor of Cumberland County was Elmer Fisher of Bridgeton, who had a flair for showmanship. Fisher was a convincing speaker and tried to give value for money received. He became associated with Jack Moulan, a successful medicine man of the time. At the death of Moulan, Fisher took over his equipment and toured the country.

Boys of Bridgeton would give their versions of the traveling medicine show about a week later. These shows were usually a good burlesque of the original, and their medicine consisted of a harmless preparation of licorice and water.

The medicine show provided a pleasant break in the routine of a small community even though it accomplished little for the health of the populace.

BRIDGE GIVES CITY NAME

Prior to 1716 a bridge of logs resting on pilings was built across the Cohansey River near the uppermost portion of the waterway. This span connected the north and south settlements of the area for the first time, and the community thus formed became known as Cohansey Bridge, later Bridgetown, and finally the city of Bridgeton.

Because of its centralized location Cohansey Bridge soon became a popular crossroads village in the South Jersey system of roads, and a stagecoach stop for wagons on the Philadelphia-Salem route.

Among the first to see the business potential of The Bridge, as it was commonly called by first settlers, were Silar Parvin, Elias Cotting, and William Doubleday. Parvin, for whom Parvin State Park is named, opened the first country store in the area. In 1716 all three men obtained liquor licenses and conducted taverns in the budding town. These inns were gathering places for farmers, businessmen, and wood cutters anxious to learn the news of Philadelphia and New York brought by stage riders.

When Cohansey Bridge was named county seat after the creation of Cumberland County in 1748, the residents of Greenwich, a much larger village, did not take kindly to the idea, and ill feeling delayed the erection of the first county courthouse until the summer of 1752. Court was held there on August 25 with John Brick, a former assemblyman, presiding as judge. Most cases concerned runaway indentured persons, although a horse thief was tried, convicted, and hung in 1758. In 1759 the courthouse burned to the ground. It was replaced by a brick building with a cupola on top, housing a bell which arrived from Bridgewater, Massachusetts, in 1763. This bell became known as South Jersey's Liberty Bell when it rang out news of the Declaration of Independence on July 4, 1776. It can still be seen in the county courthouse.

In 1800 three to four hundred persons resided at Cohansey Bridge and 9,526 in the entire county, according to the census of that year. Bridgeton today has a population of approximately 20,000.

Educational facilities in Cohansey Bridge settlement began in 1773, when a private school was started by John Westcott. The Reverend Andrew Hunter, pastor of the Greenwich Presbyterian church, conducted a classical school in Cohansey Bridge in 1780. Mark Miller, who had already deeded land for a church, gave another plot for the establishment of a school at Giles and Academy streets in 1792. Five years later a group of citizens joined with the Brearley Lodge of Masons to erect Harmony Academy on Bank Street. Laurel Hill Academy was started on Pearl Street in 1822.

The public school system dates from a frame building erected on Bank Street in 1847. West Jersey Academy for Boys, on the site of the present high school, opened in 1852. Ivy Hall Seminary for girls was launched in 1861. The West Jersey Baptist Association opened a boarding school for boys and girls in 1870. These last three schools gained distinction in the field of education and lasted to the turn of the century.

In the first city election held after the effective date of the incorporation of the city in 1865, James Hood, Republican, was elected mayor over his Democratic opponent Adrian Bateman by

Cobb's Band was one of several musical organizations in Bridgeton in the late 1880s. Many of the early instruments are on display at the Bridgeton Historical Museum. (Courtesy of Cumberland County Historical Society)

a majority of twenty-nine votes. Bridgeton exists today under a modified form of commission government. It is the center for glassmaking, ironcasting, clothing factories, manufacturing, vegetable and fruit packing.

LUMBER AND GLASS

While the city of Millville could be said to have emerged from a small 1755 log cabin settlement known as Shingle Landing, its possibilities as a town were not realized until Colonel Joseph Buck, a soldier and adventurer under George Washington, was mustered out of the Continental Army following the surrender at Yorktown in 1781 and came to live in the area. He plunged into Cumberland County politics and from 1787 to 1790 served as sheriff of the county. About 1795 he envisioned a city of mills along the Maurice River with manor houses farther uptown. To this end he dealt in real estate and laid plans for a town. Among early land purchasers were James Sweatman, Nathan Leake, Jeremiah Stratton, Ezekiel Foster, David Nicholas, Jeremiah Seeley, and James Ware. Although Colonel Buck bought and sold much acreage, he did not live to see his dream come true. There were less than twenty dwellings in Millville when he died in 1803.

Two other men prominent in the affairs of Millville arrived in 1790. Henry Drinker and Joseph Smith formed the Union Company and purchased 19,563 acres of land in a survey made for Thomas and Richard Penn. The company built a dam, raised a pond known as Union Mill Pond, and established lumber mills.

In 1806 James Lee from Port Elizabeth started a window-glass factory on the site of the present American Legion hall. In company with Ebenezer Seeley and Smith Bowen, Lee erected a dam across the Maurice River to provide power to a new paper mill project. This enterprise failed. Meanwhile Lee's original glass factory and another plant operated by Frank Schetter of Baltimore were absorbed by the Whitall Tatum Company, which in turn was taken over by the Armstrong Corporation in 1939.

Millville's most historic structure still standing is the Mansion house built in 1804 by David C. Wood, who in 1814 erected an iron foundry in Millville with Edwin Smith as a partner.* Charcoal was the fuel used, and the large tracts of land covering the northern and eastern parts of what was then Millville township and extending into Gloucester County, owned by the company, furnished the necessary supply. Smith soon sold his interest, and Wood carried on alone. The Lee and the Wood factories brought new people to Millville, and the town showed its first real progress.

One of the great glassmakers of Millville was Dr. T. C. Wheaton, born in the small Cape May County hamlet of South Seaville in 1852. He arrived in Millville in 1884 and opened a drug store at 18 West Broad Street. With a diploma from the Philadelphia College of Pharmacy and the University of Pennsylvania Medical School, Wheaton hung out his shingle as a physician, later opening a second drugstore at High and Sassafras streets.

Wheaton became friends with William Shull and Eugene Goodwin, operators of a small glass factory nearby. When the firm faced financial difficulties, Dr. Wheaton loaned the partners several thousand dollars. In 1888 he took over personal direction of the eight-pot furnace and gave up his practice to devote his whole time to glassmaking.

Dr. Wheaton died on September 30, 1931, and his son Frank H., who started in his father's business at $5 per week, took over. Today the Wheaton plant covers a large part of Millville's third ward and is the top industry of the town. Blood plasma bottles, first used in World War II, were turned out at the Wheaton plant.

Millville Township, created by an act of the legislature on February 14, 1801, attained city status on February 26, 1866. On

* The Mansion house, now the home of the Millville Historical Society, is constructed of New Jersey iron stone mined in the Cumberland district. Richard D. Wood, brother of David C., was the second owner. Richard D. established a textile plant, built a dam, brought the railroad to Millville, and engaged in many community activities. His son George next occupied the house. The last member of the Wood family to live there was George Wood Furness, who left Millville in 1958, thus completing one hundred and fifty years of continuous occupancy of the house by one family.

An early picture of the crew and original building of the Wheaton glass factory which today covers a large part of Millville's third ward. (Courtesy of Millville Historical Society)

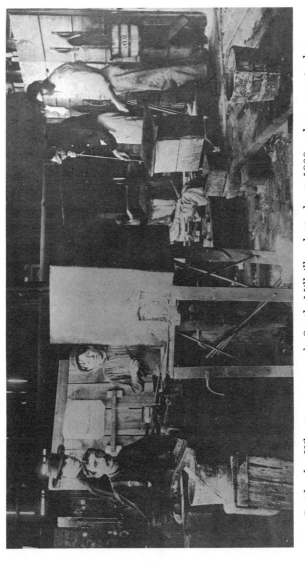

Inside the Wheaton company's South Millville plant about 1900, when expert glass blowers earned from $6 to $8 per day. An early historian has identified the workers as Albert Felmey (seated), blower; William Cox (rear), grapher; Ken Hickman, snapping-up boy; Andy Bittle, mold boy; William Peek and Ralph Compton, blowers. (Courtesy of Virgil Johnson)

March 13 the first municipal election was held with James M.
Wells being named mayor. At that time the city's population was
not quite five thousand. The city fathers first met at Ludlam Hall,
for which the city paid $100 annual rent. In 1881 the first city
hall was erected at the northeast corner of Second and Sassafras
streets at a cost of $10,000. Many of the taxpayers disapproved
of spending that much money for a hall and threatened to ride
the city officials out of town. The building served as city hall,
fire and police headquarters.

Millville's first police force consisted of three men, a city
marshal and two constables. They were not furnished badges,
although the council passed an act granting them permission to
"wear badges of their office at their own expense." The new
policemen also had to furnish their own uniforms. William L.
Earle was the first town marshal, Abram Donnelly and William
Carey constables. They received no salary but were paid fees, a
system that lasted until 1927.

THE HOLLY CITY

A visitor entering Millville drives past a stone wall entranceway
on which is a setting of ornate letters reading MILLVILLE, THE
HOLLY CITY. The wall is flanked on either side by two large holly
trees. Each Christmas season thousands of visitors flock to Millville to see its elaborate holly displays and the world's largest
holly plantation.

The giant holly farm on the property of the New Jersey Silica
Sand Company was not originally a commercial enterprise. In
fact, it may have been the most costly single hobby in existence.
At any rate, it completely changed the lives of the two men most
concerned with it.

Clarence Wolf, a native of Highspire, Pennsylvania, arrived
in Millville as a teacher in the city's public school system. In 1918
he became principal of Millville High School. During the course
of his principalship he met Burdette Tomlin, who became a

prosperous businessman in South Jersey and for whom Burdette Tomlin Memorial Hospital in Cape May Court House was named.

In 1921 Tomlin offered Wolf a partnership in a new sand business he was launching with headquarters at Millville. Upon the Death of Tomlin in 1923, Wolf bought the remaining shares, gave up teaching, and became president of the firm known as the Silica Sand Company.

During clearance of land for expansion, workmen uprooted numerous holly trees growing in profusion on the property. Wolf decided the holly was worth keeping and designated a part of the land owned by the company for the replanting of the trees. In 1926, as Christmas approached, he hit upon the idea of cutting back the holly trees and sending gift boxes to his customers.

The response was so enthusiastic that the following year Wolf doubled his output of holly. This practice continued for some years until a frost one season killed most of his trees. Wolf decided this would not happen again and embarked upon plans for better protection of his holly; in 1939 he launched a real holly orchard.

About that time Daniel Fenton, a native of Gloucester County, arrived at Millville as a vocational-agricultural teacher in the Millville schools; he and Wolf found a common bond in their interest in holly. Again a teaching career lost as Fenton joined Wolf as supervisor of the holly plantation.

There are more than sixteen varieties of American holly in the Millville farm, plus English, Chinese, and Japanese holly. Fenton estimates that there are 6,400 trees twelve to twenty feet high and 8,500 trees up to eight feet.

In the center of the plantation is Holly House, a showroom containing the largest collection of hand-painted holly glassware in the world, featuring the leaves and berries in many forms and arrangements. The collection is composed entirely of gifts sent to Wolf and Fenton by friends from all parts of the globe.

Wolf left his imprint upon Millville in many ways. He served on its school board, civic committees, was responsible for the large YMCA and gave the association a tract of land along the Port Elizabeth-Cumberland Road for a summer camp. In 1946 he was named Millville's outstanding citizen. A year later he founded the Holly Society of America; its original membership of eight has expanded to several thousand.

Lafayette College of Easton, Pennsylvania, from which he graduated in 1911, conferred an honorary Doctor of Science degree upon him in 1957. Wolf died in May of 1966 at the age of seventy-nine. At his death Fenton took over as president of the company and the holly experimental farm.

On April 8, 1971, the farm was sold to the American Holly Products Company, to be operated as a commercial venture. Fenton continued as head of the parent operation.

There is no doubt of Millville's pride in its title Holly City, for in addition to the familiar sprig of holly on official city stationery there are such Millville institutions as Holly City Corporation, Holly City Service Station, Holly City Music Center, Holly City Glass, Inc., Holly City Tire Company, Holly City Real Estate, Holly House Restaurant, Holly Park Motel, and a barbershop quartet which has taken part in national competition under the title The Holly City Four.

THE TWO-FACED CLOCK

One of the unusual reminders of another day that Bridgeton has succeeded in preserving is a two-faced clock located in its tiny but highly interesting Nail House Museum.

The clock, a grandfather type made in 1830, is anchored in the wall of Nail House, once the business office of a small firm calling itself the Cumberland Nail and Iron Company. This timepiece is so placed that one face shows inside the office, for the benefit of officials no doubt, while the other face is on the outside wall of the building, where ironworkers reporting to their jobs could check their hours.

John Whitehead of Haddonfield constructed the two-faced clock according to the best information available. However, while Whitehead's name appears on the outside face of the clock, that of J. C. Harris of Bridgeton is on the inner wall face. It is generally thought that Harris, who worked in Bridgeton at clock repairs, placed his name thereon during a repair job.

The Cumberland Nail and Iron Company was launched in 1814 by Benjamin and David Reeves of Camden. Production began the following year, continuing through several owners until the late 1890s. The plant was located on the Cohansey River flowing through Bridgeton. A footbridge connected two parts of the operation, a rolling mill on one side and nail-making machines on the other. Workers carried the sheets of iron from the foundry across the bridge to the machines, one of which is on display at the Nail House.

Near the turn of the century the city of Bridgeton bought the factory and surrounding land of 1,100 acres to preserve part of the Cohansey River watershed as a park. The Antiquarian League of Bridgeton was formed to preserve and restore the historic building. Through the efforts of the league, headed by Mrs. Jonathan Moore, old nails and other items relating to early Bridgeton have been collected to create the Nail House Museum.

FRUIT, EGGS AND INDUSTRY

After developing Hammonton and Sea Isle City, Charles K. Landis conceived the idea for a settlement on the border of the great metropolitan markets with fruit culture as its mainstay. In 1861 when but twenty-eight years old, Landis selected a tract of land in Cumberland County containing about forty-eight square miles. He bought twenty-two thousand acres from Richard D. Wood of Philadelphia and the remainder from other individuals, making a total parcel of thirty-two thousand acres.

In the center of this tract, Landis planned Vineland. On August 8, 1861, he felled the first tree to make way for Landis Avenue, a street ten and a half miles long and one hundred feet wide. Landis stipulated in leases that a house must be erected upon land bought from him within a year's time, that it must be set back twenty-five feet from the street, and that shade trees should be planted along the front of each place. No fences were allowed.

Shipping strawberries to the big-city markets from Vineland in 1868. (Courtesy of Cumberland County Historical Society)

Landis Avenue today is one of the big shopping centers of southern Jersey, but its residential section, stretching several miles, is still the way Landis planned it, and is declared by many the most beautiful of the area, with substantial homes, well set back on carefully tended lawns, and large shade trees whose limbs meet over the avenue.

The railroad came through Vineland in 1862 although a station was not built until some years later. Planks in the mud provided a temporary platform. In December of 1862 the first public schoolhouse was opened. Here were held town meetings, as well as services of the Presbyterian, Episcopal, and Methodist congregations. On Christmas day seventy-five settlers gathered for a celebration to mark the rapid progress of the city.

By 1864 more than a thousand acres had been sold in the new community. In that year an antifashion conclave was held with delegates from all parts of the east attending. The lady delegates daringly agreed to cut four inches from the length of dresses. A contemporary report of the event records that the conventioneers were given a rousing cheer from male on-lookers.

There were big doings in Vineland on November 29–30 of the year 1868, when the town found itself the center of a women's suffrage crusade. A gathering was held in Vineland with Lucretia Mott, a national leader of the movement then sweeping the country, as its principal speaker. The town seemed to have had a particular fascination for crusaders, and among those appearing at gatherings in Vineland within the next few years were Horace Greeley, Susan B. Anthony, Julia Ward Howe, and Dr. Russell Conwell, of "Acres of Diamonds" fame.

When Charles K. Landis died on June 12, 1900, Vineland was well on its way as the most populous community in the county. Although Landis's initial grape-raising plans did not come up to his expectations, agriculture did and still does predominate within the boundaries of the community, which is one of the great chicken and egg centers of the East. It is also a truck-farm area.

While its poultry and farming pursuits are sizable, Vineland is also the center for the manufacture of glass, clothing, truck bodies, bottles, canned goods, chemicals, paper products, and fertilizers. The city received a boost in population and area when it was consolidated with Landis Township on July 1, 1952.

Besides the Landis Avenue shopping district, Vineland now has several other shopping centers with nationally known chain stores, a number of fine restaurants (several specializing in Italian dishes), public and parochial high schools, and a new municipal building completed in 1970.

Vineland is the largest city in the state in area, possessing a total of sixty-eight square miles of land. Its 1971 population was placed at 48,000. The town is the site of the New Jersey Memorial Home for veterans and the Vineland State School for the mentally handicapped. In Vineland is also located the Institute for Mental Studies, a private foundation in which author Pearl Buck takes an active part. The Vineland Historical Society maintains one of the larger historical museums of the area open to the public.

FROM BACKYARD TO COMMUNION TABLE

One Sunday morning in the fall of 1869 there was an unusual feature of communion service of the Methodist Church of Vineland, New Jersey, as a result of which a million-dollar business empire was founded, the last thought in the minds of the two men involved, a minister and a dentist, both more interested in an ideal than in financial gain.

Until this particular Sunday morning, wine had been served in the Methodist church service despite the feelings of the minister that intoxicating beverages should not be used in church ritual.

This matter was discussed on numerous occasions by the Reverend A. K. Street, who was appointed in 1869 to the church, and Dr. Thomas B. Welch, a Vineland dentist, who was also communion steward of the church. Both felt there must be a substitute for what was then the accepted format of the service. Dr. Welch had for some time been growing grapes in the backyard of his home and, on the urgings of his minister, began experimenting with the preparation of unfermented juice of Concord grapes for the communion table.

In 1869 dentist Thomas Bramwell Welch developed a process which preserved unfermented grape juice so the Methodist Church of Vineland could use a nonintoxicating beverage in its communion service. He soon gave up dentistry and founded the Welch Grape Juice Company. (Courtesy of Welch Grape Juice Company)

As the result of these experiments, grape juice replaced wine in the Methodist church for the first time in history. As far as the two men were concerned, they had supplied their immediate needs and that was the end of the story. Then other Methodist ministers of southern Jersey, hearing of Dr. Welch's new grape juice, started sending in orders. The dentist began filling these requests on a personal basis, but the demand soon got out of hand.

Dr. Welch was an ardent follower of Pasteur and his theories of sterilization at a time when most of the world scoffed at the Frenchman. In the process of pasteurization Dr. Welch saw the possibility of bottling grape juice so it could be kept in unfermented form. He labored arduously on his experiments in the kitchen of his home and finally developed a practical bottling method. As word continued to spread among churchmen, the Vineland dentist was soon squeezing more grapes than pulling teeth.

Grapes were first squeezed by hand, but as the workload increased Dr. Welch built a small brick factory and invested in two power pressers. The grapes used were grown in his own vineyard or in the surrounding area. In 1876, six years after Dr. Welch had introduced grape juice, his clientele remained largely clerical; his advertising was confined to circulars sent through the mails. At this time Dr. Welch was still not impressed with the prospects of his grape juice beyond church use and he wrote to his son Charles, then a dentist, in Washington, D.C., "Stick to dentistry; forget grape juice."

Charles didn't agree and urged his father to try wider advertising. They chose a church periodical, the *Christian Advocate,* and inserted a one-inch announcement. The younger Welch went a step further. He gave up his dental practice and bought his father's interest in the business. This was in 1873, when Dr. Welch's Grape Juice was still being delivered to the Vineland express office by wheelbarrow.

In 1896 the elder Welch reinvested in his son's grape juice business and, with the funds on hand, father and son launched a three-year advertising campaign in magazines. This was the breakthrough, and the young company coined the slogan "Welch's Grape Juice, the National Drink."

Vineland, headquarters of the company for thirty years, was deemed too small for future expansion, and the operation was moved to Watkins, New York, in 1896; one year later it was relocated at Westfield, New York, where it built a new plant. Some three hundred tons of grapes were pressed that year and Concord grape cultivation became the chief agricultural pursuit of the New York community.

Dr. Thomas Welch lived to see his son Charles well established in the business. He died in 1903 shortly after the enterprise was incorporated in New York state.

On April 22, 1913, the Welch product received international publicity when Secretary of State William Jennings Bryan gave a dinner for James Bryce, retiring British ambassador, and served grape juice instead of the customary champagne. Another publicity windfall occurred in 1914, when Secretary of the Navy Josephus Daniels issued an order forbidding liquor on battleships and in Navy yards. Satirists of the day with much glee dubbed the fleet "The Grape Juice Navy."

Until his death in 1926 Charles Welch was the guiding spirit of the firm which had blossomed into an international institution. Today more than one hundred thousand tons of Concord grapes from nearly thirty thousand acres are processed yearly by Welch plants in New York, Pennsylvania, Michigan, Arkansas, and Washington. Vineland's part in the story now exists only in history.

REVOLUTION IN THE KITCHEN

In 1810 Nicolas Appert, a French confectioner, published his principles of food preservation through sterilization. His theory was that heat would preserve fruits, meats, and vegetables by arresting natural tendencies of spoilage. Appert was awarded a 12,000-franc prize by the Emperor Napoleon, who during his war campaigns had many times asked French scientists if they could come up with a way to preserve food so it would keep while his army was on the march.

John L. Mason, born in Vineland, who in 1858 patented a jar with a porcelain-lined metal screw top which made it possible to preserve food without refrigeration. (Courtesy of Glass Containers Manufacturers Institute)

But it was not until November 30, 1858, that the full practical potential of Appert's theories was realized. On that date John Mason patented the first Mason jar, which soon revolutionized the eating habits of millions of people.

Son of a Scottish farmer, John L. Mason was born in Vineland in 1832. As a young man he moved to New York City and established a metals shop on Canal Street. It was there that he first envisioned his famous jar.

At that period South Jersey was the axis of a glass empire of twenty-eight glass factories. One of the well-known glass-producing operations was that of Samuel Crowley, at Crowleytown on the Mullica River, a short distance from Batsto on the Burlington County side of the river.

In October of 1858 Mason the tinsmith visited Crowley and outlined his idea of a fruit jar with grooves into which a porcelain-lined metal screw top would fit. Could Crowley make such a jar? Crowley could and did.

The first such jar was blown by Clayton Parker of Bridgeton, principal glassblower of the Crowley works.* Mason returned to New York and secured a patent for his Improved Jar which carried the notice that was to be inscribed on preserve jars for the next three-quarters of a century, "Mason's Patent, November 30, 1858."

* Jonathan Parker, brother of Clayton and also a glassblower, worked at the Crowleytown glass factory. In 1954, when ninety-two years old, he gave this interesting picture of the operation to Meade Landis of the *Bridgeton Evening News:*

"I started to work in the Crowleytown plant at the age of ten. I was paid ten dollars per month for twelve hours work a day, six days a week. When I was old enough to cut wood for the furnace I was paid one dollar per day. During the six years I worked in Crowleytown, I never saw a dollar in cash because the factory store extended credit on book, and by the time payday came around I had used up all my pay on book account. When I started work the blower did everything. The Mason jar required a tight-fitting top, and the rim had to be ground on a grind-stone. This was kept in motion by a horse hitched to a long pole which went around and around to generate power.

"By 1885 after working in Bridgeton, I went to Woodbury to organize the Woodbury Glassworks. I returned to Bridgeton and joined Clayton and my other brothers Benjamin and Joseph in a glassmaking operation of our own."

During the winter of 1858 Mason moved his business operations to 257 Pearl Street, New York, and formed a partnership with T. W. Frazier, Henry Mitchell, and B. W. Payne. Mason and his partners made the molds; various glass factories produced jars according to the original Mason plans.

The Civil War interrupted the new enterprise, and Mason's name disappeared from New York City directories until 1865, after which Mason moved his business to Spring Street. In 1873 he moved to New Brunswick, New Jersey, where he married and raised a family. There Mason became associated with the Consolidated Fruit Jar Company, which acquired rights to his first two patents. These patents expired in 1875 and entered the public domain. On February 8, 1876, Mason assigned remaining rights in the jars to Consolidated.

In the words of J. E. Pfeiffer of Swedesboro, an authority on South Jersey blown glass, "It was a Jersey operation all the way. Mason was a Vineland man, Crowley a Burlington County industrialist, Parker from Bridgeton and finally the Consolidated Fruit Jar Company, a New Brunswick firm."

A good exhibit of Mason jars is to be found in the glass museum at Batsto, the restored iron town of Cumberland County, New Jersey. John Adams, Atlantic City publisher, had one of the most complete collections of Mason Jars in the state; at his death it was given to the Wheaton Museum in Millville.

THE SEABROOK ENTERPRISE

In the early 1880s Arthur P. Seabrook, a hard-working dirt farmer, prided himself on the quality of peas, green beans, spinach, and lima beans he was able to coax from the soil of his 57-acre farm near the city of Bridgeton, Cumberland County.

In fact, farmer Seabrook had so much confidence in his produce that after harvesting it he packed it onto an old wagon and sold door to door in the nearby area. His needs were small, his methods by today's standards crude. But vegetables from the Seabrook farm became known for quality, and soon there were

The main plant of Seabrook Farms in Cumberland, including the employees housing development (upper left) and one of the experimental fields (top center). (Courtesy of Seabrook Farms)

demands from a wider circle than farmer Seabrook could service in his horse and wagon. By 1900 Seabrook was shipping fresh vegetables to Philadelphia, Baltimore, and New York.

In 1912 his son Charles F. took over the management of the farm and its growing market. Young Seabrook is described by those who knew him as a man with the green thumb of a Burbank and the business acumen of a Rockefeller. An advocate of controlled irrigation, which his father had started in a small way, Seabrook soon had his farm prosperous and green while others of the area were burning up in the drought.

He also installed a cold storage plant and warehouses and was one of the pioneers in controlled atmospheric storage, now practiced on a wide scale by most South Jersey agriculturists.

By World War I, with its increased demands for food, Seabrook built the 57-acre farm into one of 3,000 acres. In 1922 he added a cannery to the property.

Within a decade Seabrook was to produce his first quick-frozen vegetables. The chapter that led to this development started in Canada, where Clarence Birdseye of New York was studying the eating habits of the Eskimos and hit upon the process which was to make his name a household word.

Birdseye came to Seabrook Farms in the late 1920s to further his experiments. Under an arrangement with Seabrook, Birdseye handled sales while Seabrook concentrated upon seed development and processing. When General Foods acquired the Birdseye patents in 1929, Seabrook was given the job of producing frozen lima beans.

In 1944 Seabrook Farms established its own brand and began to do its own marketing of frozen foods. By 1956 the annual sales had grown to a multimillion-dollar figure.

John Seabrook, son of Charles, took over the booming farm business in the early 1950s. In 1957 Seabrook Farms introduced its Miracle Pack prepared food line, which makes it possible for a housewife to serve elaborate dishes such as chicken cacciatore and beef goulash in a few minutes.

Meanwhile another big company in the food line, Seeman Brothers, Inc., of New York, was on a program of expansion. In March of 1957 it acquired Francis H. Leggett and Company with its wholesale grocery operations in New York, Pittsburgh, and Cincinnati. White Rose Ceylon tea was its top seller. In May 1959, Seeman Brothers acquired Seabrook Farms and changed the name to Seeman Brothers, Inc.

Charles Seabrook died in 1964, but the ideas he fostered are still the backbone of the Seabrook enterprise.

Seabrook Foods, Inc., which now conducts the farming part of the vast complex, is a combine of seven different companies with holdings throughout the United States.

As part of its scientific farming program, Seabrook does not plant or harvest by the calendar, a system used by farmers since the dawn of planting. Based on data accumulated over a period of years, the company uses early and late plantings, slow and fast growers, in a system that keeps a flow of matured produce on a daily basis. As a result, the processing plant and the freezing plant operate close to capacity every day from April through late November. The last of the spinach is cut by December 1.

Seabrook Farms practiced ecology when the word was still buried in the dictionary. All natural organic waste is placed back in the earth to build soil elements. Seabrook Farms' work in soil conservation is recognized and studied throughout the agricultural world.

The Seabrook Farms processing center now covers more than 120 acres. Cultivated acreage has increased to 20,000 acres, yielding approximately 120 million pounds of products annually. Three hundred and fifty independent farmers provide additional products for the Seabrook operation. The company not only furnishes these farmers with seeds but also oversees the scheduling of planting and harvesting. In this way it keeps maximum quality control and is able to synchronize harvests. It is estimated that 2.5 million pounds of seed are planted each year.

For its irrigation needs, the farm uses more than 450,000,000 gallons of water yearly, which comes from Seabrook's deep wells on its farm land. During peak season Seabrook employs 2,000 workers. Contract farmer payments exceed $3,500,000 a year.

Seabrook Farms is the largest farm-freezing operation in the world.

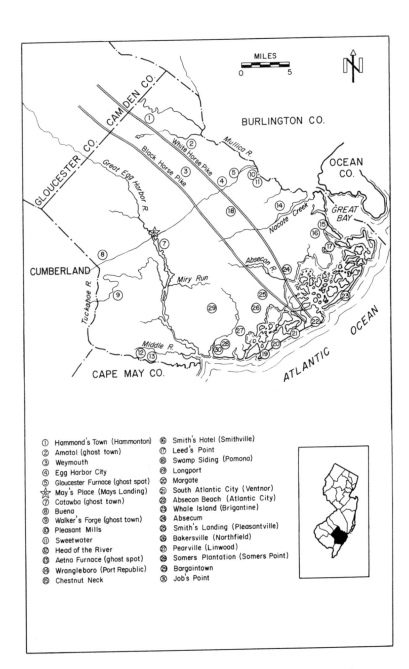

MILES
0 5

N

BURLINGTON CO.

OCEAN CO.

GLOUCESTER CO.

CAMDEN CO.

White Horse Pike

Mullica R.

Black Horse Pike

Great Egg Harbor R.

Nacote Creek

GREAT BAY

CUMBERLAND

Tuckahoe R.

Miry Run

Absecon R.

ATLANTIC OCEAN

Middle R.

CAPE MAY CO.

① Hammond's Town (Hammonton)
② Amatol (ghost town)
③ Weymouth
④ Egg Harbor City
⑤ Gloucester Furnace (ghost spot)
☆ May's Place (Mays Landing)
⑦ Catawba (ghost town)
⑧ Buena
⑨ Walker's Forge (ghost town)
⑩ Pleasant Mills
⑪ Sweetwater
⑫ Head of the River
⑬ Aetna Furnace (ghost spot)
⑭ Wrangleboro (Port Republic)
⑮ Chestnut Neck

⑯ Smith's Hotel (Smithville)
⑰ Leed's Point
⑱ Swamp Siding (Pomona)
⑲ Longport
⑳ Margate
㉑ South Atlantic City (Ventnor)
㉒ Absecon Beach (Atlantic City)
㉓ Whale Island (Brigantine)
㉔ Absecum
㉕ Smith's Landing (Pleasantville)
㉖ Bakersville (Northfield)
㉗ Pearville (Linwood)
㉘ Somers Plantation (Somers Point)
㉙ Bargaintown
㉚ Job's Point

ATLANTIC COUNTY

ATLANTIC COUNTY

The original people of Atlantic County were the Lenni-Lenape Indians, who called their summer camps along the shoreline portion of the area Absegami, meaning Little-Sea Water. When Dutch sailors from the ship *Fortuyn* landed in 1614, they called the river and area Eyren Haven (Little Egg Harbor), perhaps, as tradition has it, because of the number of birds' eggs they found along the banks of the river. Later the river name was changed to Mullica, to honor early Swedish settler Eric Mullica and to avoid confusion with Great Egg Harbor River to the south on the boundary between present Atlantic and Cape May counties.

Among the first permanent settlers of the county were Peter Steelman, Thomas Clark, Elisha Smith, and Edmund Iliff, who purchased acreage along the seacoast from Philadelphia land speculator Thomas Budd in 1695.

In 1696 Peter Steelman's brother James was appointed overseer of highways for the seacoast section of Gloucester County, of which the area was then a part. He was ordered to construct a road from Gloucester City, on the Delaware River, to the coast, and he followed an old Indian trail along Great Egg Harbor River which eventually became part of the Mays Landing-Somers Point highway.

By 1775 small communities were flourishing at Pleasant Mills, Leeds Point, Chestnut Neck, and Wrangleboro along the south side of the Mullica and at Mays Landing, Head of the River, and Somers Point on the Great Egg Harbor River.

The settlers increased in such number that on February 7, 1837, the legislature set off Egg Harbor, Galloway, Hamilton, and Weymouth townships as a new political division which became known as Atlantic County.

The first court session under the new jurisdiction was held on July 25, 1837. Isaac Smith was the first sheriff, serving until 1840. Robert K. Matlock of Woodbury became the first prosecutor. The new county's first clerk was James H. Collins.

Because of its central location, Mays Landing was chosen as county seat. It has remained so despite several attempts by Atlantic City to move it there.

MAYS LANDING

Woodsmen, shipbuilders, and those who followed the sea erected log houses on the waterfront at Mays Landing in 1695, but the first permanent settler was Peter Steelman, who purchased 110 acres in the vicinity of Gravelly Run on November 20, 1706. His brother Eric bought 50 acres nearby on May 31, 1708.

Another early arrival was Elisha Smith, who started a gristmill in 1739 about three miles from Mays Landing on a stream called Mill Run on old deeds and Miry Run on present-day county maps. Edmund Iliff of Blackbird Creek, Delaware, made extensive land purchases in the area in 1735.

George May, for whom Mays Landing is named, purchased land from Edmund Iliff in 1749. There is no record, however, of May's settling there until 1760, when he was appointed an agent of the West New Jersey Society.

During the Revolution the closing of New York harbor and blockade of Delaware Bay made two South Jersey waterways, the Mullica and the Great Egg Harbor rivers, important to the colonials. Supplies for the army and the Continental Congress began arriving early in 1776. The little knoll of ground in Mays Landing today known as Sugar Hill was the site of a temporary storehouse for cargoes of sugar and molasses brought up the river by privateers, then taken across the state in open wagons to the various colonial encampments.

Originally the community was called May's Place and The Landing. In 1778 privateers Thomas Leaming and Thomas

Sinnickson offered cargoes for sale in advertisements designating the place as May's Landing. In September of that year John Stokes, a marshal of the state's court of admiralty, advertised a sloop for sale at May's Landing.

The same year also saw the establishment of the area's first stage line, operated by Samuel Marryott from Cooper's Ferry (which became Camden) on the Delaware River to Mays Landing.

Cannon for the War of 1812 cast in the furnaces of Walker's Forge, Weymouth, and Batsto were handled for shipment at Mays Landing.

Although many ships had been built there in the late 1700s, this industry did not reach its peak until 1840, when Captain George Wheaton built shipways at the easterly end of the present county park for the mass production and repair of vessels. Later, when shipbuilders began to build their larger vessels elsewhere, nearer open water, the slack in commercial activity was taken up as the town became crowded with lawyers and clients there for several days at a time attending court sessions. Shortly after 1837 Mays Landing had eight hotels and taverns.

Lake Lenape, now a recreational center in the heart of the town, was created in 1846 by the erection of a dam.

Mays Landing prospered as an industrial center until the bog iron furnaces began to close down in 1860 following the discovery of iron and coal in Pennsylvania.

In 1867 George Wood and Sons incorporated the Mays Landing Water Power Company, and the community became a cotton mill town. Houses were built for the workers, a coalyard was established for them, as was a company store. Most workers seldom used currency, the store handling transactions on credit. The company continued until February, 1949, when the bottom dropped out of the cotton market and the plant closed, throwing its 300 employees out of jobs. As there were no prospects of securing other employment in the town, many workers departed. For a while it looked as though Mays Landing would become one of the ghost towns of the country. Finally the town decided upon a day of prayer. On March 29, 1949, the townspeople met with delegates from other communities to ask for divine guidance.

Believing that personal sacrifice and investment were also needed, twenty-eight local businessmen began a series of meetings, as a result of which $10,000 was put up to purchase the old water plant. A volunteer committee set out to secure a new industry. Undersheriff Phil Gravatt succeeded in convincing Philadelphia dress manufacturer Harry Rosenberg that the town was a good location for his factory. On January 22, 1950, the Rosenberg company formally moved in. At a town ceremony the Reverend Edward Zelley, Methodist pastor, said the achievement was an answer to the prayers and the spirit of people working together.

THE *SKUNK*

Many tales are told of derring-do among the privateers operating near Mays Landing and the upper reaches of Great Egg Harbor River during the Revolution. One concerns the *Skunk*.

This skunk was not the familiar species but a small vessel with sails and a weapon as dangerous as the one possessed by its animal counterpart. It was a camouflaged craft, with a well-covered cannon mounted on the stern, where one would not expect to find such a weapon. The job of the *Skunk* was to keep British ships from approaching the storehouses of Mays Landing and Sugar Hill.

The *Skunk* had a crew of twelve men commanded by Captain Samuel Snell, an officer in the militia who did a little privateering on the side and who, prior to his military service, had resided in the Thompson Town area of Mays Landing, where he operated a tavern between 1767 and 1770 according to a license on file.

The tactics of the *Skunk* were simple. It would approach a British vessel making its way up the river, turn tail, throw off coverings, and blast the Britisher with its cannon, escaping in the resulting confusion.

For a time this kept British shipping from venturing too far up the Great Egg Harbor, and Captain Snell was the hero of Sugar Hill.

One summer afternoon in 1778 a British merchantman sailed up the river seemingly a prize for the taking. The *Skunk* swung about from its concealed cover and made for the craft. Just as the *Skunk* was within firing distance and before it could uncover its cannon, the merchantman sprouted guns and blasted. Captain Snell found that he had tackled a 74-gun frigate.

Realizing the British had played his own game, Snell accomplished what may have been one of the fastest retreats of the war. Under full sail and with the crew bending on oars, Snell made for shallow water, where the frigate could not follow. The *Skunk* was safe for the day, but its career of surprising was over. However, in its short career it had been responsible for the capture of nineteen British craft.

JOHN UNDERHILL, BENEFACTOR

John W. Underhill came to Mays Landing from Iowa about 1905 and opened a barbershop in the Temperance House, a hotel located on Main Street across from the present courthouse. He was the only Negro resident of the town at that time.

A philosopher, skilled conversationalist, well read on civic subjects, Underhill was soon taken to heart by the townsmen and their children, especially when he enlarged his activities to include a store featuring penny candies. As he was quite a storyteller, one could often find a group of youngsters about his store, listening to his tales.

Underhill had a firm belief in the value of real estate as an investment. The story is told that he employed the services of Mays Landing's only cab driver to take him to various spots in the nearby township when land was for sale. Thus he accumulated considerable acreage of undeveloped woodland, including the site of the present Atlantic City Race Course.

When the land boom of the 1920s hit, Underhill sold quietly and at considerable profit. Others whom he had advised to go into land buying also profited. But the town knew little of these activities as Underhill was daily behind the counter of his store.

On the morning of October 24, 1925, a customer, finding the store closed, investigated. In the small living quarters to the rear he discovered the storekeeper dead.

On the bureau of Underhill's room township officers found a will. Mays Landing was amazed when it was discovered that Underhill had an estate worth in the neighborhood of $100,000 which he left, save a small sum to a half sister in Iowa, to the town that had befriended him.

Underhill directed that most of the money be used to build the best gymnasium possible adjoining the Mays Landing school —for "my children." He asked town officials to use what money was left to erect a fountain and to put benches and shrubbery in the park across from his store.

These requests were carried out, and today Mays Landing has a fine school gymnasium, a beautiful park, and an athletic field all dedicated to the man from Iowa. In addition, a large marble shaft in Union Cemetery, Mays Landing, erected with contributions from friends, has an inscription which reads: "John W. Underhill, Public Benefactor."

THE ATTACK ON CHESTNUT NECK

Between 1776 and 1782, according to title expert Paul Burgess of Brigantine, a total of 452 privateers were commissioned by the colonial authorities in Philadelphia to harass British shipping along the Atlantic Coast. The greater number of these privateers operated from Mays Landing, Toms River, and Chestnut Neck. Many of the Chestnut Neck vessels were built in nearby Nacote Creek shipyards—an area known at various times as Wrangleboro, Unionville, and Port of the Republic—at a mill owned by Patrick McCullum and Micajah Smith, who had received their charter from George III.

In the summer of 1778 several of these craft captured British merchantmen *Venus* and *Major Pearson* off Sandy Hook in New York Bay. The vessels were taken up the Mullica River to Chestnut Neck, where the cargo—estimated to have been worth

$500,000—was removed, the ship equipment was sold at public auction, and the hulls were set afire. The *Pennsylvania Packet* for September 3, 1778, carried the following sales notice:

By way of Public Vendue on Monday the 14th. instant at the Forks of Little Egg-Harbor and Chestnut Neck, New Jersey. A very valuable Cargo of the Ship "VENUS" (bound from London to New York) lately captured and brought there by Capt. David Stevens, consisting of fine coarse broadcloaths, fine and course linens, Callcoes, Lawns, Silks, and Sattins, Silk and threat stockings, Men and Womens Shoes, a great variety of Medicines, etc. The vendue to begin at 10 o'clock in the forenoon and to continue until the whole is sold. Attendance will be given and conditions made known by, John Stokes, Marshal.

This action seems to have focused British attention upon the Chestnut Neck privateers, for Rear Admiral Gambler wrote to the British War Office from New York: "Because I judged it expedient to annoy the rebels at Egg Harbor [Chestnut Neck] from whence their little privateers sally to intercept the trade bound hither, I have ordered . . . an expedition under the command of Captain Ferguson. . . ."

A fleet of nine vessels was collected in New York harbor: the sloops *Zebra*, *Vigilant*, and *Nautilus*, with two galleys and four other armed boats. Captain Henry Collins of the *Zebra* was in command of the fleet, and Captain Patrick Ferguson of the 70th Regiment British Foot was in command of a detail of 300 men of the 5th Regiment British Foot, an old regiment of the British line, and 100 men of the 3d Battalion New Jersey Volunteers, a group loyal to the crown. On September 30 the fleet passed outside Sandy Hook and ran into strong winds, which delayed arrival off the bar at Little Egg Harbor until October 6.

Meanwhile, having learned of the expedition and its purpose, General Washington ordered Count Casimir Pulaski and his mounted unit to make a forced march from Red Bank (Monmouth County) to Middle of the Shore (Tuckerton), thence to Chestnut Neck. Governor William Livingston of New Jersey held an emergency session of the Safety Council at three o'clock on the morning of September 30, following which riders were sent to warn settlers to be ready to oppose the invaders.

Captain Collins and his fleet were still waiting for favorable winds on October 6 when a Tory spy reported that Pulaski was on the way there. In a conference with Captain Ferguson it was decided that they could not afford to wait. Galleys and armed boats were quickly launched and filled with troops.

A heavy fog settled as the vessels approached the shore, where they were greeted by gunfire from the colonials in the tall meadowgrass. But the British landed, formed a solid line, and charged.

Confronted by trained soldiers, the colonials retreated far into the woods, leading the enemy to exhaust their supply of ammunition. But the Tory Volunteers set fire to the shipping in the harbor—eight sloops and schooners plus a number of whale boats —the wharfs, the homes, the Daniel Mathis tavern, and the storehouse.*

While at Chestnut Neck, Captain Ferguson learned of an important saltworks at Bass River. He destroyed it, a sawmill, all the buildings belonging to Eli Mathis, and twelve houses of colonials.

He had been ordered to burn the warehouse and buildings at the Forks of the Mullica (Pleasant Mills). But, not knowing the exact whereabouts of Pulaski and fearing to encounter what might be a superior force, he returned to the fleet, and the expedition sailed for New York.

Some privateer operations continued from Chestnut Neck. In November and December of 1778 the *Pennsylvania Packet* and *New Jersey Gazette* ran advertisements announcing the sale of captured ships. But most of the villagers resettled at Wrangleboro.

On October 6, 1911, through the efforts of the General Lafayette Chapter, Daughters of the American Revolution, a tall

---

* Although most writers have reported that all houses of Chestnut Neck were destroyed, one survived—the Benjamin Johnson homestead, which was occupied by his direct descendants until 1956. A few years ago his great-great-great-granddaughter Sara Wilson told me the legend of why their house was spared. When young volunteer James Bell approached the building with a torch he saw Benjamin Johnson's daughter Michele run inside. While he was still trying to find her, he and his companions were ordered to return to the beach. After the Revolution, unable to forget the incident, he returned to Chestnut Neck, sought out the girl, and married her. At that time he learned how Michele had been able to elude him in 1778. She had escaped through a secret tunnel from the basement to the nearby creek.

monument overlooking Chestnut Neck harbor, depicting a Continental soldier on guard, was dedicated "in honor of the Brave Patriots of the Revolutionary War who defended their liberties and their homes in a battle fought near this site October 6, 1778."

On October 6, 1928, there was an hour-long reenactment of the Redcoat landing, firing of buildings, and the retreat and chase into the woods.

A few miles from Chestnut Neck, in the northeast corner of Atlantic County, on Nacote Creek, is the small settlement of Port Republic, to which most of the former residents of Chestnut Neck retired after the sacking of the neck by the British. At various times in its history it was known as Wrangleboro, a name suggesting some of the goings-on in nearby taverns and Unionville when the Methodists built Union Chapel there in 1837.

Port Republic's beginnings can be traced to March 11, 1774, when Evi Smith, Hugh McCollum, and Richard Wescoat, owners of lands on both sides of Nacote Creek, obtained a royal charter to erect a dam and build sawmills and a gristmill. The dam is still in existence.

One of those who fled Chestnut Neck was innkeeper Daniel Mathis, whose tavern was put to the torch. Mathis took over the Micajah Smith property and refashioned it into a tavern he called the Franklin Inn. This place is still in existence and is now a private dwelling.

PLEASANT MILLS

Pleasant Mills on the Mullica River at the edge of the Wharton State Forest today is a rustic setting for a dozen private dwellings and the beautifully preserved "Kate Aylesford Mansion."

Elijah Clark established Pleasant Mills plantation in 1762 and that name was retained as the property passed to Richard Wescoat and Edward Black in 1779 and to Batsto ironmaster Joseph Ball in 1787. Some writers attribute the name Pleasant Mills to the advent of the cotton mill there about 1822, but the name was in existence long before this as established in the Batsto papers in a letter written by Samuel Richards of Batsto during August 1796 which reads: "I have purchased Pleasant Mills from Mr. Ball."

In view of the present scene of tranquillity, it is hard to imagine the activity of early days. Privateers operating on the lower Mullica River brought captured cargoes to warehouses at the Mills. Residents helped shape cannon balls for the rude firing pieces used at Princeton and Monmouth. General Benedict Arnold was in military command of the village. Count Casimir Pulaski camped his tired troops at the Mills after his unsuccessful dash to save Chestnut Neck. Sailor Boy Tavern, built by the Widow Cullen in 1750 on the old Egg Harbor Road, was headquarters for blockade runners and privateers. And on a nearby island in the Mullica, Captain Teech (the fabled Blackbeard) is said to have once made his camp when pursuit became too hectic on the open seas.

The center of early social activity was the Kate Aylesford mansion, so named after the heroine of Charles Peterson's best-seller of that name. The structure restored by artist Ray Baker and his wife was originally the Elijah Clark house, built in 1762 by Colonel Clark, commander of the 3d Battalion, Gloucester County Militia. As applied to the house, the name Aylesford is purely fictional as is the name Major Gordon, Kate's lover in the novel. Many people still believe they once existed.

Pleasant Mills was the scene of an event which may have helped set General Benedict Arnold on the road to treason. Arnold was headquartered at the village because it was on a direct line between General Washington and the privateers of Chestnut Neck. Vast stores of captured goods were on hand; it was Arnold's job to see they remained safe.

In September of 1778, learning the British were planning a raid on Pleasant Mills and Batsto coupled with a third on Chestnut Neck, Arnold acted quickly without consulting higher authority, commandeering twelve public wagons and teams to move the goods to safety. Some of his superiors took exception to the act after complaints by the team owners, and General Arnold found himself facing court-martial on a number of charges, including one that he profited personally in the disposal of the goods in Philadelphia. His hearing, which began at Middlebrook, New Jersey, on June 1, 1779, extended to January 26 of the following year.

While acquitted of most charges against him, Arnold was reprimanded by General Washington in general orders of April 6, 1780. Arnold bitterly resented the reprimand, declared himself the victim of petty staff jealousies.

During the Revolutionary War period outlaw Joe Mulliner was a frequent unwanted and uninvited visitor to Pleasant Mills, keeping the settlers in a state of terror. Mulliner was finally hunted down, captured, taken to Burlington where, after a trial, he was hanged in the yard of the old jail. His body was brought back to Atlantic County and buried near Pleasant Mills.

The historic Methodist church of Pleasant Mills, built in 1808, is the outgrowth of a log cabin church erected in 1758 by Colonel Elijah Clark. In his journal of 1775 the Rev. Philip V. Fithian, a Presbyterian minister, mentions that he preached at "Clark's log cabin meeting house." John Brainerd, who followed his brother David in converting the Indians, records in his diary a visit to the cabin church in 1774.

The Rev. Charles Pitman, for whom Pitman, New Jersey, is named, was a frequent preacher at Pleasant Mills. C. A. Malmsbury, who wrote on Pitman's life, tells of quarterly conference crowds of such size that the church could not accommodate them. On such occasions William Richards of Batsto would send a large flat wagon on which a pulpit was erected.

An interesting sidelight on the character of two early church trustees was told to me by Charles F. Green of Pleasant Mills. Simon Lucas was an extremist in keeping of the Sabbath, and would not compromise. However, one Sunday morning a large run of herring appeared in nearby Atsion Creek, and the male population turned out to land them.

Another church trustee, Jesse Richards, and one of his daughters passed the stream on the way to church. The young lady was shocked and thought the men should be chased from the stream.

Her father replied, "I don't think anyone has the right to, but I'll ask brother Lucas."

The daughter was more shocked by Simon Lucas's reply: "The time to catch herring is when the herring is here!"

In 1822 a cotton mill was erected by Benjamin Richards and named "Pleasant Mills of Sweetwater." This is the earliest use I have found of the name Sweetwater in connection with Pleasant Mills proper.

The mill was destroyed by fire in 1856. Five years later it was rebuilt as a paper mill, but in October of 1878 it once more burned to the ground. In 1880 the present mill building was constructed and operated by the Pleasant Mills Paper Company. It ceased operations in April 1915. The mill had a brief return to life in 1951–52 as a remodeled summer playhouse. A part of the structure is now a private home, the remainder a set of picturesque ruins which attracts artists.

IRON FORGES OF ATLANTIC COUNTY

Weymouth Furnace

Weymouth Furnace, in Weymouth Township on the road to Hammonton near the junction of Deep Run Creek and Great Egg Harbor River, was established in 1801 by Charles Shoemaker, George Ashbridge, Morris Robeson, and John and Joseph Paul, who purchased the 78,060-acre tract from the West Jersey Proprietors on November 6, 1800.

Weymouth turned out a variety of ironware, such as stoves, iron pipe, and plates. An early description of the furnace states that it produced about 900 tons of castings annually, and it is said some iron pipe still used in Philadelphia bears the imprint of the works—a raised W.

There were also a sawmill, a gristmill, and a company store, plus workmen houses at the Weymouth works, which at various times employed more than one hundred men.

In 1808 ownership passed to Samuel Richards of Atsion, linking the Weymouth enterprise with the Richards iron empire. A canal was dug from the ore ponds to the furnace in 1818.

In 1846 there was a wooden tramway from Weymouth to Mays Landing to speed passage of wagons carrying ore to a shipping point at the head of the Tuckahoe River. Weymouth Forge was destroyed by fire in 1862; three years later the furnace suffered the same fate.

In 1866 Stephen Colwell built a paper mill on the site and operated it until 1887, when it was closed permanently and abandoned. It disappeared following a series of fires. Today Weymouth ruins—with stone arches bridging a swiftly running stream, a chimney stack from the paper mill, and two original workmen's houses—is a picnic area maintained by the county.

Aetna (Tuckahoe) Furnace

Aetna Furnace, on the north side of the Tuckahoe River, just south of Head of the River road, was operated between 1816 and 1832 under the management of Joshua Howell and John R. Coates.

The Aetna Furnace on the Tuckahoe River (not to be confused with the Aetna Furnace of Charles Read in Burlington County at Medford Lakes) was 25 feet high, with a 14-foot clearance at the top. It was enclosed by a wall consisting of five layers of brick 3 feet thick. At the back of the furnace a long inclined roadway leading to the top was used to haul the materials which charged the fires.

Aetna Furnace went the way of all other such endeavors in the South Jersey woods: when the fires were extinguished, the workers scattered. As late as 1898 the main stack was still intact, although trees had begun to sprout from its sides. A 1960 visitor to the spot failed to uncover a single remaining brick.

Gloucester Furnace

Gloucester Furnace, on Landing Creek near the Mullica River in what is now Egg Harbor City, dates from 1785. George and Mark Richards and Benjamin Jones bought Gloucester Furnace in 1825 and five years later sold it to Thomas Richards of Philadelphia and John Richards of Gloucester County. The latter was manager of the works.

By 1855 Gloucester Furnace had seen its heyday. There is no trace of the furnace site today. There is some argument about the exact location, although the state has placed a marker near where the furnace is thought to have been.

Walker's Forge

Walker's Forge, on South River in Weymouth Township three miles from Mays Landing, was founded by Lewis M. Walker of Berks County, Pennsylvania, about 1816. Walker was also part owner of the Speedwell and West Creek forges.

In addition to his forge Walker built a sawmill and was successful for many years, employing up to a hundred men. The forge disappeared about the same time as the collapse of the South Jersey iron industry.

THE AMERICAN ALMANACK OF DANIEL LEEDS

Leeds Point, near Great Bay and once the ferry connection between the mainland of old Gloucester County and Brigantine Island, was founded by Daniel Leeds, who arrived from Leeds, England, in the ship *Shield* in December of 1678 and settled in Burlington, where he married Ann Stacy, daughter of a local tanner in 1681. In 1682 he was appointed to the Provincial Assembly and began a survey of land in the Great Bay area including "all the land from James B. Smith's place, near Smithville, running north to Holly Swamp Creek, to Wigwam Creek, to Mott's Creek to Duck Creek and then to Lower Island [one of the names by which Absecon Island was then known]." Following the death of his wife in childbirth, Leeds married Dorothy Young and moved to Jackson, in Burlington County. But as soon as he filed his survey he received a grant for the land from the Council of

Proprietors and moved to Leeds Point, which he named for his son Japhet.

Although New England historians claim proof of an almanac compiled by mariner William Pierce and printed by Stephen Daye in 1639, others credit Daniel Leeds's *The American Almanack*, printed in 1686, as the first almanac published in this country. *Poor Richard's Almanack*, published by Benjamin Franklin from 1732 to 1758, refers to Leeds in its 1735 printing as the "first author south of New York." Leeds's almanacs, hand printed in the shop of William Bradford in Philadelphia at first, later in New York, were published yearly by Daniel Leeds until 1716, when the work was taken over by his sons Felix and Titan. Later editions carried the line "Printed and sold by William and Andrew Bradford in New York."

For a time Leeds was deputy for Edward Hyde, Lord Cornbury, governor of New York and New Jersey. In 1708 Lord Cornbury was recalled by Queen Anne because of his unpopularity in the colonies, and Leeds bowed out of public life. He died in 1720 at the age of eighty-six.

As the anchor of a stageline between Cooper's Ferry (Camden) and the seashore operated by Christopher Rape, Leeds Point was also a port of entry for Brigantine Island and site of a small bay ferry to the island.

A carriage house for the stageline was located on the Leeds Point road about halfway between the Point and Smithville. With the end of stagecoach days, the house was abandoned. However, in the early days of World War II it came again into public prominence following a raid by the FBI which disclosed its use as a radio transmitting station by Nazi agents. Although the Nazi had fled, supposingly picked up by a submarine in one of the nearby inlets, plenty of evidence of their presence remained. When I visited the house, which has since been converted into a private home by Mr. and Mrs. Jack Mooney, I found empty food cans, household articles and radio equipment, all bearing the swastika. Radio wiring to the rear of the building was still in place.

Leeds Point today is a residential settlement with several of the older homes restored.

THE JERSEY DEVIL

No history of South Jersey would be complete without a mention of its great folklore monster—the Jersey Devil.

Both Estelville and Leeds Point in Atlantic County claim him. In an effort to reach a friendly compromise, those who know about such things say the devil was born in Estelville and then flew out the window and across the county to the swamps surrounding Leeds Point, where to this day he resides.

The Jersey Devil, or Leeds Devil as he is sometimes called, is one of the best-known pieces of folklore in the state, and his legend has persisted in twice-told tales since the late 1700s.

According to the legend, Mrs. Leeds of Estelville, finding that she was expecting her thirteenth child, in anger shouted, "I hope it's a devil!" She got her wish. Her child was born with horns, tail, batlike wings, and a head resembling that of a horse. According to superstition, its appearances precede an outbreak of war. Before World Wars I and II frequent appearances of the devil were reported by allegedly sober citizens.

At one time a reward was offered for the capture of the Jersey Devil by a man who claimed it was a rare Australian bat. A state guidebook issued in 1939 made the Jersey Devil the official state demon. The WPA book compiled on New Jersey had this to say of the Jersey Devil: "Only old Judge French showed any kindness to the demon and every morning for years it is said the judge and the devil engaged in lively discussions of Republican politics, while breakfasting together on ham and eggs." Area Republicans are quick to point out that the book was compiled by a Democratic administration.

Professor Fred R. MacFadden, Jr., of Coppin State College, Baltimore, has found mention of the *devil* in Burlington as early as 1735. He believes it is the same Jersey Devil, that at that period the word *Burlington* was used to designate any place from the town of Burlington to the Atlantic Ocean, and that Atlantic County's claim to the devil is legitimate.

In 1966 it was proposed that the Jersey Devil be placed on a

U.S. postage stamp as part of a folklore series. While the devil has not been seen lately, folks up Leeds Point way say that there is no indication he has left the area and that he may reappear at any time.

TOWNE OF SMITHVILLE

Smithville on the Shore Road, Atlantic County—not to be confused with the "bicycle town" of the same name in Burlington County—was the site of the first Quaker meeting house in the county. Built in 1744 after the Quakers of that section decided the trip to Tuckerton meeting via Quaker Bridge was too long and dangerous, the meeting house was located off the old Moss (Morss) Mill Road, a few hundred yards from where the Smithville Inn now stands. In those days there were no lines dividing Smithville and Leeds Point, the entire area being known as Leeds. The Smithville meeting flourished until 1855, when activities were transferred elsewhere. The original structure is gone, but a stone tablet marks the spot where it stood.

Between the years 1787 and 1789 James Baremore of Brigantine Island built an inn on land owned by John Smith at Smithville. The land was purchased by Smith from Daniel Leeds on April 20, 1784. The Baremore inn was about 75 feet long and 20 feet wide, with a leanto kitchen in the rear. There were four rooms, each with its own door leading to a small covered porch which faced Shore Road and extended the length of the structure.

In its first years the inn was the only licensed one in the area, selling Yankee rum in pewter cups for three cents. Township meetings were held at the inn until the erection of the first township hall in 1876 on land adjoining the old cemetery. This hall is now a restored private dwelling. Galloway Township's new hall is located at Germania, a more central location.

Smithville's inn passed to various Smiths and was conducted as a tavern until 1880, when it became a private dwelling. By 1900 the building was empty, fast falling victim to the encroaching woodlands.

The Smithville Inn, shown as it was before restoration in 1951, served during the nineteenth century as a principal stop on the stagecoach line from Cooper's Ferry to Leeds Point and as a center for Galloway Township meetings, elections, and court sessions. (Courtesy of the Library of Congress)

In 1951 Mr. and Mrs. Fred Noyes, operators of a small antique shop in Absecon, discovered the old building and began restoring it. They operated it as a restaurant featuring early South Jersey dishes. In 1957 the Cranmer General Store of New Gretna, abandoned and falling apart, was brought to a spot near the inn and restored. This store, about 110 years old, was the beginning of the Smithville village of today, with a total of more than forty-two old South Jersey buildings.

Smithville has its own airfield and, in deference to its beginnings, a horse-drawn stagecoach takes guests from the airfield to the inn. A sleigh is used when there is snow.

Almost directly across from the inn is the Emmaus Methodist Church, built in 1790 and still in use.

Among the many stories told of the old inn is the one about its "political fence," which it is claimed helped popularize the phrase "mending one's political fences." At the time of the incorporation of Galloway Township in 1798, the Smith Hotel was the township's polling place. Election was an all-day event and picnic. However, as the day wore on and the liquor flowed freely, arguments between voters of rival parties erupted into fights until the whole place resembled an Irish donnybrook.

Township officials decided to halt this annual cracking of skulls and ordered the constable to erect a fence down the middle of the Smith Hotel yard. It was his job to see opponents stayed on their own side of the fence.

This structure stood for many years. Just before election day the constable would get out hammer and nails and say: "It's about time to mend our political fence."

SUMMER HOME OF THE LENAPES

Absecon was a favorite camping spot of the New Jersey Lenape in their summer pilgrimages to the seashore. The Indians erected temporary lodges of skins or cedar bark and feasted throughout the summer on food from the nearby waters. Fish and oysters were dried in preparation for the winter inland, and shells were collected for use in bartering. A large mound of shells about four feet high once stood near Buttonwood Hill on Absecon Creek as attested in a deed of April 7, 1799, in which a boundary is traced "to a shell heap at meadows edge near Absequan Bay."

The first recorded transaction citing Absecon is a real estate deal of December 2, 1695, when John Reading of Gloucester sold two hundred acres to Thomas Budd, merchant of Philadelphia. Reading referred to his acquisition as Mount Eagle and to present Absecon Creek as Reading River.

The year in which Peter White and his family became the first permanent residents of Absecon cannot be ascertained with any accuracy. However, a deed and survey made in 1704 by Daniel Leeds describes a boundary as "between Thomas Budd's one thousand acres whereon Peter White now dwells." Between 1726 and 1734 White's name appears frequently in Quaker meeting records.

During the Revolution, Absecon was the site of a number of clashes between roving Tory bands and patriots. British land parties would come up Absecon Creek and demand provisions. One such party was wiped out by sharpshooters who disappeared into the woods as quickly as they had appeared. Captain Patrick Ferguson, brother of Scottish philosopher Adam Ferguson, was sent with a command to fire the village and avenge the deaths of the seamen. Once again South Jersey woodsmen drove the British back to sea.

During colonial times village life in Absecon centered around Absecon Tavern, a rambling structure at the crest of a hill overlooking the countryside. With the establishment of the first stageline, the inn became a principal stop.

On April 4, 1774, when Galloway Township was formed from Great Egg Harbor, Absecon Creek and Bay were dividing lines and the village of Absecon referred to as part of the township. It was finally set off from Galloway on February 29, 1872.

The first meeting of the proposed Camden and Absecon Railroad, later the Camden and Atlantic, was held in the Absecon store of John Doughty in 1851. Dr. Jonathan Pitney and General Enoch Doughty presented the first draft of a charter. On March

19, 1852, the charter was granted by the legislature, and on July 1, 1854, the first train, nine cars drawn by the locomotive *Atsion*, puffed into the Absecon station, dooming the stageline and bringing a new era to the country town.

Absecon was incorporated as a city on January 1, 1903, with Edward Armstrong as first mayor. Today the city stands as the gateway to Atlantic City and is a traffic junction for shorebound motorists.

GHOST TOWNS

Catawba

Once located on the east side of the Great Egg Harbor River about four miles south of Mays Landing, Catawba is the most unusual ghost town of Atlantic County. For years Catawba has been called a mystery village, and tales of strange deaths, hidden treasure, and such happenings, growing with each retelling, have beclouded its real history.

Two years ago when I attempted to locate the town I was unable to do so. A nearby woodchopper offered help but warned, "The place is hexed."

Catawba was the dream of George West and his wife Amy. West, a prosperous merchant of Burlington, New Jersey, came to the area and secured two land deeds, one dated June 11, 1811, the other July 1, 1813. He laid out a town plot he called Catawba —I could find no reliable explanation for the name—and erected a mansion which rivaled that of Joseph Bonaparte in Bordentown and drew the curious from all parts of the woodlands.

A Methodist church was constructed by West, and about twenty families were attracted to his settlement. Nearby Mays Landing, still in its heyday as a shipbuilding center, offered jobs. In fact, Catawba seemed to have a good chance of success until May 17, 1826, when the first of a series of deaths occurred in the West family. Thomas Biddle West, fourteen, the youngest son, died about forty-eight hours after he was suddenly stricken. James S. West, twenty-three years of age, died on August 24, 1829, after a sudden illness. George West, the father, died after a sudden attack on September 3, 1829. His wife died on September 10. Oldest daughter Charlotte Biddle West, oldest son Joseph E. West, and daughter Marie Inglis West survived.

According to the legend that developed a few years later, the deaths were attributed to poisoning, and the finger of suspicion pointed to Joseph West, who was reported to have locked the mansion and disappeared. This was not true. Joseph continued to occupy the house, which he mortgaged to the Board of Free-holders for $6,000. In 1837, when he could not pay off the mortgage, the property passed to other owners. In 1865 it belonged to General Enoch Doughty of Absecon, one of the founders of the Camden and Atlantic Land Company and the Camden and Atlantic Railroad. Doughty needed lumber for some building he was doing in Absecon and demolished the mansion.

Joseph West moved to Burlington, where he engaged in real estate business. As the result of one deal he landed in jail. After serving his term he returned to Mays Landing, where he stayed a short time, then moved to Philadelphia, where he was admitted to the bar of Pennsylvania. When he died in 1885 he still owned considerable property.

More practical stories attribute the deaths of the Wests to a plague or epidemic never further identified. Inasmuch as Mays Landing was a port in the West Indies trade, some people believe the disease may have been carried by one of the seamen and contracted by the Wests, with whom the seamen were in daily contact.

Most of these facts I have cited are based on the research of Kenneth Scull of the Chelsea Title Company of Atlantic City, who devoted considerable time to the study in an attempt to disprove the mystery element of the legend and give the real story its proper place in Atlantic County history.

Catawba began to disappear with the end of the shipbuilding era in Mays Landing. The church was carted away piecemeal by people in the neighborhood. Time and encroaching vegetation did the rest. Until about six years ago, some of the gravestones of the cemetery were still to be seen. But vandals broke most of the stones, and today they have all disappeared. While there are homes in nearby woodlands, there is now no such place as Catawba.

Belcoville

A town does not need a hundred years to vanish. It can disappear overnight. Belcoville, near Mays Landing, is a ghost of World War I. It was laid out in 1917 as a community to house six thousand munitions workers of the Bethlehem Loading Company. Plans also called for a proving grounds for big guns with a range of twenty miles, but the combined political power of Atlantic City hotelmen and Atlantic County poultrymen killed that proposal. Instead a shell-loading plant was erected and in February, 1918, the construction of homes began.

The plant was not ready for production until October 24, 1918. Although the Armistice was signed on November 11, 1918, and the plant produced little to justify the expenditure of millions of dollars, construction activity continued until December 1, when the project's 1,800 employees were dismissed. Actual shell loading on a small scale was continued until January 21, 1919. On July 1 of 1919 the town and plant, consisting of 206 dwellings and 84 factory buildings, were abandoned. Many of the structures were torn down immediately; others were left to rot. Some of the properties were sold to the Mays Landing Water Power Company and the village vanished.

Amatol

On the White Horse Pike, near Hammonton, Amatol was another boom town of World War I, the site of a munitions depot employing several thousand workers. Following the Armistice the plant was closed and everything movable was carted away.

Shortly thereafter Frank Gravatt, Atlantic City real estate man, bought the 6,000-acre Amatol tract and the federal government displayed an interest in the location for lighter-than-air craft experimentation. But nothing came of that idea, and Amatol settled back in the pines until 1926, when industrialist Charles M. Schwab picked Amatol as the site for a wooden bowl speedway. Schwab

On May 1, 1926, the Amatol Race Track near Hammonton opened with a 500-mile race on the wooden oval built by industrialist Charles M. Schwab. For two years the track featured as many as seventy-five cars in a single race, with drivers from all over the world. But Schwab lost interest in the venture, and the facility was demolished in 1933 after standing idle for several years. (McMahon Collection)

poured millions of dollars into the undertaking, and on May 1, 1926, the first auto race was held with a crowd of several thousands attending. Harry Hartz, hero of the Indianapolis Speedway, won the first and second 500-mile races. The last big event at the track was a combined stock car and motorcycle race on May 30, 1928. Schwab lost interest in racing and leased the place to auto companies seeking a testing ground.

In 1933 the big oval was torn down and the six million feet of lumber in the grandstands and track and the three miles of fencing were sold. Today not a board of the oval is left and I found difficulty even tracing the path of the original track.

The administration building was remodeled, and it now houses Troop A, New Jersey State Police. It is known as Hammonton Barracks.

Thompsontown

A number of towns in Atlantic County were really family settlements. This was the case with Thompsontown, which appeared on some maps as Thompson Town, near Mays Landing, between the main highway leading from Gravelly Run to Catawba. During the late 1700s and early 1800s it consisted of several houses and a general store. It was also the site of a ferry across Great Egg Harbor River, operated by Edward Dowers from a place called Dowers Dock. It was later run by a man named Morris who lived on the west side of the river. A bell on the east side was sounded by customers wishing to be taken across.

Adamstown, Risleytown, Lakestown, and Smith's Landing—also family settlements—have been absorbed into Pleasantville.

Hewittville, Higbeeville, and Johnstown, a group of family settlements in the vicinity of Smithville, became part of Galloway Township.

Weymouth, once scene of an iron foundry and mill, has also settled back into the woodlands, the mill site now a picnic area. Gigantic City, in the woods near Pomona, was never more than a realty broker's dream.

There are many others in the pines which have disappeared either through absorption by other communities or abandonment.

HOME OF THE LAKE FAMILY

Pleasantville, on the mainland across the meadows from Atlantic City, is the homestead of the remarkable Lake family—inventors, clergymen, land speculators, farmers, and founders of Ocean City.

The origin of the name Pleasantville is part of one of those South Jersey fables which, for want of a better explanation, tend to be accepted and repeated. According to this tale, Daniel Lake had a small store on the southeast corner of Shore Road and Adams Avenue. One day he crossed the intersection to Daniel Ingersoll's blacksmith and wheelwright shop to buy a board on which to paint a sign for his store. Ingersoll said, "I'll give you the board if you let me paint it." It was agreed and, as Lake watched, Ingersoll painted LAKE'S STORE, and under it PLEASANTVILLE N.J. Lake placed the sign over his establishment, and other residents took a liking to the sound of Pleasantville and started using it. In 1888, when the town was incorporated as a borough, this name was used.

The date of the incident has never been established, but the community can be traced to the seventeenth century, when Daniel Smith arrived from England and purchased farming land along the old Shore Road. The original Shore Road was a stagecoach route in 1716 and was altered considerably in 1731 by surveyors from Burlington and Gloucester counties who laid out the present route bearing that name.

William Lake, pioneer of the clan, settled in Great Egg Harbor, as the area was then called, prior to 1702. When he died in 1716, he was the largest realty holder in the shore district.

The Lake family has always been a large one, with descendants scattered throughout South Jersey. Two Lakes, Daniel and Simon, served in the Revolutionary War. The second Simon Lake put up the money necessary for the founding of Ocean City by his sons on October 21, 1879, and was active in the association that launched the "Christian resort."

James Edward Lake, seventh son of Simon, was born on January 19, 1845, and was the developer of Absecon Highlands.

Daniel Lake's son Jesse, who was born in Pleasantville in 1803, was the inventor of the caterpillar tractor.

Jesse, and John, Lucas, David, and Simon Lake were charter members of the group which constructed the first turnpike across the meadows to Atlantic City in 1853.

Simon Lake, the grandson of the first Simon Lake, was born in Pleasantville in 1866. At the age of twenty-eight he invented the first workable submarine. When the federal government seemed more interested in the underwater boat of J. P. Holland, Simon took off for Europe and spent several years advising and designing underwater vessels for the governments of Russia, Germany and Italy. This Simon Lake is also credited with the invention of a device for capping tin cans whose use was opposed by the cappers' union because it would throw men out of work. Lake was belatedly recognized by the Navy Department in 1964, when the world's largest submarine tender was named the U.S. *Simon Lake*. Lake did not live to see this recognition, having died on June 23, 1945.

John Lake Young, builder of the Million Dollar Pier on the Boardwalk in Atlantic City, is another member of the Lake family.

The Lake name is preserved on the tabernacle ground in Ocean City, where a memorial records that resort's founding by the Lakes.

A Simon Lake monument stands in a small park adjacent to the city hall in Pleasantville.

TWO BEGINNINGS FOR HAMMONTON

Hammonton, the only officially designated "town" in Atlantic County, had two beginnings, each distinctive.

Located on the borderlines of Atlantic, Gloucester, and Burlington counties, Hammonton traces its history from the arrival of William Coffin of Green Bank in 1812 to build and operate a sawmill for landowner John R. Coates. The mill was located at a body of water now known as Hammonton Lake, at the crossing of trails between the iron towns of Batsto and Weymouth and the shipbuilding center of Mays Landing.

In 1817 Coffin also went into partnership with Jonathan Haines in a glass factory. Among the principal products of the firm were whiskey flasks known by such names as Weeping Willow, Eagle, Old Glory, Bunch of Grapes, and Sheaf of Rye. According to Rhea Mansfield Knittle in her book *Early American Glass* (1927), at least fourteen varieties of flasks from the Coffin and Hay plant have been authenticated. (In 1836 Coffin leased his glassworks to his son Bodine and his son-in-law Andrew K. Hay, the firm afterward being known as Coffin and Hay.) Charles Miller of Hammonton has a number of the Coffin and Hay flasks.

Coffin was a developer; he built a company store, small houses for his workers, and a school which was also used by visiting clergymen for services. As his community began to take on the appearance of a village, Coffin named it Hammondtown for his son John Hammond Coffin, replacing the earlier name of Coffin's Glass Factory. The original spelling of Hammondtown was later changed to Hammonton.

After William Coffin's death his son continued the operation, but by 1850 the wheels of the old mill had ceased to turn and the glassworks had fallen into decay.

Hammonton's second lease on life came in 1850 when Richard J. Byrnes, a young Philadelphian, finished business school and started as a banker with Charles K. Landis, founder of Vineland. Byrnes and Landis bought considerable land in the Hammonton area with the intention of selling it in bulk. A good slice of this land was bought from actress Charlotte Cushman, who had purchased it as an investment.

In 1856, the original bulk plan having been discarded, Byrnes and Landis made direct appeals to prospective settlers through newspaper advertisements.

On May 15, 1857, the first purchase of land was made by Matthew Seagrove of Philadelphia, who bought four acres and an old house which was a remnant of the Coffin glassworks. In the summer of the same year Captain Abraham Somerby of Newburyport, Massachusetts, purchased a piece of property at the foot of what is now Central Avenue and erected the first house in the "new" Hammonton.

The town quickly fulfilled the dream of its developers and became known as Peach City because of its large peach orchards. A peach festival attracted thousands each year. But changing soil conditions wrote finis to the peach era. Today blueberries are the top crop, covering approximately 3,500 acres. The Hammonton Fruit Auction, through which passes the greater part of the crops, has a season business of more than a million dollars. A government blueberry testing farm is located in Hammonton.

Hammonton remained a part of Mullica Township until 1865, when it applied for a charter. The new town was incorporated on March 22, 1866; its population was 1,500. In territory Hammonton is about $11\frac{1}{2}$ miles long and $4\frac{1}{2}$ miles wide.

On July 16, 1865, some Catholics gathered to celebrate the feast of Our Lady of Mount Carmel. Through the years the event has grown into one of the largest religious pilgrimages in the nation, from 30,000 to 50,000 persons now gathering annually at Saint Joseph's Catholic Church for masses, parades, and fireworks.

Fifteen clothing factories now operate in Hammonton, plus a brewery and several chemical plants.

Some of Hammonton's better-known sons were stage star Victor Moore, born there in 1876; Andrew Rider, the cranberry king and founder of Rider College in Trenton, and George Washington Pressey, inventor of the Pressey Brooder (forerunner of the chick brooders now in use) and the American Star Bicycle, which revolutionized the cycling industry.

ANDREW RIDER, TRAVELING SALESMAN

Although he founded Rider College in Trenton, Andrew J. Rider wanted to be remembered as the salesman who brought the Jersey cranberry into international prominence.

It was about 1889 that Rider bought his first cranberry patch, a small bog in Hammonton. This holding he increased to five hundred acres and then resigned as president of the college bearing his name to devote all his time to cranberries.

At that point in agricultural history the Jersey cranberry was not the popular item it is today; in fact most growers found difficulty selling their product. Rider devoted his unique selling talents to promoting the berry and in the fall of 1893 sailed for London to create a European market.

To publicize the berry he carried a number of crates with him, using the ship's dining hall for his first demonstration. In London he found the English did not know how to prepare cranberry sauce. To overcome this he wrote and published the first cranberry cookbook.

Rider soon discovered that, to become popular with the English people, any new product must first be accepted by royalty. Through the Prince of Wales he sought to get his cranberries into Windsor Castle. Once Queen Victoria had tasted and approved them, the whole of London wanted cranberries. A year after Rider sailed back to the United States, England was importing five thousand barrels of Jersey cranberries annually.

ENGINE WHISTLE VIRTUOSO

You may have heard many railroad songs—but have you ever listened to one played on the whistle of a locomotive?

According to old-timers of the Hammonton area, William "Whistling Bill" Wardoff, engineer of the old Reading Railroad line which once ran through Hammonton, Egg Harbor City, and the South Jersey woodlands, began his impromptu whistle concerts in the early 1900s.

His specialties were "Yankee Doodle," "Home, Sweet Home," and "How Dry I Am." It is reported that on Sundays he played popular hymns like "Rock of Ages."

The whistle of his engine would carry for several miles, especially at night. People would stand on the Hammonton station platform and applaud his efforts as Bill rode through.

However, nonmusical residents objected to such concerts and in 1924, when Wardoff was forty-five years old, he was officially requested by the Reading Railroad to discontinue his concerts when at the throttle of passenger trains. The ruling carried an exception in Bill's favor—he could continue to play his whistle offerings while piloting freight trains.

"Whistling Bill" made his home in Audubon, New Jersey. He died on November 17, 1940.

THE WINE CITY

Egg Harbor City is a town that was planned one way and turned out another. In colonial days the region was inhabited by backwoodsmen, Tory refugees, charcoal burners, and Pineys. Legend has it that the outlaw band of Joe Mulliner, active during Revolutionary War days, camped where present Philadelphia Avenue is located, in the heart of the city.

The history of Egg Harbor City as a town really began on July 4, 1854, when the first regular train to Atlantic City passed through. As the wood-burning engine stopped for water and more fuel at Cedar Bridge (Pomona), a group of German businessmen from Philadelphia, making the trip as guests of the railroad, stepped out to help with the refueling as passengers often did on early train runs. While thus occupied, Dr. William Schmoele, Henry Schmoele, P. M. Wolsieffer, J. H. Schoemacher, and A. K. Hay were impressed with the countryside. In an inspirational reaction they visioned the founding of a "dream city" settled by their countrymen, where traditional customs, speech, and recreations could be preserved.

On their return to Philadelphia they sold their idea to other Germans and, after a more thorough inspection of the area, formed an association. In December 1854 the association purchased thirty thousand acres from Stephen Colwell and ten thousand from William Ford, most of the land being the old Gloucester Furnace tract.

The plan was to have the area laid out in 20-acre farms with

The pride of the Egg Harbor City fire department in 1918 in front of the American Hotel, a favorite stopping place on the White Horse Pike between Philadelphia and Atlantic City. (Courtesy of the Henry Warker Collection)

a city at each end of the development, one depending on the new railroad, and the other on the reliable Mullica River. In 1856 Dr. Schmoele completed the layout for Egg Harbor City with avenues named for famous Germans and German cities. Wide streets were to assure room for German carnivals and fairs. This planning saved Egg Harbor from the traffic problems today besetting other cities.

The city received its charter on March 16, 1858, and on June 8 the first municipal election was held with thirty-five registered voters. P. M. Wolsieffer, later assemblyman from Atlantic County, became the first mayor. The city had bright prospects with German settlers arriving from all parts of the nation.

The German language was widely used, and Egg Harbor's first newspaper, the *Egg Harbor Pilot* (1858), was printed in that tongue. It has long since been out of existence. Cultural halls sprang up including the Aurora, Stutzbach's Apollo, and the Concordia. The Aurora Singing Society had its birth in 1857 and was active until World War I. Egg Harbor's first band was organized in 1860 and played for the first Atlantic County Fairs held in that city. One of the best-known bandmasters of the town was Jacob Oberst, who presided at all civic functions, playing a silver cornet with one hand and directing with the other.

Following the Civil War the original Town and Farm Association became a memory. While the town served by railroad continued to grow, the one by the Mullica River never materialized, and the area is still a wilderness. Egg Harbor City continues to elect a harbormaster each election but possesses no harbor.

In 1859 John Wild started a small winery which was the beginning of an industry which would put Egg Harbor City on the wine map of the world. Schuster, Butterhoff, Saalman, Hinke, Kayser, and Bannihr were among early family names in the winemaking business of the town.

But Egg Harbor's lasting fame as a "wine city" can be attributed to Louis Nicholas Renault, vintner for the Duke of Montebello at Rheims, France, who came to America in 1864 as an emissary of the duke. Stranded in America at the end of the Franco-Prussian War, Renault started a search for a soil that would grow grapes like those produced near Rheims; he found it in Egg Harbor City.

He produced his first champagne in 1870. Today L. N. Renault and Sons, also called the House of Renault, is internationally known, and the 600 acres of grapes adjacent to Bremen Avenue, Egg Harbor City, are basic in the production of more than 240,000 gallons of champagne a year.

The winery left the hands of the Renault family in 1919, when it was purchased by John D'Agostino, who operated it until 1968, when it was taken over by a corporation headed by William R. Carroll with Dr. Curt D. Degener as operations manager.

The firm is continuing the hospitality tours started by D'Agostino. It includes a museum containing more than four hundred champagne glasses, representing three centuries of the glassmaking art, assembled by Miss Marie D'Agostino.

Caught in the whirlpool of tight money in the 1930s, most of Egg Harbor City's older business establishments boarded up. A concerted effort by the town's banking establishments brought new business ventures, including a boat-building firm, to reestablish the basic industrial foundation of the city.

BARGAINTOWN

Between the middle 1700s and the 1800s Bargaintown, a few miles inland from Somers Point on Bargaintown Lake and Patcong Creek, was a stagecoach stop, the only post office between Somers Point and English Creek, and a political center of Egg Harbor Township.

Early records show that Samuel Somers, grandson of Richard Somers of Somers Point, built a sawmill and a gristmill near the pond prior to 1750. A second gristmill was constructed in 1758 by Japhet Ireland.

There is evidence that Bargaintown received its unusual name as early as 1760 through David Howell, a blacksmith known for his love of a bargain who worked as hard at selling land as he did at his forge.

Another widely circulated story concerns James Somers, who owned a home bordering the millpond, which then was just a swamp. This swamp was a barrier to easy access to those living on the other side of it. Somers is said to have offered his women slaves their freedom if they could build a roadway across the swamp. Carrying stones in their aprons, the women constructed a crude dam and road. Somers kept his bargain and thus, according to legend, the place became known as Bargaintown.

There are at least three other versions of the name, including one stemming from the farmers' trading center in the community.

One of the colorful figures of early Bargaintown was Captain Return Babcock, from whom Somers purchased much land. Babcock spent most of his life at sea. During one of these voyages his vessel and other merchant ships were overrun by pirates in the Mediterranean. The attackers ran the ships aground, plundered them, and left the crews to die on a small deserted island. Babcock gained both the admiration and hatred of the pirates by his swordsmanship during the attack, and the pirates decided that, instead of being killed, Babcock should lose the use of his sword arm. Holding him fast, the buccaneers severed his arm above the elbow.

Babcock was left to bleed to death, but one of his crew scrambled to a burning boat, secured pitch and a kettle. He plunged the stump of Babcock's arm into the heated pitch, thus saving his life. The captain returned to Bargaintown and spent his remaining days there.

Church life in Bargaintown centered around the Zion Methodist Church on Zion Road, established in 1764 and known as the Blackman Meeting House, later the Cedar Bridge Meeting House. Services were conducted by missionary John Brainerd.

Patcong Creek, much deeper than it is now, flowed through Bargaintown to the Great Egg Harbor River. In 1800 Christopher Van Sant built a full-rigged vessel on the creek.

At the turn of the century Bargaintown was the center of a now long-vanished business—ice cutting and storage. Bargaintown Pond was the mainstay of this occupation. Daniel S. Collins operated this business into the early 1900s, and his ice wagons were familiar sights in Atlantic City.

Evidence that Bargaintown was once favored by the Indians for clambakes was uncovered, according to florist Charles Fischer, when his nurseries were first constructed. In turning the soil his men found many piles of clamshells and arrowheads.

Bargaintown is now the site of many estatelike homes. Several restored houses near the pond are all that is left of the original village.

A CONVINCING PREACHER

In its early days Atlantic County attracted a number of itinerant preachers, many sincere, some only looking for a night's free lodging and a couple of meals.

In 1780 David Sayers, a former captain in the Continental Army and a prominent resident of the area known as Head of the River, at the headwaters of the Tuckahoe River, was known for his dislike of these itinerants and vowed publicly to shoot the first one to cross his yard.

During a heavy snowstorm a man knocked at the Sayers door, introduced himself as the Rev. Mr. James and asked shelter. Sayers answered, "I don't take to preachers. Get!"

History does not detail the remainder of the conversation. It does record the fact that the Rev. Mr. James stayed the night with Sayers; in fact, he stayed several days. The wandering preacher must have had strong arguments for religion because shortly after his visit Sayers began a move to organize a Methodist congregation. William and Jeremiah Smith, Revolutionary War officers who operated a lumber mill at Head of the River, permitted services to be held in the meal room of the mill every Sunday. Preachers riding through the area were invited to speak.

Many people were arriving at the river town because of shipbuilding activities there. Soon the mill was overcrowded on Sundays, and the need of a regular church became evident. The Smith brothers and Daniel Benezet of Philadelphia, whose son lived at Head of the River, gave land, lumber, and labor for a small church which was finished in 1792. Sayers was one of the first trustees. The Rev. Mr. James seems never to have returned.

Around the church sprang up a cluster of homes, a one-room

schoolhouse, and the Teapot Inn, which was not entirely welcomed by the church people but was a favorite of the seamen and later the Aetna Furnace iron workers. The inn is the only house left in the vicinity of the church and is now a private dwelling. The school was moved to Aetna Drive, a few miles away, and in time disappeared.

In 1792 the area was officially known as Tuckahoe but was called Head of the River by its residents. Today Tuckahoe, a Lenni-Lenape name meaning "where the deer are shy," is on the Cape May County side of the Tuckahoe River, and Head of the River church is located in Atlantic County on part of the vast Estell Manor tract.

The Head of the River church reached its peak about 1827 after the start of the Aetna Furnace nearby. At that time it had a membership of 172, the largest congregation on the Methodist circuit.

In 1832 Aetna Furnace closed down, the shipbuilding activities of the Tuckahoe River moved closer to open water, and regular preaching at the church was discontinued, although records show revival meetings were held in 1842 and 1846. By the early 1900s the church ceased to function as such; but, because of the historic importance of the structure, a new board was formed for its preservation. Today the church is beautifully restored, and anniversary services are held once a year. The site bears a New Jersey State historical marker.

SOMERS PLANTATION

Somers Point, known first as Somers Plantation, is rich in both historical fact and legend. It was founded in March of 1693 by John Somers, a follower of Quaker George Fox, who left England because of religious persecutions.

Somers first settled in Dublin, Pennsylvania, later moving to the edge of Great Egg Harbor Bay, where he purchased three thousand acres of land, most of which was waterfront property, from Thomas Budd, Philadelphia merchant and land speculator.

Others who arrived about the same time were Jonas Valentine, John Gilbert, Sr., Jonathan Adams, Peter Covenhoven, John Scull, and James Steelman. Together they established the earliest community of what is now Atlantic County. Deeds of these men were recorded in Burlington on November 29 and 30, 1695, along with the Somers deed.

Although the land deeds are dated 1695, John Somers was in the area in 1693 as attested by a Cape May County document of March 20, 1693, which reads: "The Court of Portsmouth, Cape May County, appoints John Somers supervisor of roads and constable for Great Egg Harbour [Atlantic County]."

On October 2, 1695, John Somers was granted permission by the Grand Jury of Gloucester County to link Great Egg Harbor and Cape May County by means of a ferry across Great Egg Bay. The permit set exact passage price to be extracted: "every single person twelve pence per head, and for sheep and hogs, four pence per head and for all manner of grain two pence per bushel." The ferry left from Job's Point, named for a son of John Somers, near the old homestead. A marker designates the spot.

John Somers was already married when he settled in South Jersey in 1684. According to records of the Great Egg Harbor-Cape May Monthly Meeting of Friends, his son Richard was born in the same year. In fact, seven of his ten children were born on the plantation. The Somers mansion was built by Richard sometime between 1720 and 1726. John Somers became a representative of the Fourth Assembly of the Province of Nova Caesarea, which met at Perth Amboy in 1708. He died in 1723 and was buried on his own plantation, as was the custom.

But it was Richard Somers, the great-grandson of John, born at Somers Point on September 15, 1778, who brought fame to the family name. In 1798, when he was twenty, Richard and his close friend Stephen Decatur received warrants as midshipmen. He was assigned to the *United States,* the fourth vessel of the new U.S. Navy to sail.

In 1804, when the nation was at war with the Barbary coast powers, Commodore Edward Preble's squadron of six vessels was dispatched to Tripoli. Somers had command of the schooner *Nautilus,* his first and only command. The young officer distinguished himself in action and was promoted to the rank of commander.

On September 4, 1804, Commodore Bainbridge's frigate *Philadelphia* ran aground in Tripoli harbor, and the commodore and his crew were taken prisoner. In a daring maneuver Stephen Decatur burned the *Philadelphia* and escaped.

The success of this action led Commander Somers to propose a similar plan for destroying the enemy's flotilla and rescuing the crew of the *Philadelphia* in the resulting confusion. He fitted a ketch, loaded it with 100 barrels of powder, 150 shells, and a quantity of broken iron. The crew was to sail the small craft into the harbor, aim it at the pirate flotilla, light a fuse and escape in rowboats.

At nine o'clock on the night of September 4 the ketch set sail. About ten o'clock there was an explosion that lit up the harbor. The ketch had disappeared. A search by fleet small boats for survivors proved fruitless. Later some bodies were washed ashore and buried in the sand, but the body of Somers was never recovered.

Congress erected a monument to Commander Somers and his crew at the Washington Navy Yard. In 1860 it was moved to the Naval Academy grounds at Annapolis. Somers Point honored its son with a monument near the New York Avenue school.

Somers Point was the original port of entry for Great Egg Harbor, a customhouse being established with Daniel Benezet, Jr., as collector, commissioned March 21, 1791. The office was abolished on June 30, 1912.

During the War of 1812 a small fort stood on an embankment overlooking the Great Egg Harbor River. John R. Scull was captain of a company of about a hundred men known as the 1st Battalion, 1st Regiment, Gloucester County Brigade, New Jersey Militia, Volunteers, which manned the structure. There is no record of the group's being in combat. The company was disbanded in 1815. No reminder of the fort is visible today.

Somers Point was incorporated as a borough in 1886 with a voting population of 48. By 1900 the point had 308 voters; it was incorporated as a city on July 7, 1902, with George Anderson as mayor.

A ferry operated between Somers Point and Ocean City until 1912, when the first wooden bridge between the two communities was constructed. A toll of twenty-five cents was charged. In 1922 the state took over operation of the bridge, eliminating the toll. The present concrete span was built ten years later.

The Somers mansion remained in the hands of heirs until April 8, 1937, when it was conveyed to the Atlantic County Historical Society. On October 8, 1941, the mansion became the property of the State Commission on Historic Sites, which operates it as a museum.

SHIPBUILDING TOWNS

The Shore Road town of Northfield had its start as a boatbuilding settlement called Bakersville, named for Daniel Baker, son of a Nantucket whaler, who built a shipyard on the east side of Shore Road between Mill Road and the post office in 1815. He launched his ships in a ditch large enough to float anything he could produce. One Baker ship was christened *Atlantic County* in honor of the new county created from old Gloucester. Baker persuaded Pardon Ryon, a Yankee peddler from Connecticut, to settle and open a store at Bakersville.

Christopher Van Sant, another Bakersville shipbuilder, is credited with the construction of a full-rigged vessel at Patcong Creek, Bargaintown, and floating it down to the Great Egg Harbor River. Most of Bakersville ships were of the 30-ton, two-masted schooner class, constructed to carry cordwood to New York markets.

Shipbuilding and the sea were so important to Bakersville that, when a school was opened in 1817, navigation was a required subject. Emaline Huntley of Connecticut was one of the first teachers. She was paid $10 a month and boarded free with families of the children she taught.

Records do not show when the name was changed from Bakersville to Northfield but, according to historian Frank Butler, it was around the turn of the century. Daniel T. Steelman, who later became superintendent of schools of Gloucester County, is credited with suggesting the name Northfield, which seemed appropriate because a large part of the town was in the north field of the old Ireland family estate.

The community was incorporated as a city on March 21, 1905. Walter Fifield was first mayor. Today Northfield is the home of Birch Grove Park, one of the largest on the mainland of Atlantic County, with a total of three hundred acres. It was constructed entirely with volunteer help. Northfield's sea-faring past is kept alive in the many small boatyards and marinas which dot the boulevard from the city to the Margate Bridge, across the meadows to Absecon Island.

In the days of sail the Shore Road community of Linwood was a typical port town and had a special type of house still found there—a three-story bread-box design, without ornament, topped by a cupola known as Widow's Walk or Captain's Walk.

This walk offered an unobstructed view of the entrance to the bay and various docks of the waterfront. It was there, by "sea windows," that the women kept watch for their husbands' ships returning across the mouth of the bay. The glass-enclosed walks were reached by a small stairway, usually with a locked door. An era passed, but the cupola remained.

First settlers of the area were the Quakers, mostly farmers. As early as 1750 a log meeting house was built and a cemetery established.

In 1848 at the height of Linwood's boat-building activities, Captain Elmer English conceived the idea of a seaman's church, and constructed the Bethel Methodist Church, popularly referred to as the Mariners' Church. Captain John Walter Tilton, returning from a long voyage in 1859, also became interested in the building of a centrally located church. Together with his friend Francis Somers, who donated the land, he was responsible for the Central Methodist Church completed in 1860.

Linwood was originally known as Leedsville, deriving its name from Leed's Store, a central gathering place. In 1880, with the advent of a post office, postal authorities refused to accept the name Leedsville because of another town of that name in the state. At a meeting in the schoolhouse a vote was taken, and Linwood was adopted as a name. The city was incorporated on April 27, 1931.

Like its sister city of Northfield, Linwood is still much of a boating community, with several marinas located there.

PIRATES, SHIPWRECKS, AND STORMS

Any place named Brigantine is likely to stir up visions of pirates, shipwrecks, and windjammers. The island to the north of Atlantic City is just such a place, where fact and fancy run headlong into each other until it is hard to verify the former or ignore the latter.

In the late summer of 1698, according to Brigantine legend, the barkentine which served as the flagship for the notorious Captain William Kidd of Greenock, Scotland, anchored near the mouth of Brigantine Inlet. Captain Kidd, his mate Timothy Jones, and several of the crew came ashore in a long boat, on the bottom of which rested a heavy leather and brassbound sea chest which they buried among the dunes of the island. Later, according to the story, Kidd and Jones returned, dug up the chest, and re-interred it elsewhere. A fight ensued, and Jones was killed by Kidd, who buried his former mate beside the chest before departing. The alleged loot has never been found.

Brigantine's first landowner of record was John Adams, who received a 50-acre grant in 1724. In 1802 James Baremore, who had been one of the operators of the Sailor Boy Tavern at Pleasant Mills and had built the original Smithville Inn, became the first permanent resident of Brigantine Island, building a home he called Baremore's Plantation on a site now several hundred feet out into the ocean.

Legend has it that during the War of 1812, while James Baremore was away from the island, a British landing party came looking for food. James's twelve-year-old son Daniel defied the invaders and chided them for taking his father's vegetables, to which a British officer replied, "Here is money for them, but tell your father we will be back for the whole island later and that time we will not pay for it!" But the British did not return.

The Baremore home, threatened by the sea many times, was washed away in a storm in 1830. Baremore salvaged what he could and built farther inland. Tradition has it that during one storm the tide swirled around the Baremore house and would have floated it away but for an old cow which scrambled to the porch, giving the structure the additional weight it needed to keep to its foundation. Baremore died in 1852, at the age of ninety, leaving the plantation to his grandchildren.

Over three hundred vessels have been wrecked on the shoals of Brigantine since the late 1700s. One of these wrecks was that of the Scottish bark *Ayrshire* with two hundred passengers during the night of December 29, 1849. The wreck is important in that it marked the first use of a breeches buoy, the apparatus perfected by William Newell, a local advocate of government action to protect shipping. John Maxen threw the line which was responsible for saving all passengers. For his part in the rescue he was awarded a medal by the United States government.

A far different fate befell the packet *Powhatan,* which went aground in a nor'east storm of April 15, 1854, at five o'clock in the afternoon. The vessel broke in two, and all aboard perished. Brigantine residents gathered forty bodies from the beach and buried them at Rum Point. Many more bodies were seen floating in the bay. Isaac and Robert Smith of Smithville fished them out and buried them in a common grave in the old Quaker cemetery at Smithville.

During the early 1800s Brigantine was served by boat from the Inlet wharf in Atlantic City. In 1880 the sailing sloops were replaced by the first motor launch on a regular schedule.

The same year the Ocean Island and Brigantine Development Company, headed by Congressman A. C. Harmer of Philadelphia, developed the upper half of the island; the Brigantine Improvement Company developed south of the island's center.

In 1885 Brigantine had its first post office and a mailboat between the island and Atlantic City. Alfred Holzkom was postmaster, operating from a small building on Brigantine Avenue, now beyond the low-water mark as are many sites of old island buildings because of a drastic change in the shoreline after the turn of the century.

In 1892 Brigantine seemed to be in a wave of prosperity. The first land companies merged. A trolley line was established with double-deck sight-seeing cars in operation. Boatloads of visitors from Atlantic City came to the island for a day's excursion among the sand dunes.

Pavilions were constructed on each end of the line, which continued until 1908.

Brigantine has been the scene of many development plans. In 1900 a group envisioned the island as a modern Venice, with canals for streets; another attempted to create an exclusive artists' colony. These projects failed, people moved away, and for a time the island was principally a home for a U.S. Coast Guard Station.

The Island Development Company tackled the task of rejuvenation in 1923. In 1924 Brigantine had its first direct connection to Atlantic City via a bridge costing $1 million. This was a toll span until 1925, when it was sold to Atlantic County. On September 21, 1938, the bridge was destroyed by a hurricane, and Brigantine residents returned to a ferry connection with Atlantic City. The span was rebuilt, but on September 14, 1944, a hurricane hurled tons of water at the structure, and it again collapsed. It was rebuilt, but in 1969 it was declared unsafe and heavy traffic forbidden. A new high-level span was completed in 1972 at a cost of $10 million, and the old bridge was closed.

One of the worst disasters of recent date to strike the island was the storm and flood of March 1962. Houses floated across streets, piers slid into the sea, and a state of emergency was declared. But the people swept up, rebuilt, and, within the past ten years, three thousand new homes have been added to the island.

FROM ARROWHEADS TO JETS

It is a long step from Indians to supersonic jets, but Pomona, adjoining Egg Harbor City in Galloway Township, made such a step.

During the land boom on Brigantine Island about the close of the nineteenth century, the Brigantine Transit Company had sixteen trolley cars in service. The line was dismantled in 1908. (Courtesy of the Conover Collection)

At various times in the past the community was known as Swamp Siding, Cedar Bridge, and Doughty Station.

On January 12, 1897, it was the site of an interesting archeological discovery. While fox hunting in the area, George W. Sneft and some friends from Egg Harbor City saw an opening in the dense brush only a short distance from a road. Upon investigation they found an Indian hut made of hickory wood still in good condition. Further search revealed four additional huts around which were many arrowheads and pieces of pottery.

Ten days later two Italian woodchoppers working in the same area came across a skeleton, tomahawks, and stone darts.

Thorough examination by experts indicated that the artifacts were the remains of a permanent village of the Lenni-Lenape Indians, who lived in the vicinity before the arrival of the white man.

Today Pomona is primarily a farming community, the home of the 300-acre truck and berry farm of the Liepe Brothers, the $3.5 million plant of the Lenox China Company built in 1954, and the Atlantic City Municipal Air Terminal. On land which was used as a naval air station during World War II the government built the enormous and important National Aviation Facility Experimental Center, where every safety device to be used in the operation of the nation's airports is tested before installation.

THE UNUSUAL COLONEL McKEE

McKee City, which is not a city but a sprawling expanse of small farms, scattered homes, and a shopping center, located half in Hamilton Township and half in Egg Harbor Township in the heartland of Atlantic County, was originally a tenant-farmer settlement, brainchild of Colonel John McKee of Philadelphia, reportedly the first Negro colonel of the Pennsylvania National Guard.

Born in Alexandria, Virginia, in 1821, McKee arrived in Philadelphia in 1842 and operated a restaurant said to have been located at Eighth and Market streets, before acquiring a block of row houses in the Quaker City.

His big dream was a vast farm complex under his direction, plus a military college for orphan Negro and white children organized along the lines of Girard College. In keeping with this ambition Colonel McKee first visited South Jersey and bought land in Atlantic County in 1884 (Deed Book 96, page 459, Atlantic County Clerk's Office, Mays Landing). Between that time and his death on April 6, 1902, he had recorded forty deeds to various parcels of property in the two-township area. It is said his holdings amounted to more than four thousand acres. Searches were underway on additional property when he died.

The McKee property was located along the Newfield Branch of the Pennsylvania and Reading Railroad right-of-way. About one third of it was in Egg Harbor Township, the remainder in Hamilton Township. Streets were laid out by McKee personally and saltbox-type houses built. The developer also constructed his own sawmill, at which lumber used in house construction was cut. There were about eighteen farms of 50 acres each along the railroad between English Creek Road and the Reega flag stop of the rail line. Along Harding Highway there were some 100-acre farms; one was leased by Arthur Boerner, who became well known in the area for his county agricultural activities.

Leases on these farms show Colonel McKee to have been a man meticulous about the tiniest detail. One such lease, dated March 4, 1899, stipulated that the lessee was to clear ten acres of land a year for five years. So there would be no misunderstanding of the word *clear*, McKee included this paragraph: "A strip, five hundred twenty-five feet or two and one-half lengths of rope deep, extending the whole width of the farm is to be cleared by cutting off the wood and brush and burning the same; taking out stumps of trees and hauling them in a pile in back of the house."

McKee also decreed that, in the first year, two and one-half acres of rye and timothy seed should be sown in the fall and the same amount of clover in the spring and "No hay, straw nor fodder will be sold off the farms."

If the tenants carried out all instructions in the first five years they could lease for another ten at $50 per year, payable semi-annually. McKee kept tight rein on his lands. A detailed search of county records failed to disclose any land sales by him in his lifetime.

McKee lived in Philadelphia and visited McKee City about every two weeks, renting a horse and buggy from Michael Hopkins, who had stables at English Creek Road. At Christmastime the colonel would send a car filled with presents to be distributed among his tenants. A community hall at the corner of English Creek Road opposite the McKee City Store was the scene of a big Christmas party staged by the colonel.

McKee built the first schoolhouse in the vicinity—a frame one-room structure.

The community had a large freighthouse since practically all merchandise was delivered by rail. A post office was housed in the freighthouse for many years with Alex Heggen, Sr., holding the postmastership for forty-five years.

McKee City was so named by Colonel McKee himself, who insisted that all leases be drawn to list land "in McKee City." The place was not incorporated, but the name appears on all maps of the area. A roundabout on the Black Horse Pike is called McKee Circle.

Besides his lands in South Jersey and Pennsylvania, Colonel McKee—according to Paragraph 19 of his will—also owned lands in Russell, Logan and Cabell counties in West Virginia, plus a tract of forty-nine thousand acres in Franklin County, Georgia. A further search of records revealed additional lands in Martin, Lawrence, and Johnson counties in Kentucky.

McKee instructed that the lands remain unsold "as long as they seemed likely to increase in value." This suggests that McKee intended the revenues from his properties to be used to support his military college project, which he intended for Pennsylvania.

Although McKee did not live to perfect his college plan, he made provision for it in a 13-page will dated December 8, 1899. After a few family bequests, McKee directed that the remainder of his estate be handled by the Most Rev. Patrick John Ryan, Archbishop of the Catholic Diocese of Philadelphia and his successors in office, with full authority to collect rents (in McKee City) and profits from his other acreages.

The Bishop's office was also charged with the erection of the college "and an iron statue of myself [McKee] astride a horse in my full uniform worn by me as Colonel of the Thirteenth Regiment, National Guard of Pennsylvania. The said esquestrian statue and pedestal on which the same is to be erected, shall be of the same size, material, color, style and pattern in every way as that erected to the memory of General F. Reynolds, on the north side of the new city hall in the city of Philadelphia. There shall be cut in large letters: COLONEL JOHN McKEE, FOUNDER OF THIS COLLEGE."

McKee's integrated college was never erected, the trustees finding that the fund given them was inadequate to accomplish the establishment of such an institution. Because of the colonel's laudable objective, the trust created instead a scholarship fund for the needy of the Philadelphia area.

The estate is believed to be the largest ever left to charity by a Negro. According to a memorandum filed in 1971 to the Orphans Court Division, Court of Common Pleas of Philadelphia, the estate is now valued at $1,250,000.

One important fact about Colonel McKee's life is not known— how he acquired the money it took to amass such a land empire.

QUEEN OF THE COAST

In 1695 the Council of Proprietors informed land speculator Thomas Budd that the only way he could acquire the West Jersey land he wanted was by taking additional acres on islands between Little and Great Egg Harbor rivers.

"I don't want that swampland at any price," Budd told the surveyor general. "It will never be good for anything but sea gull nests." Budd was speaking of Atlantic City!

Despite his reluctance he completed the transaction (which included the first survey of Absecon Island on which Atlantic City is located dated October 11, 1695) for 440 acres.

At that time the area called Absecon Island consisted of three islands, noted on early maps as Sand Hills, Inside Beach, and Cedar Beach. Budd paid forty cents an acre for his farmlands on the mainlands and four cents an acre for his island swamp and sand dunes.

Budd planned a colony along the Little Egg Harbor (Mullica) River, but the plan never got beyond the talking stage. While Budd accompanied the surveyor in plotting his grants, that was about his only physical contact with the land; he preferred to conduct all business from his Burlington office.

Later surveys of Absecon Island show the lands owned by Daniel Coxe and Jacob Spicer of Cape May County, Andrew Steelman, Peter Conover, and Daniel Ireland of Gloucester County, and John Scott of Rhode Island.

Andrew Steelman made his first purchase of land—180 acres—in 1727 and eventually acquired most of the beachfront. John Ladd, Jr., Philadephia merchant and land speculator, became owner of 318 acres on March 4, 1739, later that year annexing another 717 acres, all on Absecon Beach.

It is impossible to name with any degree of accuracy the first white inhabitant of Absecon Island. Daniel Ireland, William Boice, and George Stibbs, all prominent in mainland communities during the Revolution, spent time on the island, but mainly for fishing and hunting.

Jeremiah Leeds of Leeds Point, credited as Absecon Island's first permanent settler, made his initial land purchase in 1804 from James Steelman IV, and Sarah and Henry Smith by deed dated July 7 of that year recorded in the Atlantic County clerk's office at Mays Landing (Book H).

Jeremiah, a direct descendant of Thomas Leeds, who came from Leeds, England, to Shrewsbury, Monmouth County in 1676, had moved to Absecon Island in 1783, when he was twenty-nine years old. He built a log cabin near what is now Arkansas and Arctic avenues, and proceeded to plant corn and rye. During his occupancy of the island, it was known as Leeds Plantation. Jeremiah married twice. Among the children of his second marriage were Chalkley Steelman Leeds, who became the first mayor when Atlantic City was incorporated, and Robert B. Leeds, who became the first postmaster. Over the years the Leeds family contributed to the growth of Atlantic City. They developed two small frame hotels into the impressive Haddon Hall-Chalfonte Hotel complex.

Dr. Jonathan Pitney of Absecon, generally referred to as the "father of Atlantic City," was the first to see the area's possibility as a bathing spa. Active in the civic life of South Jersey after his arrival in Absecon in 1820 to set up a medical practice, Dr. Pitney in 1837 led the successful fight for the divorcement of Gloucester and Atlantic counties.

The island across the meadows from his home, which still stands on Shore Road, Absecon, seemed to draw him. In 1851 he joined with Samuel Richards and General Enoch Doughty in a petition to the state legislature for the right to build a railroad into South Jersey. Richards hoped the project would provide cheaper means of transportation for his bog-iron products in Weymouth and Batsto. General Doughty hoped to promote development of the twenty-five thousand acres of land he owned in lower Atlantic County.

On March 19, 1852, the legislature sanctioned the building of the railroad. On June 24 work started on a single-track line from Camden to Absecon based on a preliminary survey made by Richard Osborne, a Philadelphia civil engineer. By August of 1853 the road was completed to Absecon and tested. That same year officers of the Camden and Atlantic Railroad Company formed a land company to acquire an Absecon Island bathing beach, which they intended to promote as an asset to the new railroad.

In December of 1853 Osborne was called upon to map the "bathing village." A controversy developed over a name, some people favoring Ocean City, Seabeach, Strand, and Bath. Osborne submitted his city map to the board in January of 1853. Here is his account of what happened as delivered in a speech at the twenty-fifth anniversary celebration of the railroad:

When before the board, I unrolled a great and well finished map of the proposed bathing place, they saw in large letters of gold, stretching over the waves, the words ATLANTIC CITY. This title was greeted with enthusiasm by the board. The name was unanimously adopted and that day Atlantic City came into existence on paper.

It is a proud name for the nation . . . and I may be permitted, without egotism, to say I am proud of having christened her.

When the Camden and Atlantic Railroad made its first trip into Atlantic City in 1854 the tracks ran down Atlantic Avenue, the principal thoroughfare, and the steam engines looked like this one named "The Curlew." (Courtesy of Edward T. Francis)

The city was incorporated on March 3, 1853, and operated under that charter, despite some glaring boundary errors, until 1902, when Governor Franklin Murphy granted a new charter raising the original debt limit and resetting boundaries.

The first election was held on May 1, 1854, with twenty-one registered voters. Chalkley Leeds was named mayor at a meeting of city council in the United States Hotel. For the next twenty-one years the council met at various hotels. The young resort made steady progress. More hotels were built. Two more rail lines came shoreward. Philadelphians and New Yorkers flocked to its beaches. In 1870 this activity was capped by a development that began a new era for Atlantic City—the Boardwalk.

Up to 1870, Atlantic Avenue, principal thoroughfare of the resort, was the focus of visitor interest. With the railroad running down the middle of the street, passengers could alight in front of their favorite hotels, all of which faced Atlantic Avenue. The beachfront was undeveloped. Sea-bathing hours were from 6 A.M. to about 11 A.M., after which the hotels and their band concerts and dances were the center of attraction.

Early boarding houses lacked refinements until Charles McGlade took over the Mansion House and installed an elaborate lobby—all gold, mirrors, and glitter—and furnished it with comfortable chairs, sofas, and costly carpeting. Mansion House became the talk of the town, and other hotelmen soon provided similar pleasant accommodations. But they soon found that guests returning from hikes on the beach tracked sand which ruined carpeting and furnishings. Alexander Boardman, a hotelman who doubled as a conductor on the Camden and Atlantic Railroad, found that even upholstery in passenger cars was being ruined by beach sand.

In the spring of 1870 Boardman and Jacob Keim, operator of the Chester County House on South New York Avenue, invited a group of hotelmen for a discussion of the problem. Out of the meeting came the idea of a walkway of boards which could be put down on the sand in the summer and stored in the winter.

While the city council approved the idea there was no money available for lumber or workmen. It was estimated that such a walkway from the Absecon Lighthouse in the Inlet to the Sea

In 1889 the Chalfonte Hotel in Atlantic City was moved a half block to the present site of the Chalfonte-Haddon Hall complex on the Boardwalk. (Courtesy of Mall Dodson)

View Excursion House at Missouri Avenue would cost $5,000.

Brown and Woelpper, a Philadelphia lumber firm which also held controlling interest in the United States Hotel, agreed to furnish the necessary lumber for scrip instead of cash.

On June 26, 1870, the walk of boards was finished and dedicated with appropriate ceremonies. The first walk was constructed of wide boards 1½ inches thick, nailed to joists set crosswise 2 feet apart. Sections in 12-foot lengths for easy handling were attached to guide posts in the ground about 18 inches above the sand. In September of 1870 crews removed the walk and stored it on one of the high spots of the island. The next season it was again put upon the sand, a procedure followed for eighteen years.

By 1880 the first walk had become so battered that a new one 14 feet wide was built. By this time the walk's possibilities as a business center were apparent, and the city passed legislation regulating business establishments bordering the promenade. This ordinance was also responsible for the development of another Atlantic City institution—the ocean pier.

The first was Howard's Pier at Kentucky Avenue in 1882. In 1884 Applegate's Pier at Tennessee Avenue was added. It was later and better known as Young's Ocean Pier, the resort's pioneer amusement man, Captain John Lake Young, having bought it from the original owners. The Iron Pier, which was destined to be more famed as Heinz Pier, made its appearance in 1886. The Steel Pier opened in 1898, the Steeplechase in 1899, and the Million Dollar Pier in 1906.

The piers started a new phase in resort history as the glamorous world of show business took over the area. Soon such people as Sarah Bernhardt, Lillian Russell, Victor Herbert, David Belasco, Sigmund Romberg, Flo Ziegfeld, Earl Carroll, W. C. Fields, Ed Wynn, George White, John Philip Sousa, Eddie Cantor, and Al Jolson were familiar figures at the resort. George M. Cohan used the Shelburne Hotel piano to polish his songs. The year 1920 saw the amazing total of 168 Broadway-bound shows opening in the resort's three main theatres—the Apollo, Globe, and Garden Pier.

Between 1870 and 1896 the walk underwent five changes and

About 1900 the Boardwalk at Atlantic City was much narrower than it is today. This view taken near New York Avenue shows numerous concessions and attractions now gone, such as the Academy of Music. In those days it was fashionable to avoid the sun, hence the many umbrellas. (McMahon Collection)

Atlantic Avenue, Atlantic City, during the Golden Jubilee celebration in 1904. The old city hall (on the right with a Victorian tower) and the trolleys have long since disappeared. (McMahon Collection)

emerged in its present form. On August 17, 1896, the walk was formally designated a street and given the name Boardwalk.

In the fall of 1920 the Boardwalk became the scene of the first big beauty contest, outgrowth of a floral parade started in 1914. The first beauty queen of Atlantic City was not a Miss America but Viola Walsh, resort resident who was crowned Queen of Carnival in 1914.

The first of the present series of pageants was staged to help prolong the season. In 1921 it was agreed to name the beauty queen Miss America. There were eight contestants that year with Miss Margaret Gorman, sixteen, from Washington becoming the first of a long line of Miss Americas.

In 1929 the gigantic Atlantic City Convention Hall, occupying an entire block from the Boardwalk to Pacific Avenue, was built at a cost of $12.5 million, an impressive figure, particularly in a year that saw the beginning of the depression.

On November 30, 1970, a new West Hall, costing $13 million, added 200,000 square feet of exhibit area, making a total of 500,000 square feet available to conventions. As part of the dedication ceremonies attended by convention officials from all parts of the nation, a helicopter took off, hovered, and landed again on the floor of the main auditorium of the hall complex.

In July 1911 President William Howard Taft, in Atlantic City to address a Christian Endeavor convention, dined at No. 1 Atlantic Ocean, on the new Million Dollar Pier, with members of his staff and the family of pier owner John L. Young. (McMahon Collection)

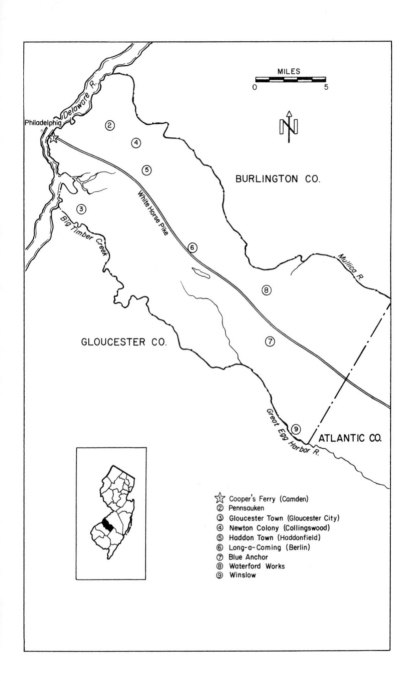

MILES

0   5

N

Delaware R.

Philadelphia

BURLINGTON CO.

White Horse Pike

Big Timber Creek

GLOUCESTER CO.

Mullica R.

Great Egg Harbor R.

ATLANTIC CO.

☆ Cooper's Ferry (Camden)
② Pennsauken
③ Gloucester Town (Gloucester City)
④ Newton Colony (Collingswood)
⑤ Haddon Town (Haddonfield)
⑥ Long-a-Coming (Berlin)
⑦ Blue Anchor
⑧ Waterford Works
⑨ Winslow

CAMDEN COUNTY

CAMDEN COUNTY

From its twelve miles of Delaware River waterfront, Camden County now spreads southeast through agricultural areas to the Atlantic County line.

My first impressions of Camden County were received as a youth when I rode along the old Gloucester toll road with my father, taking our vegetables in a covered farm wagon from Woodbury in Gloucester County to the old Dock Street market in Philadelphia. Among these early memories are the tollgate houses where one secured a bit of "medication" against the cold, as my father so aptly put it, and the long waits in the freezing temperatures for the ferry boats. However, I was a latecomer. Camden's first visitors arrived in the 1600s.

Samuel Norris purchased considerable land in this area from Edward Byllynge and trustees in 1678 according to early realty records.

Camden County owes much of its later development to the initiative of William Roydon, who in 1688 secured a license from the general court of Gloucester to operate a ferry between the Jersey and Pennsylvania shores. A year later Roydon sold the ferry to William Cooper, for whom the community that is now Camden was named.

The area was still part of Gloucester County during the Revolution. At times detachments of both English and Hessian troops camped within its borders. The state legislature met in Haddonfield in 1777 because Hessian troops occupied Trenton. Commencement exercises for the College of New Jersey (later Princeton University) were held at Cooper's Ferry in 1766 as British forces were in Princeton.

First seeds of the movement which resulted in the formation of Camden County were sown in 1825, when residents of the

Cooper's Ferry district banded together to try to force removal of the county seat of Gloucester County from Woodbury to Camden. The fight was bitter, and the Cooper men lost. Waterford and Gloucester areas closed ranks, with Newton favoring the change. Camden lost by 876 votes.

In 1827 a public meeting was held at Vauxhall Gardens in Camden to petition the legislature to unite the townships of Waterford, Camden, Newton, Union, and Gloucester into a separate county to be called Delaware. This move also failed, and the proposal for a new county lay dormant until 1843. That campaign was successful, and the county was created on March 13, 1844, by taking a generous slice of Gloucester County, including parts of Waterford, Gloucester, Newton, Camden, Union, Delaware, and Washington townships. But it was called Camden County rather than Delaware.

With the creation of this new unit, there began a series of bitter struggles over the county seat. Abraham Browning, John W. Mickle, and others who had spearheaded the drive for the new county wanted the county buildings in Camden. However, the other districts joined forces and began campaigns for Haddonfield, White Horse, Mount Ephraim, and Long-a-Coming. Before it was over there were four elections, a directive from the Supreme Court, and two amendments to the original act. Finally an order from the Supreme Court directed the Board of Freeholders to erect a courthouse at Camden. The original structure was completed in 1855 at a cost of $40,000. It was of brick and located midway between Market and Federal streets, extending to Sixth Street, to the new line of Broadway. After nearly fifty years of service the old building was torn down in 1904. A new building was erected, its official opening was on April 24, 1906. The structure was turned over to the county on February 13, 1907.

There are 37 municipalities in the county today, the largest of which is Camden City. About 95 percent of the estimated 438,000 population is urban.

In addition to two bridges leading to Philadelphia which have replaced the old ferries, Camden County is crossed north-south by the New Jersey Turnpike. The county has many miles of interstate highway and the high-speed Atlantic City Expressway from Turnersville to the seashore. Camden County is served by the Pennsylvania-Reading Seashore Lines and the Jersey Central railroad. Its mass transportation facilities were recently augmented by the inauguration of a high-speed line from Lindenwold to Philadelphia. The White and Black Horse pikes also cross Camden County, feeding into the two bridges to the Quaker City.

Cherry Hill, one of the fastest-growing townships in Camden County, is the former Delaware Township which was incorporated on February 28, 1844, an offshoot of Waterford Township. This community derives its name from a large farm occupied for many years by the Abraham Browning family. The name of the district was changed to Cherry Hill by popular vote in 1961. It is the site of a giant shopping center, several nationally known inns, and numerous industrial sites.

HADDONFIELD

Haddonfield, on the Kings Highway just south of Camden City, is one of the oldest towns in South Jersey. It dates to 1683, when land holdings were first acquired there by Richard Mathews and Francis Collins. When the Kings Highway was laid out in 1681 from Burlington to Salem, it ran through what became the Mathews tract, north of Ellis Street to Cooper's Creek. The Collins land was to the southwest, from the head of the middle branch of Newton Creek to the south branch of Cooper's Creek.

In 1698 John Haddon of London acquired approximately five hundred acres of what is now Haddonfield. In 1701 his daughter Elizabeth left England to take care of her father's lands in America. Her motivation was not confined to business. Elizabeth had become infatuated with young Quaker missionary John Estaugh, who had sailed for America previously. They met in the new land, and Elizabeth convinced John that "The Lord hath commanded me to love thee." They were married on October 1, 1702. Henry Wadsworth Longfellow heard of the love story and commemorated it in his poem "Theologian's Tale."

Elizabeth Haddon first made her home in a house built by John Willis. In 1713 she supervised the building of a mansion which the young couple called New Haddonfield. Constructed of brick and boards, the house stood about a third of a mile from the center of Haddon Town; it was destroyed by fire on April 19, 1842.

The couple made several trips to England. In 1720 Elizabeth brought back her nephew Ebenezer Hopkins, who was to remain in Haddonfield and become a man of prominence in the community. Elizabeth survived her husband by twenty years and died in 1762. In the Friends cemetery in Haddonfield there is a bronze plaque upon which is engraved:

In memory of
Elizabeth Haddon
Daughter of John Haddon of London
wife of John Estaugh

She was a Founder and Proprietor
of Haddonfield, N.J.

Born 1680   Emigrated 1701
Married 1702   Died 1762

Buried near this tablet
Originator of the Friends Meeting
here established in 1721

A woman, remarkable for resolution,
prudence, charity

John Kay settled in the area about the same time as Elizabeth and John Estaugh. He operated the Free Lodge Mill, later known as Evan's Mill, near Cooper's Creek.

The Quaker meeting house was built near the intersection of Ferry Road and Kings Highway in 1720.

The oldest and smallest house in Haddonfield still standing dates to 1742 and is located at 23 Ellis Street. It was the home of Sarah Haddon, sister of Elizabeth.

The growing community of Haddonfield, like many others of that time, had one major fear—fire. Thus the formation of Friendship Volunteer Fire Company on March 8, 1764, was one of the first civic actions of the settlers. Each of the twenty-six members of the fire company was required to furnish two buckets. The association itself provided six ladders.

Haddonfield was the center of considerable activity during the Revolution, much of it centering around the Indian King (Creighton) Tavern. The town was occupied at various times by both Continental and British troops. A guardhouse was kept by the American forces on the grounds of William Griscomb. When British forces marched through the town they fired the guardhouse and Griscomb's home. An adjoining house belonging to Thomas Redman also was burned. British officers quartered their troops with the inhabitants of Haddonfield, who had little say in the matter. Many of the foot soldiers camped on the grounds surrounding houses occupied by their officers and used fences for firewood.

One tale that survives is of a man named Miles Sage, who was attached to the Continental Army guardhouse unit. Sage was sent on a mission and returned not knowing the Americans had been driven from the area. He rode up to the headquarters to find it occupied by British officers. As he remounted, British guards drew up in three ranks to block the street. The rider charged the Redcoats, but his horse stumbled and fell. The British guards laughed at the fallen horseman and inflicted a number of bayonet wounds. They would have made short work of Sage had they not been stopped by a Scots officer, who ordered the fallen man taken to a nearby house and his wounds treated. Sage lived to resume his service with the Continental forces.

The Hessians, under Count Carl Emil Kurt von Donop, camped at Haddonfield on their way to the battle of Red Bank, the count making his quarters in the John Gill house. Haddonfield was also the camping ground of Major John Simcoe and his Queen's Rangers. At that time Simcoe was trailing General Wayne, who, learning of Simcoe's presence at Haddonfield, planned an attack; Simcoe retreated from the town.

Haddonfield again saw British troops during the retreat of General Howe from Philadelphia in June 1778. It took Howe's forces four days to pass through the town.

The borough of Haddonfield was incorporated on April 6, 1875, the first borough commission consisting of five members: John H. Lippincott, Joseph F. Kay, Alfred W. Clement, Nathan Lippincott, and Samuel P. Hunt. Headquarters of the borough government remained in the old town hall on Haddon Avenue until March 21, 1924, when a town meeting authorized the purchase of property on Kings Highway. This land was owned by George Horter, a public-spirited citizen who, among other gifts to Haddonfield, provided a stone watering trough for horses at Tanner Street and Haddon Avenue. The present town hall, built in 1927 on a bond issue of $175,000, was opened in 1928.

Manufacture of pottery was one of the earliest industries of Haddonfield. The first plant, said to have been on Ellis Street, was laid out in 1798. A small pottery plant was built in 1805 by John Thompson, who purchased property at what is today 50 Potter Street from Charles French and John Brick. The former factory is now the attractive two-story home of Mr. and Mrs. Harry Becker. It bears the original dates in the stone part of the walls.

Potter Street was also famous for its row of open sheds for the use of wagons from the seashore. The famed Egg Harbor wagons carried clams and fish from the waters of the Atlantic Ocean and Great Bay. The glasshouse wagons were pulled by teams of six to eight mules with a bell on each animal warning that glass was being transported and to approach with care. Charcoal wagons from the pine belt also used the Potter Street sheds.

The Coffin name, prominent in Atlantic and Camden counties, turns up in Haddonfield history because William Coffin, Jr., moved to the town about 1852 and built a home on Kings Highway. He dealt in Haddonfield real estate.

The old Friendship Volunteer Fire Company continued its informal service until February 21, 1857, when it became the Haddonfield Fire Department with Richard W. Snowden as president. The company passed into the control of the borough commission and became known as Haddon Fire Company No. 1.

The Society of Friends was responsible for the first school in Haddonfield, built in 1786 on the southwest corner of the burying ground. The Grove school house was built in 1809 on Grove

Street on land donated by William E. Hopkins. School rooms were also provided in the first town hall. The first stone school was completed in 1869.

For more than a century after Haddonfield's beginnings, the Society of Friends conducted the only religious activities. The Baptists began services in 1817 with the preachings of John Sisty of Philadelphia.

Haddonfield is now a town of 13,118. Its streets are still lined with giant buttonwood trees. Houses dating from the 1700s are still to be found on the quiet streets, each house with a plaque authenticating the date of its construction.

A TAVERN STATEHOUSE

Haddonfield takes justifiable pride in picturesque Indian King Tavern at 233 Kings Highway. Dating from 1750, this building is one of the best-preserved examples of the early colonial tavern in the state. It is now operated as a museum under state supervision.

This house was built by Mathias Aspden, a Philadelphia merchant and shipowner, on land purchased from Timothy Matlack, one of the early settlers of Haddonfield. It was sold to Thomas Redman on May 1, 1775. On May 5, 1777, he sold it to Hugh Creighton, who put up his sign CREIGHTON HOUSE.

Creighton entered the tavern business through his marriage to Mary French, a widow who, under her own name, operated a tavern at Kings Highway and Potter Street called the Indian King. An apartment building now occupies that site.

It is generally believed that the sign INDIAN KING was removed from the Mary French tavern when it ceased to operate and was then hung in front of the Creighton House. In documents of the Revolutionary period, the name Creighton House is used.

The Creighton House not only served as headquarters for the Provincial Assembly when the Hessian troops occupied Trenton but after independence was declared it became the temporary meeting place of the state legislature. It was in the upstairs meeting room of Creighton House that the word *colony* was struck and the word *state* inserted in official Jersey documents. It was also here that the Great Seal of the State of New Jersey, designed by Francis Hopkinson of Burlington, was accepted, although it was not then officially adopted.

In January 1777 the Council of Safety, which dealt with traitors and British sympathizers, was formed at the Creighton House. The inn was headquarters for such colorful figures as General Anthony Wayne, Count Pulaski, "Light Horse" Harry Lee, and, as the tide of war changed, British plunderer John Graves Simcoe.

There has long been a controversy as to whether or not a secret tunnel existed between the tavern and the guardhouse across the street. This bit of romanticism started when a sealed-up recess was discovered in the basement of the tavern on the Kings Highway side. It is now generally thought that this was a wine cellar rather than a secret tunnel. Why the entranceway was closed is not known.

The historical connection of the Creighton House was not confined to the Revolutionary period. Hugh Creighton was the uncle of Dolly Payne, better known as Dolly Madison.[*] Young Dolly Payne was a familiar figure in Haddonfield and had her pick of available swains of the town before she met and married John Todd, a wealthy Quaker lawyer of Philadelphia who died of yellow fever in the epidemic of 1793. Instead of going into mourning, Dolly became a dazzling figure of society and married promising young Virginia congressman James Madison. When he became President, Dolly made her own place in history by saving vital state documents when the British burned the White House.

There is a Dolly Madison bed on the second floor of Creighton House. While the young lady did own this piece of furniture, it was not used at the inn but in a nearby home. At that particular point in history, ladies did not stay overnight at taverns, although they did take part in social affairs there.

[*]Although numerous references spell her name Dolley, an authenticated facsimile of the will of Mrs. Madison, in her own handwriting (once in my possession, recently donated to the Camden County Historical Society, where it is on display), begins "I, Dolly Madison . . ." It is signed "Dolly Madison," leading me to believe that this was her choice of spelling.

Creighton continued as owner of the inn until 1790, when he sold it to John Burroughs. The old tavern was also operated under other names: Old Tavern House, the American Tavern, Roberts Hotel, and, after Haddonfield voted to ban liquor, Temperance House.

According to some sources, in the years between 1800 and the Civil War the tavern was used as a way station of the underground railroad which spirited runaway slaves to Canada and safety.

After serving as a wayside inn, general store, and rooming house, Creighton House was abandoned sometime before 1900. The state of New Jersey acquired possession on June 15, 1903, and embarked upon an extensive restoration program. It was decided to retain the name Indian King although there have been periodical discussions of a possible restoration of the Creighton name. The large second-floor room where the colonial legislature met is still used for meetings.

NEWTON COLONY

Collingswood, formerly Newton Colony, bordered on the north and south by Cooper and Newton creeks, is a true suburb of Philadelphia and Camden, adjoining the border line of the latter city. Although it dates official beginnings to 1888, when voters agreed to incorporate 1,340 acres of prime farmland into a political subdivision, Newton Colony's roots extend back to the voyage of an English fishing boat, *Ye Owner's Adventure,* under the command of first mate John Dagger.

The vessel, known in marine language as a "pink," a narrow-sterned coastal craft with a forty-six foot keel used during the seventeenth century to transport passengers from the British Isles to the New World, had been at sea nearly two months before sighting the shoreline of Salem on the Delaware River, on November 19, 1681. Its twenty-one passengers included Thomas Thackara, Mark Newbie, William Bates and thirteen children, George Goldsmith, and Thomas Sharp.

The new settlers were met by Robert Zane who, along with his Indian wife Alice, later became prominent in the business life of Newton Colony.

In March of 1682 the group sailed north up the Delaware to the mouth of the creek since named Newton, and founded a colony with boundaries extending from Gloucester to Cooper's Creek, including parts of Haddon Township. A meeting house was erected in 1684 and served the colony until it was destroyed by fire in 1817.

The name Newton does not appear in early records, but some local historical buffs believe the colony was named for Sir Isaac Newton, famous English mathematician and philosopher. An alternate possibility is that the name is a slurring of New Towne.

In 1728 Thomas Atmore was named constable and Joseph Ellis and Robert Hubbs road supervisors. Ferry Road, running through the settlement, was laid out in 1792 and became the country's first toll road under the name of the Haddonfield-Camden Turnpike. Tolls were collected until Camden County took over the road in 1909.

Newton Colony was the scene of forays by both British and American forces during the Revolution. When this harassment became unbearable, a unit of militia was formed, the Quaker residents putting aside religious scruples to fight for their crops and livestock.

In 1881 a town meeting was held at the store of James Riggins and the name Collingswood adopted for the community, honoring John Collings, a pioneer whose farm appears on a map of the area drawn in 1700 by Thomas Sharp.

Collingswood's first and only tavern, operated around 1860, was owned by Thomas Zimmerman, according to Raymond Bancroft in his detailed *Collingswood Story*. It was known as Half Way House and was located at the corner of Haddon Avenue and what is now Woodlawn Avenue.

The first real development of Collingswood was planned by E. C. Knight and R. T. Collings in 1874 at the Collings farm in Elk River, Maryland. Two years later Collings returned to Collingswood as agent for Knight and purchased the Burton farm, a vineyard of 112 acres which later became a golf course and is now Roberts Park.

In March of 1886 the town was treated to its first big-scale land sales promotion with special trains from Philadelphia to the sales site. Lots sold at $250. In 1888 residents held a special election and voted to incorporate Collingswood as a borough. Josiah Stokes was elected mayor under a provisional form of commission government. A new borough act in 1896 converted the town to councilmanic format with Henry Tatem first mayor under this system, which served the borough until 1917, when voters approved a return to the commission format in use today.

The town's first street lighting was by kerosene lamps which were extinguished for economic reasons during the period of full moon.

Although several small enterprises started in Collingswood, the town remains primarily residential. In 1903 a glass factory occupied the site of the present police station; it was destroyed by fire. For a time the federal government conducted a wireless station on the Kalium Springs property within borough limits. Kalium Springs Improvement Company offered spring water as a cure-all with the advice "drink six to eight glasses a day." Maurice Murphy's "Dew Drop Ice Cream" was also a popular product.

Shortly after World War II Mayor Arthur E. Armitage made the statement that Collingswood's future was "up—not out," referring to its land limitations. Almost as if in answer was the building of the Park View Apartments, largest multistory apartment structure in the state at that time. The project met heavy opposition from Collingswood resident as did any move to detract from the residential aspects of the place. In 1963 residents were still protesting to city officials on high-rise buildings. At the time Collingswood received its name the population was approximately 20; today it is a community of more than 20,000.

FERRY TO PHILADELPHIA

According to records on file at the Camden County Historical Society, a ferry service across the Delaware connecting the growing city of Philadelphia with Jersey began in 1688, when the County Court of Gloucester authorized a public ferry at "some proper place between ᵞe mouths of Cooper's Creek and Newton Creek." William Roydon was the first ferryman; he provided transportation at rates of six cents for each passenger, twelve for man and horse.

The first ferry slips were merely planks on pilings, without overhead shelter. Often the passengers waited for the boats in nearby bars, where they could satisfy their thirst. Many of these bars were owned by the ferrymen, who thus profited from delays in service.

The first ferries were wherries holding about twelve people and manned by a crew of three or four. Locomotion was by sail if there was a fair wind or by rowing if there was not. All boats were fitted with skids or handles by which the passengers and crewmen could drag the boat across the ice to open water when necessary.

Horses, wagons, and carriages were transported across the river in a scow ferry which could be operated only in favorable weather. Because of this uncertainty, most farmers of the Camden area hauling their vegetables to the Philadelphia market would unload at the Camden wharf, place the goods aboard one of the smaller boats, and leave horses in nearby stables, also operated by ferrymen.

The first improvement on these primitive forms of transportation was the teamboat, so called because power was furnished by a team of horses walking a treadmill attached to a set of paddles or a single-paddle shaft. There was no protective covering for passengers.

Initial ferry landings on the Camden side were made at Cooper's Point, at Cooper Street, and at Kaighnton. The Cooper's Point landing was established about 1708 with the Philadelphia terminal in a section known as Kensington. This route was later changed to Arch Street, Philadelphia, with alternate trips to Poplar Street, Philadelphia. Ferries also were in operation from a Vine Street, Philadelphia, terminal. About 1800 Abraham Browning, Sr., established a ferry at the foot of Market Street, Philadelphia.

Between 1785 and 1807 John Fitch, Colonel John Stevens, Oliver Evans, and Daniel Large built steamboats to provide ferry

About the turn of the century when this photograph was taken, it was possible to take a trolley car or drive a rig to Camden's West Jersey Ferry, where the horse could be left with attendants in the open stalls (at right) while the traveler continued by boat to Market Street, Philadelphia. The opening of the Delaware River (Benjamin Franklin) Bridge in 1926 marked the beginning of the end for the Camden ferries. (Camden County Historical Society)

service on the Delaware River. Large, Joseph Bispham, and several others ran a line from Middle Ferry at the foot of Cooper Street, Camden, to Market Street, Philadelphia. Their *Camden* tied up sidewise rather than bow first, as in the case of later steam ferries. She was an open craft with no superstructure and thus no protection for passengers. The first covered ferryboats appeared about 1835.

During the heyday of the ferry service there were five boats on the Delaware by the name of *Camden,* including one made of iron which many people believed would not float.

The *New Jersey* caught fire in midstream on Saturday night, March 15, 1856, and more than sixty lives were lost.

Other early ferryboats were the following: *Beverly* (1882), *Wenonah* (1882), *City of Reading* (1889), *Philadelphia* (1896), *Cape May* (1901), *Ocean City* (1903), *Margate* (1906), *Hammonton* (1906), *Wildwood* (1911), *Salem* (1913), *Bridgeton* (1913), *Delaware,* later renamed *Atlantic City* (1914), *Haddonfield* (1921), *Millville* (1921), *Ventnor* (1922), *Haddon Heights* (1922), *Chelsea* (1923), and the second *Ocean City* (1923).

The end of the Camden ferries began in 1926 with the opening of the Delaware River Bridge (later renamed the Benjamin Franklin Bridge), although some held on for several years. The Pennsylvania and Reading railroads continued using the ferries as part of their service until 1952.

Ferry Obituary

Vine Street ferry, discontinued September 14, 1926.
Shackamaxon Street ferry, discontinued November 1, 1926.
Chestnut Street ferry, discontinued June 11, 1936.
South Street ferry, discontinued April 30, 1938.
Market Street ferry, discontinued March 31, 1952.

A TOWN DESTINED TO THRIVE

Philadelphia merchant Jacob Cooper, son of William and Deborah (Medcalf) Cooper, was perhaps the first man to realize the possibilities of building a town at the present site of Camden, New Jersey. On April 23, 1764, he obtained from his father a tract of a hundred acres located between the lands of Jacob's nephews Daniel and William Cooper. The north end of the tract was the old bridal path leading to the ferries, which in 1761 had been laid out as part of the road from Haddonfield to the Cooper Street ferry.

In 1773 Jacob Cooper plotted forty acres of his tract in town lots, naming his project Camden in honor of Charles Pratt, Earl of Camden, a champion of constitutional rights for the colonies at a time when such thinking bordered on treason in Britain. By 1781 Cooper had sold 123 of the lots; he sold the remainder to his nephew William.

Joshua Cooper, son of Daniel, created the next addition to Camden. In 1803 he laid out lots in a tract to the south of the original development. Further expansion came on April 10, 1820, when Edward Sharp mapped a town plan called Camden Village from the part of the estate of Joshua Cooper adjoining Camden on both sides of Bridge Avenue. His map was recorded on July 3, 1820. Sharp, who had come to the vicinity from Philadelphia in 1812, was one of the first to propose publicly the building of a bridge across the Delaware River to Windmill Island, then located in the middle of the river opposite present-day Spruce Street, Philadelphia. He presented a petition to the legislature seeking authority for such a span, the eastern end of which would be at Bridge Avenue, Camden. A newspaper reported "The Windmill Island Bridge Bill passed the Senate January 22, 1820, and the House February 18, 1820," but the project never materialized.

Various sections of Camden have been identified by special names over the years. For example, south of Cooper Street was called Daniel Cooper's Ferry, while the popular name for Cooper's Point was Samuel Cooper's Ferry; at various times these two sections were known as Lower Billy's Ferry and Upper Billy's Ferry. The Kaighn's Point settlement, named for land developer Joseph Kaighn, was also known as Kaignsborough, shortened in 1801 to Kaighnton. Tenth and Federal streets were called Dogwoodtown. There were also Ham Shore and Pinchtown, small groups of fishing shacks between Bridge Avenue and Spruce

Street. Other sectional names were Cooper's Hill, rising from a marsh west of Fourth Street and South of Bridge Avenue and owned by Richard M. Cooper of the State Bank of Camden, Nanny's Woods, Stockton, Centreville, Kaighnville, Liberty Park, and Sweet Potato Hill. Districts within the eleventh and twelfth wards had names such as Wrightsville, Fettersville, Boothmanville, Cramer Hill, Pavonia, Cramer Heights, Fairview, North and South Spicerville, French Tract, Rosedale, Bailytown, Deep Cut, and East Camden.

The first volunteer fire organization in Camden dates to March 15, 1810, when Perseverance Fire Company No. 1 was organized. It had one engine, a secondhand one, from the Pat Lyon shop in Philadelphia. Known as "the Silk Stockings," the members of this company had uniforms of white capes, dark trousers, and the usual glazed hats.

On November 13, 1826, a move for city government was started at a meeting in the hotel owned by Ebenezer Toole. The legislature, however, did not act upon a city charter until February 14, 1828. On March 13 the first meeting of city council was held at the John M. Johnson hotel, site of the Vauxhall Gardens on the West side of Fourth Street below Market. It was a stone building two stories high with an attic which served as jury room when county courts were held there prior to the erection of county structures. During its first days, the city council met at various places including Toole's Hotel, the Vauxhall Gardens, Alderman Smith's house, Cake's Hotel, and the Baptist meeting house.

In 1830 the second volunteer fire company came into being. This group was known as the Fairmount because the engine had once been the property of the Fairmount Company of Philadelphia. The name was later changed to Weccacoe Fire Company. Headquarters were in a frame building belonging to Ebenezer Toole at Third and Plum streets.

The burning of the Vansciver Carriage Factory on Front Street in 1834 pointed the need for better fire-fighting equipment. At a town meeting on December 14, 1834, it was decided to obtain $800 for this equipment from the state bank. Disagreements as to how the funds should be used resulted in all but $400, which had been spent on a horse cart and hose, being returned to the bank.

The Mohawk Company was organized in 1849, but after a score of charges against members, including those of deliberate fire setting, the company was ordered disbanded by city council. The Shiffler Hose Company came to the scene on March 7, 1849. The Independence Fire Company dates to April 3, 1851. Two other companies of this era were the United States Company No. 5, incorporated on February 10, 1854, and the Weccacoe Hose and Steam Company No. 2, organized on March 15, 1858.

By 1871 it was decided that the original city charter of 1828 was inadequate to care for the changing needs of the growing city, and city solicitor Alden C. Scovel was given the job of drafting a new one. This revised charter, approved on February 14, 1871, extinguished the ancient township of Newton. The latter had lost land to Camden in 1831, to Haddon Township in 1865, and what was left was annexed to Camden by the 1871 charter. The area within the bounds of Camden City was now six and a half square miles; population at the time was 28,482. A move for the erection of a larger city hall was started in 1868. Work actually began in 1874, on the site of the original hall; it was completed in 1876.

Camden was destined to be an industrial complex because of its port facilities for shipping on the Delaware River and its proximity to Philadelphia, already a trade center. Emergence into the field of big-time manufacturing can be traced to the arrival of Richard Esterbrook in 1858 to launch the first steel pens in America at his Esterbrook Steel Pen factory, which is still in existence. Joseph Wharton established the nation's first nickel works in Camden in 1862. The industrial image of Camden was enlarged in 1869 by the start of a vegetable-packing factory operated by Joseph Campbell and Abram A. Anderson, which was the forerunner of the Campbell Soup Company.

In 1894 Eldridge R. Johnson started producing talking machines in his repair shop, improving Thomas A. Edison's invention and laying the foundation for the Victor Talking Machine Company, which, as the RCA-Victor company, is today one of the largest of Camden's industries.

In 1899 the New York Shipbuilding Company occupied a 160-acre tract extending to the south end of Camden. Shipbuilding hit its full stride during World War I. With patriotism running high, those turned down by the army stormed the gates of the New York Shipbuilding Company to add their bit to the war effort. I remember men working in the "York Ship" who had never previously spent a day at hard labor—clerks, bartenders, shop salesmen, packers, clergy. My father left a comfortable job in Philadelphia to do his share by helping to build ships, although he had never before been inside a shipyard. As youngsters we were allowed to watch from outside a high iron fence as soldiers with mean-looking bayonets, patrolled the vast yards, in which action continued day and night. With the sudden termination of the war, production dropped like a rock. Giant cranes were stilled. Most of the workers returned to peacetime pursuits. Others faced long layoffs. The transatlantic liners *Manhattan* and *Washington* were among the ships constructed on a postwar schedule. When World War II began, the yards returned to production with special contracts with the Navy Department. With peace came another cutback from which the shipyards have not yet recovered.

The 1820 dream of Edward Sharp to span the Delaware River finally came true on July 5, 1926, when the Delaware River Bridge, now called the Benjamin Franklin Bridge, was dedicated by President Calvin Coolidge. The bridge, then considered an engineering marvel, cost $40 million. Soon after the first span was put into operation, a move was started for a second bridge across the Delaware. This culminated in the Walt Whitman Bridge, opened to traffic on May 16, 1957. It was three years and eight months in the building and was financed through a $100 million bond issue.

Camden is also the site of the Camden campus of Rutgers—The State University of New Jersey, Camden County Community College, and the Camden County Vocational School. The Camden County Historical Society maintains a comprehensive library and museum.

Today, with a population of 102,551, Camden has an ever growing complex of apartment houses and shopping centers to care for the workers of its own plants as well as the thousands who cross the two bridges each day to work in Philadelphia.

THE GRAY POET

Walt Whitman, "the gray poet" as he was called because of his preference for gray attire, made Camden his home in later years. Born in Huntington, Long Island, New York, on May 31, 1819, the second of nine children, Whitman came to live with his brother George and family in Camden in 1873 after suffering a paralytic stroke. He was fifty-four years old at the time.

Although his poetry caused controversy in literary circles, by 1884 Whitman had enough income from his writing to buy a small house at 330 Mickle Street, which he furnished with a bed, a few chairs, and tables made from packing boxes. It is said that he revised *Leaves of Grass* at this house.

Whitman enjoyed South Jersey and spent holidays at Laurel Springs, a town a few miles southeast of Camden. Camden friends provided him with a horse and buggy, and he made many trips through the pinelands, having a lifelong love of natural beauty.

Whitman died in Camden on March 26, 1892. He had planned his tomb in Harleigh Cemetery, including the inscription which appears on the tomb: "For That of Me Which Is To Die."

Camden has heaped many laurels upon the poet, including naming after him the Walt Whitman Bridge over the Delaware River from Philadelphia to Camden, the Walt Whitman Plaza, and the Walt Whitman Hotel.

His admirers purchased his house on Mickle Street and turned it over to the state, which now operates it as a historical site.

DIVIDED ISLAND

The Delaware River between Camden and Philadelphia was not always an open stretch of water. Opposite Spruce and Pine streets in Philadelphia, there was an island known as Windmill Island because of the structure built upon it by John Harding in 1746.

Ferryboats skirted the island until 1838, when increased traffic resulted in a channel being cut through. The half north of the cut became known as Smith's Island, named for owner John Smith, who sold boat ballast. In the 1880s Jacob Ridgway built an amusement park there and ran special boats from Camden. The half south of the cut retained the name Windmill Island.

In May 1890 the two isles were declared a menace to navigation and a detriment to the establishment of Camden and Philadelphia as leading ports of the Delaware, and the federal government assumed control.

In 1891 there began the removal of twenty-one million cubic yards of material downstream to League Island in a project which cost $3,635,000, the largest dredging project undertaken by the government to that time. The project was completed in 1897.

PENNSAUKEN

Pennsauken Township, a business center in Camden County just south of the Benjamin Franklin Bridge, has been in two counties and four townships. In 1686 it was part of Gloucester County, which was divided into five townships in 1695, the area comprising Pennsauken becoming a part of Waterford Township. At another division in 1844, it was placed in Stockton Township. On February 18, 1892, Pennsauken was created a separate township by act of the state legislature.

The township can trace its history to 1633, when fifteen English colonists arrived and built a fort on the eastern shore of what is now Pennsauken Creek. They named the site Fort Eriwomac after a local Indian chief and settled awaiting the arrival of their patron, Sir Edmund Plowden of London, England. Sir Edmund had dreams of a colony in which religious freedom was guaranteed. However, his plan for a colony collapsed, mostly due to a lack of financial support. After four years the Pennsauken settlers abandoned the fort.

A group of Swedes took possession of the vacant fort, holding it until 1664, when the king of England granted five hundred acres near Pennsauken Creek to Samuel Jennings, who became deputy governor of West Jersey in 1681. First settlers on this plot included William Cooper, Samuel Cole, Samuel Spicer, John Kay, and Henry Wood.

The first Pennsauken trails were made by Indians. They were later followed by stagecoaches on trips to and from New York and Philadelphia which included a stop near Tippin Pond. According to township records, a tollgate was located in the vicinity of the Woodbine Swim Club. The Camden and Amboy Railroad was built across the area in 1830 followed by the Camden and Atlantic line in 1854.

Because of its accessibility to nearby metropolitan areas, the township quickly became a center for small businesses, and many of its largest farms were cut up for residential developments. Its present population is 36,394.

GLOUCESTER TOWN

In the southwestern part of the peninsula formed by the Delaware River and Big and Little Timber creeks south of Camden, Gloucester City has been the county seat of Gloucester County, a ghost town, a business center, a gambling resort and race track site, and a family vacation spot, as well as the steady industrial and home community it is today. The name Gloucester comes from a cathedral town in the west of England, ancestral home of many of the South Jersey community's first settlers. It is of Celtic origin, *glaw caer* meaning handsome city.

Captain Cornelius Jacobsen Mey landed a group of settlers on an island in the Delaware River opposite the present city of Gloucester in March of 1623. He fixed upon Hermaomissing, at the mouth of Sassachon, most northerly branch of Big Timber Creek, as the site of a permanent colony he hoped to establish. There he built a log fort he called Nassau in honor of a town on the Rhine in Germany. Captain Mey departed when the fort was finished. Eight years later, when a second group of settlers arrived, they found the place deserted and in possession of the Indians. The exact site of the fort is still debated. In a paper read before the New Jersey Historical Society on May 16, 1850, the Rev. Abraham Messler argued in favor of the high ground at Gloucester Point, a theory that has come to be generally accepted.

By 1686 there were enough settlers in the area to consider a basic legal organization for the colony. A county constitution was drafted and adopted at Gloucester Point. Legislative records show that as the result of a petition to and action by the General Assembly on May 15, 1686, the county was legally created as of May 28 of that year.

Gloucester Town became the center of activity and county seat. In 1695 a ferry from Philadelphia to Gloucester Town was established. A year later it was found necessary to enlarge the Gloucester jail. Whether or not the two events were related is not established by the records. Crime must have been on the increase, for a short time after the building of a jail a second one was needed.

In 1722 Joseph Hugg, who had purchased five hundred acres of land from Robert Zane in 1683, began operating the ferry. In 1750 Hugg built a tavern (near the ferry slip) which soon became a center for town meetings.

About 1760 a group of young men from Philadelphia formed the Gloucester Fox Hunting Club which, for more than fifty years, had its headquarters at Hugg's tavern. Out of this organization emerged the 1st Troop, Philadelphia City Cavalry, which boasts of having acted as escort to every president of the United States from George Washington to Richard Nixon.

On November 4, 1773, Hugg's tavern was the scene of a social event which later had some bearing on history. A Quaker by the name of Betsy Griscom was married to John Ross, an artisan of Gloucester Town. Because Ross was an Episcopalian, Betsy was read out of Meeting. This opposition led the young couple to move to Philadelphia, where at her small sewing shop on Arch Street Betsy won her place in history by making a thirteen-star American flag ordered by General Washington.

During the Revolution 4,000 British and Hessian troops were stationed in Gloucester under command of Lord Cornwallis, who made his headquarters at the home of Colonel Ellis.

In 1786, following the end of the war and the transfer of Gloucester County activities to Woodbury, Gloucester Town went into almost total eclipse. Its hundred or more homes had been reduced to a half dozen when David S. Brown, a native of Dover, New Hampshire, decided to erect a large cotton mill in the town. On July 1, 1844, ground-breaking exercises were held for a four-story unit of Washington Mills, later known as Argo Mills and the first of many enterprises Brown built in the village.

Also in 1844 Camden County was cut from Gloucester County. But Gloucester Town remained in Camden County, which has confused letter writers ever since, according to postal officials.

When the first looms of the new mill went into operation on July 31, 1845, there were 363 employees on the payroll. The Gloucester Manufacturing Company, designed to bleach, dye, and print the output of Washington Mills, was incorporated by Brown and his associates the same year. A population of 2,188 was shown in the 1850 census.

In 1871 Brown further expanded his operations by building the Ancona Print Works, forerunner of the Armstrong Cork Company holdings in Gloucester, and by incorporating the Gloucester Iron Works to take over a small foundry which had been started by William Sexton and James Michellon in 1864.

Brown also had a hand in the building of the Camden, Gloucester, and Mount Ephraim railroad (1865), the Gloucester Savings Institution (1872), and the Gloucester Gas Works (1873).

In 1868 Gloucester Town citizens held a meeting and incorporated as Gloucester City with a mayor and council. These same citizens were not happy when William J. "Billy" Thompson, a former Philadelphia restaurant man, decided to build a dining spot on a municipal wharf which had been erected in 1873. Thompson promoted Gloucester as the home of the planked shad dinner and became known as "the Duke of Gloucester." Staid citizens felt Thompson was disturbing the dignified atmosphere of their town.

Seeing the possibilities of Gloucester as a playground for Philadelphians, Thompson leased the Buena Vista Hotel and made it the most popular spot on the Delaware River. When ferryboat operators refused to run boats late at night, Thompson bought them out and established twenty-four-hour service. He led the movement for a municipal water supply in 1883, started the first electric plant in an old building on Market Street near the river, and built the Camden, Gloucester, and Woodbury Railroad.

In 1890 Thompson conceived the idea of a race track. Unable to obtain an official authorization from the existing race circuit, he went ahead and operated what was known as an outlaw track. Eighteen months after its initial race the track was closed by an act of the state legislature that barred horse racing in New Jersey. This setback failed to stop the promoter. He turned his attention to the construction of Washington-Park-on-the-Delaware, a 900-acre recreational area which was opened in 1896.

Thompson was also a political boss, dominating politics of Gloucester for nearly twenty years. He was a delegate to the national Democratic conventions in Saint Louis and Chicago which nominated President Cleveland. He also served two terms in the New Jersey legislature.

Thompson was the father of ten children. He built a mansion on the waterfront at King Street which became the gathering place of leading political figures of his time. It is now a district headquarters for the United States Coast Guard.

Thompson died on July 2, 1911, while on a trip to his birthplace in Ireland. His body was returned to Gloucester and buried in Saint Mary's Cemetery. While some Gloucester citizens blamed Thompson for bringing gamblers to the city, others considered him a town benefactor. Today it is still debated whether he was saint, sinner, or perhaps a bit of both.

Gloucester always had luck in its industrial growth. As soon as one industry closed down, another took its place. One of the great industrial boons was the location of the New York Shipbuilding Company plant in Camden just over the town line in 1901. The Pusey and Jones Shipyard was an important World War I industry, employing nine thousand workers at one time. When the war ended the plant was taken over by the Ruberoid Company, the Harshaw Chemical Company, and the New Jersey Zinc Company. Shipbuilding flourished during World War II, and Gloucester City felt the effects of this large payroll. Today

Gloucester is the site of a number of small industries and has a permanent population of 14,707.

LONG-A-COMING

Long-a-Coming, about fourteen miles from Philadelphia on the original stage road from Cooper's Ferry to the seashore, was one of the most picturesque as well as best-known stage stops of South Jersey in the 1800s.

There are several versions of how it received its unusual name. According to one, weary travelers on the springless stage wagons lumbering through the pines from the iron towns of the Mullica River would look forward with anticipation to a stop where they could sip strong spirits and ease sore limbs. They would complain that the rest stop was "long-a-coming." Stage drivers approaching the place would shout with enthusiasm: "Long-a-Coming! Just ahead!"

Another version is that the crew of a ship wrecked off the Brigantine Island shoals were making their way on foot to Cooper's Landing, seeking a stream of cool water they had heard about from the Indians. After finding the water they commented it had been "long-a-coming."

At any rate the stage stop took the name of Long-a-Coming, and the road up through the pines became known as the Long-a-Coming Trail.

That there were settlers at the site prior to the Revolution is indicated by headstones in the vicinity and at Cemetery Chapel which bear the date of 1766. The chapel, originally a log hut, was erected on land donated by Samuel Scull, one of the village's pioneers, who deeded it to the Presbyterian church. John Brainerd, the Indian missionary, is said to have preached there. The chapel also served as a district school.

There were at least three taverns in the village during its stage-coach era. Upper Tavern, often called Scull's Tavern, was opened by Samuel Scull about 1761 and kept by him until his death in 1777; other operators included Henry Thorn, William Downs, and Robert Taylor. The Nicholson Tavern at Eversham and Cross Keys roads, where those roads intersected Egg Harbor Road, was kept by Joseph Nicholson about 1770. Henry Thorn took over the business in 1775. In 1778 Joseph Murrell changed the name to Murrell's Tavern. Joel Bodine had an inn in the area between 1821 and 1835.

Among other town pioneers were Peter Rich and Richard Moss, who are credited with being the first permanent settlers. Farming and logging were early industries. A charcoal-burning works was established by Thomas Wright in the 1800s. The Post Office Department gave Long-a-Coming official status by establishing a branch there in 1812. Charcoal-burner Wright became the first postmaster.

The Camden and Atlantic Railroad reached Long-a-Coming in 1853. At that time the village consisted of a group of houses centered around four country stores on Egg Harbor Road, the original stage coach road, now a principal street of the town.

The advent of the railroad ended the colorful stage days, and the stage lines began to disappear. The Mullica River mills and glassworks closed down. The Long-a-Coming Trail was no more than a memory. The stage stop of Long-a-Coming became the train stop of Magnolia on February 5, 1867. On May 7, 1867, when Joseph Shreve was postmaster, the name Magnolia was changed to Berlin, which it has remained.

The township of Berlin was created on June 11, 1910. The present borough of Berlin dates from May 16, 1927. Dr. Frank O. Stem was the first mayor of the new borough. Today's town, with a resident population of five thousand, is a far cry from the stagecoach stop of yesteryear. The leading industries are the Formigli Corporation, which makes pre-cast concrete products, and the Owens-Illinois [Glass] Company.

GLASSWORKS IN THE PINES

William Hammond Coffin and Andrew K. Hay, prominent in the development of the town of Hammonton in Atlantic County, were also responsible for the start of Winslow Township in the southeastern corner of Camden County. A glassworks established at Winslow Village in 1831 by William Coffin became important in the hollow-ware trade. Andrew Hay was responsible for the beautiful designs of the Coffin and Hay flasks made in 1836 and 1837 which are collectors' items. Hay became sole owner of the glassworks in 1851 and erected a sawmill and a gristmill to give the little community a diversity of activity.

The glassworks continued to be operated by heirs of the founders until 1884, when it was leased to Tillyer Brothers of Philadelphia, who ran it for several years before it was closed.

Winslow Township was created by the legislature on March 8, 1845, out of Gloucester Township, its most important settlement being Winslow Village, a group of homes owned by Andrew Hay. At the time the area was dense woods, and William Coffin, Jr., felled the first tree to clear land for the homes. He named the place Winslow for his son Edward Winslow Coffin. This name was retained when the township was formed, with the act providing that the first election be held at Josiah Albertson's inn in Blue Anchor and the second meeting at the Red Lion Inn of William Middleton at Clementon.

Winslow Junction was well known in railroading days for the crossing there of the New Jersey Southern Railroad, the Camden and Atlantic, and the Philadelphia and Atlantic City lines.

Nearby were two hamlets: Still on some maps, New Freedom remains a group of homes surrounding an old church and graveyard. At Conradsville a clay works flourished for a number of years under James M. Conrad. It has since disappeared.

Another well-known name in Winslow Township is Ancora, an area of farms and the site of the Ancora State Hospital for the Mentally Ill.

Another old town of the section is Blue Anchor, which takes its name from a tavern located on a prominent Indian trail to the seashore (now Route 73). The land around Blue Anchor was purchased by Abraham Bickley, a Philadelphia distiller, in 1737. In 1740 John Hider was operator of the inn, which dispensed

South Jersey applejack and became a stagecoach stop in the late 1700s and early 1800s.

At one time Blue Anchor was selected by Dr. John Haskell of Philadelphia as the site for a spiritualistic community. About twenty-five houses were built, but with the founder's death the colony fell apart. Today the area is occupied by several large farms. There is still a tavern, a produce company, and the Blue Anchor Thoroughbred Horse Farm on Thornton Avenue.

According to South Jersey legend, the origin of the name Blue Anchor stems from a visit to the area, before the establishment of a tavern, by a group of sailors from the Great Egg Harbor River who complained it was a "damned dry and blue anchorage."

WATERFORD WORKS

Today Waterford Works is a small community on the White Horse Pike in Winslow Township. It was named after a glass-producing town in Ireland by Jonathan Haines, who built a glass factory he called Waterford Works sometime between 1822 and 1824. Haines died in 1828, and the factory passed to Samuel Shreve, Thomas Evans, and Jacob Roberts. After the death of Roberts, Joseph Porter acquired all of the stock and conducted the business in partnership with his sons.

Porter had original ideas for his time. According to Charles S. Boyer of the Camden County Historical Society, Porter was the first to introduce Sunday plant closings in South Jersey. It had long been the practice to operate seven days a week, owners claiming they could not close on Sundays while glass remained in the pots. Porter made alterations that permitted a shutdown of the Waterford Works on Sunday—so his employees could attend church services—and the practice was soon followed by other glassworks.

Porter also paid the highest wages in the business. No doubt this explains the high quality of the Waterford flasks, which are prized by collectors. It also resulted in the phrase "Waterford wages," which was well known in Jersey glassmaking circles before the Civil War.

SHANE'S CASTLE

In 1760 Sebastian, Ignatius, and Xaverius Woos, brothers who had left Germany to avoid military conscription, applied to the Council of Proprietors for title to land in the dense woodlands a mile or so south of Waterford Works near a junction of Indian trails from the Delaware to the Great Egg Harbor rivers. There they built a cabin.

Shortly thereafter a priest riding the backwoods trails from Camden stopped at the cabin and celebrated Mass. This was the first of many such services at the cabin and perhaps the first Roman Catholic service of the pinelands, there being no organized congregations at that time despite the fact that a great many bog-iron workers of Atsion, Batsto, and Weymouth were Irish and German Roman Catholics. It is recorded that some Indians attended the services.

The Woos brothers, unable to speak English, declared in German that their home was *schoen,* meaning beautiful. English-speaking woodsmen corrupted the word into *shane,* and the place soon became known as Shane's Castle. One of the reasons for the popularity of this out-of-the-way site for a Catholic service may have had to do with the intolerance of the time, which often forced Catholics to meet in secret.

According to Delia Pugh, historian of the Burlington County Historical Society, the Woos brothers tried their hands at working the bog iron they found in the vicinity and even sent to Germany for laborers. A small furnace was erected. The venture failed, principally because of the larger and better-organized furnaces of Atsion, Batsto, and Weymouth.

No trace of the furnace or cabin has been found, according to Mrs. Pugh. A marker has been erected at what is thought to have been the location of Shane's Castle, describing it as the site of the first Roman Catholic Mass in Gloucester County. (At that time the land was in Gloucester rather than Camden County, boundary lines being changed at a later date.) The "castle" was never actually designated as a church.

TOMATOES, PORK AND BEANS

In 1869, when Joseph Campbell and Abram A. Anderson decided to go into the tomato preservation business, they chose Camden for their operations as it was in the heart of the South Jersey tomato-growing district with ready access to the expanding metropolitan market of Philadelphia.

John Mason of Vineland, Cumberland County, had perfected his Mason fruit jar in 1858, proving that fruit and vegetables could be preserved. The use of tin cans for the same purpose had been the subject of several experimentations by the time Campbell and Anderson started their modest business. In 1892 the firm was incorporated as the Joseph Campbell Preserve Company, later shortened to the Joseph Campbell Company. The turning point in the firm's history came in 1897, when young chemist Dr. John T. Dorrance developed a formula for condensed soups. He became president of the company in 1914.

In 1899 Campbell's first advertisements appeared on streetcar cards in New York. About the same time Grace Debbie Drayton, a Philadelphia artist, was drawing mischievous, roly-poly, fun-loving twins as a pin-money project. Campbell officials saw some of the drawings and asked Miss Drayton to develop them into art suitable for streetcar cards. In 1904 these car cards launched "the Campbell Kids" on a career that made them two of the most widely featured characters in advertising history. They became Liberty Bond salesmen in World War I and air-raid wardens in World War II.

Campell's still uses the red-and-white can design first introduced in 1898. The company entered the baked goods business in 1961 with frozen pastries under the Pepperidge Farm label. Later that year the company began marketing Delacre cookies.

In 1966 the Campbell Institute for Food Research and Camp-

Farm wagons waiting their turn at the Campbell Soup Company receiving center in Camden early in this century. Many farmers drove through the night from Atlantic, Cumberland, Gloucester, and Burlington counties to get their tomatoes to Camden for the early morning unloading. (Courtesy of Campbell Soup Company)

Producing those famous pork and beans at the Campbell Soup Company in Camden about 1908. (Courtesy of Campbell Soup Company)

bell Institute of Agricultural Research were established. Its Pioneer Research Laboratory in Cinnaminson, New Jersey, was opened the same year.

The company today is one of Camden's principal industrial firms, located in the central part of the city, near the waterfront, its original site. More than 250 separate food ingredients and supplies costing more than $300 million a year are needed for Campbell products. Campbell's markets sixty kinds of canned and frozen soups, plus a number of bean products, tomato juice, chili, corned beef hash, and sixteen different TV dinners. The company boasts of having operated at a profit every year since 1898; it sells directly to wholesalers and chain store warehouses. Current sales are reported beyond the $700 million mark.

HIS MASTER'S VOICE

A young lady by the name of Ada Crossley walked into the small studio of the new Victor Talking Machine Company in Camden on April 30, 1903, and sang "Caro Mio Ben," an Italian art song, into a big black horn. Ada Crossley then put on her hat and coat, walked out of the studio and into obscurity, having made the first Victor Red Seal Record of millions to come. That's the way the press agents tell it.

It makes a good story save for the fact that Miss Crossley was a well-known Australian contralto, famed for her oratorio work, who had just finished a recital in New York. Further checking reveals that Miss Crossley made her record, Victor No. 2185, not in Camden but at Victor Studio 826, Carnegie Hall, New York City, with C. H. H. Booth as accompanist. She made three other recordings—"Four Leaf Clover" (No. 2189); "Paysage" (No. 2190) and "New Year's Song" (No. 2191)—before departing for England, where she subsequently recorded for the Pathé Company of London.

The Crossley incident is just one of the many legends centered around the talking machine first demonstrated by inventor

Thomas A. Edison to a group gathered in his workshop at Menlo Park, New Jersey, in 1877.

In 1894 Eldridge R. Johnson, a twenty-seven-year-old Philadelphia machinist and partner in the industrial motors firm of Scull and Johnson, bought Captain Andrew Scull's interest in the firm. For a time Johnson had a contract with Emil Berliner, who had improved the effectiveness of talking machines by inventing the flat disc record. In 1901 Johnson bought Berliner's patents to supplement his own, which included a spring motor for a turntable, and formed the Victor Talking Machine Company.

According to Robert W. Wythes of the Camden County Historical Society, who has spent considerable time in researching the subject, the name Victor had an odd origin. From correspondence with Robert Hathaway, personal secretary to Johnson, just before the latter's death, Wythes learned that Johnson got the idea for the name from a bicycle popular around Camden in 1900 sold under the trade name of Victor.

In the 1890s London artist Francis Barraud had painted his fox terrier Nipper in an attentive position, head cocked to the side, seemingly listening to a voice coming from a large horn of a contraption known to the English as the gramophone. Barraud had titled the picture "His Master's Voice" and had attempted to sell it to several editors who had turned it down as unreal.

Writing for a London newspaper several years later, Barraud stated: "A friend suggested I shoot it [the painting] to a gramophone company and ask them for a brass horn to dress up the subject. This I did. Manager Barry Owen of Gramophone, Ltd., [of Hayes, Middlesex County, England] bought the painting in 1899 for an advertisement."

When Victor was formed in 1901, Johnson negotiated with Gramophone for rights to the Barraud painting in the Western Hemisphere. The English company retained European rights and still uses the picture of Nipper in its advertisements there.

In 1906 Johnson brought out the first horn fully enclosed in a furniture box, the acoustical Victrola, predecessor of the stereophonic music centers of today.

"HIS MASTER'S VOICE"

HIS MASTER'S VOICE

One of the world's most famous trademarks was originally a painting titled "His Master's Voice" by London artist Francis Barraud which showed his dog Nipper listening to a contraption known to the British as the Gramophone. In 1901 the Victor Talking Machine Company acquired the right to use the picture in the Western Hemisphere, but Gramophone, Ltd., still uses the picture in its advertisements in Europe. (Courtesy of RCA-Victor Archives)

A recording session at the Camden 5th Street studios of the Victor Talking Machine Company in the early 1920s. Mrs. Mary Molek, curator of the Eldridge Reeves Johnson Memorial Museum in Dover, Del, identifies the orchestra as that of Rosario Bourdon. (Courtesy of RCA-Victor Archives)

With his Victrola a practical instrument, Johnson launched a campaign to attract the greatest names of that golden age of music to his Camden studio. After he succeeded in recording the voice of Italian tenor Enrico Caruso, Camden became the mecca for such performers as Melba, Kreisler, Rachmaninoff, Chaliapin, McCormack, Scotti, Martinelli, and Galli-Curci.

Caruso received a royalty fee of fifty cents per record, which seemed very high at that time. His records have made more than three and a half million dollars for the Caruso heirs. In 1921, the year of Caruso's death, Toscanini made his first Victor record.

For many years the company kept a concert hall on the Atlantic City Boardwalk for the introduction of its Red Seal records.

During his later career Eldridge Johnson made his home at Moorestown, New Jersey, where he died on November 14, 1945, and to which he gave its large and splendidly equipped Community House and Trinity Episcopal Church. He was also responsible for the gift of the Johnson Foundation for Research in Medical Physics to the University of Pennsylvania in Philadelphia, the Cooper Branch of the Free Library in Camden, the Deaconess Home in Camden, and the Community Church at Dover, Delaware, where he grew up.

Johnson's personal effects, including his Camden office furnishings and most of his early models, are preserved in the Eldridge Reeves Johnson Memorial Collection established by his family and presented to the 'Delaware State Museum in Dover. The collection is housed in the largest of the Delaware State buildings, which was dedicated by E. R. Fenimore Johnson, son of the talking machine pioneer, on December 14, 1967.

Now merged with the Radio Corporation of America, the Victor company continues in downtown Camden, engaged in many kinds of electronic productions, including radios, television sets, home entertainment centers, and stereophonic recordings. The familiar Nipper trademark "His Master's Voice" is still used on many RCA-Victor products. In Victor's vaults in Camden, master records of Golden Age originals, as well as seventy thousand others, are carefully preserved.

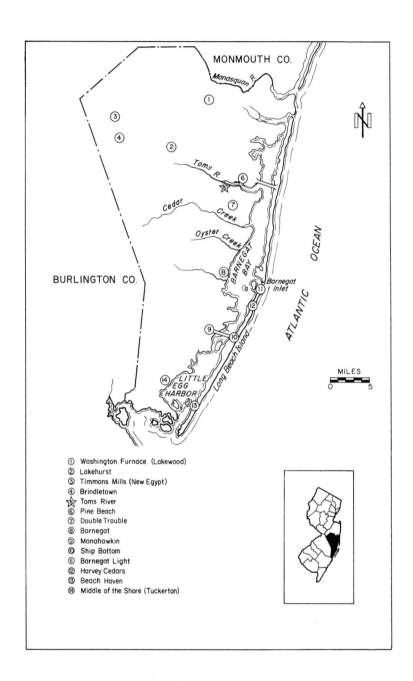

MONMOUTH CO.

Manasquan R.

BURLINGTON CO.

Toms R.

Cedar Creek

Oyster Creek

BARNEGAT BAY

Barnegat Inlet

ATLANTIC OCEAN

'LITTLE EGG HARBOR'

Long Beach Island

MILES
0   5

① Washington Furnace (Lakewood)
② Lakehurst
③ Timmons Mills (New Egypt)
④ Brindletown
☆ Toms River
⑥ Pine Beach
⑦ Double Trouble
⑧ Barnegat
⑨ Manahawkin
⑩ Ship Bottom
⑪ Barnegat Light
⑫ Harvey Cedars
⑬ Beach Haven
⑭ Middle of the Shore (Tuckerton)

OCEAN COUNTY

OCEAN COUNTY

FISH, OYSTERS, AND CRANBERRIES

Ocean County, originally part of Monmouth County, forms a right-angled triangle, the base of which is the seacoast in an almost north and south line. It runs from Manasquan Inlet on the north to New Inlet, a distance of 45 miles. The seacoast is the longest of any county in the state; there are approximately 480,584 acres within its boundaries. The northwest corner of the county, part of Plumsted Township, is crossed by the green marl belt, the most productive farmland in New Jersey.

Fishing was the principal occupation of early settlers who operated their small crafts from Toms River and Tuckerton in the pre-Revolutionary period. Their catches were carted overland to Mount Holly and Philadelphia. Due to the slow travel pace, the fish wagons advertised their coming well in advance.

The harvesting of cranberries is associated with the first days of the county. Native to the area, the cranberry grew in wild profusion in the bog lands of the Pine Barrens, especially in Ocean and Burlington counties. Today in these two counties the cranberry is a $2,500,000 business.

Privateering and shipbuilding were Revolutionary War occupations of most residents of coastal villages. The Toms River saltworks was important to the war effort.

Charcoal burning was practiced by many on the fringe of the pine belt and the charcoal burners, never too popular, were accused of laying waste to the county's vast woodlands.

The county's first big industrial move was toward the production of bog iron. Following the pattern of Burlington County, forges were established at various points of the pines. In 1789

David Wright had a furnace near what is now Lakehurst. Staffordville was opened in 1797.

Ironmaking reached its peak in the War of 1812, and furnaces were blown in at Laurelton (Butcher's), Three Partners Mill (Washington Furnace), Bamber Lake (Ferrago Furnace), and on the headwaters of Cedar Creek (Dover Forge) among others. Most of the old furnace towns vanished with the collapse of the bog iron industry. Washington Furnace was the exception, eventually becoming Lakewood.

Ocean came into being as a county by an act of the New Jersey legislature on February 15, 1850. Five townships were taken from Monmouth County to form the new political unit. A sixth township, Brick, created by the same act, was formed partly from Howell and Dover townships. At the time of separation there were about 10,032 residents in the Ocean County area. A budget of $1,800 was passed by the Board of Freeholders for its first year of operation. Toms River was chosen county seat, and a courthouse costing $9,956 was erected by June 13, 1851.

Railroads reached the beaches in 1870, and the summer resort industry was launched. Point Pleasant was laid out in 1870. In the same year Beach Haven was founded by members of the Society of Friends; Seaside Park blossomed as a Baptist meeting grounds in 1876. Island Heights was a Methodist campground in 1878, and Lakewood was on its way as a resort by 1879.

In 1891 the legislature gave Ocean County a new township, Little Egg Harbor. It was something of a left-handed gift. Burlington County, with the exception of Little Egg Harbor, was solidly in the Democratic ranks; Little Egg was just as solidly Republican. Ocean County also was Republican. The Democratic legislative leaders decided Little Egg was hopeless to them politically, and in a gesture of riddance, annexed it to Ocean County.

World War I brought a number of drastic changes in the pace of the county. The army took 493 men in the draft; nearly double that number enlisted. Men of the county who were too young for the draft formed the Ocean County Militia. In 1918 the war was brought closer to the Ocean County shore with the sinking of cargo vessels by German U-boats just off the beach.

Early in the war a chemical warfare proving ground was established at Lakehurst. Following the armistice the U.S. Navy took over the installation for a lighter-than-air program. The base is still an important part of the navy air arm.

During World War II the resort industry suffered from gas restrictions and blackouts, but the egg industry thrived with the establishment of several hundred new poultry farms, many of which are still in operation. Farm income reached about $12 million with eggs accounting for about $11 million of that figure. Boatbuilding continues as a leading industry of the county, which is the home of several giant marinas.

Today there are thirty-three municipalities in the county, ranging in size from 100-square-mile Jackson Township to ¼-square-mile Seaside Heights. Ocean County's resort business is its greatest source of income with estimates of its value ranging as high as $700 million.

LITTLE EGG HARBOR TOWNSHIP

Little Egg Harbor Township, Ocean County—not to be confused with Egg Harbor Township and Egg Harbor City of Atlantic County—was originally in Burlington County, which was Northampton Township in 1740. Born in the days when records were neither kept nor desired by most people, Little Egg Harbor —which takes its name from the river so called by sailors because of the great quantities of eggs found in gulls' nests along its banks (now the Mullica River)—had its share of privateers, smugglers, pirates, and those other legendary rascals who were part of early Jersey coast history.

The pioneers of Little Egg Harbor Township established themselves in caves along the river banks. Later they moved to log huts.

Tradition places Henry Jacobs Falkinburg, Sr., as the first white man to settle in the township. He arrived sometime prior to 1698 with a small amount of merchandise which he traded to the Indians for parcels of land. His negotiations are said to have included plots later known as Osborn and Wills islands, and the Eayre Phiphant, Elihu Mathis, and Joseph Parker farms. Falkinburg, who had a good command of the Lenape language, acted as interpreter between the Indians of the area and settlers of Burlington County.

It has never been proven whether Falkinburg arrived in Little Egg Harbor of his own accord or was hired to purchase land for others who knew of his ability to trade with the Indians. His first dwelling was a cave on his Down Shore tract, later identified in old deeds as the Parker Farm. He eventually built a substantial house, the doors of which were said to have been of solid mahogany, the wood having been secured from ships washed ashore on the beach.

Revell's *Book of Surveys*, folio 139, at Trenton, N.J., notes this on the Falkinburg holdings:

Henry Jacobs, [Henry Jacobs Falkinburg was often referred to in deeds as simply Henry Jacobs.] 800 acres, February 7, 1698. Per Daniel Leeds. Surveyed them for Henry Jacobs in his own Indian purchase near Egg Harbour eight hundred acres in two parts; Begins at pine tree and black oak for a corner back in the woods and runs thence in breadth sixty-three chains west and by south to a small creek, from which two corners it runs south by two parallel lines one hundred and two chains to two stakes in ʸe meadows taking in six hundred acres besides allowance for ways. Also two hundred acres encompassing the two great islands in ʸe meadows lying in the form of a triangle taking in same meadow within ʸe said triangle, being in all eight hundred acres as above.

Edward Andrews, his brother Mordecai, and Jacob Ong, all from the upper part of Burlington County, soon followed Falkinburg into the Little Egg Harbor area. Andrews settled on the east side of Tuckerton Creek, his farm being the land on which Tuckerton is now located. Mordecai settled on the west side of the creek. After them came Richard Osborn, who located on the island to which he gave his name, James Pharo, and Thomas Ridgway.

Those of the first inhabitants who did not farm turned to boat-building. The surrounding forests offered fine timber for hulls, and soon Little Egg Harbor ships became known along the coast for their seaworthiness.

One of the first recorded ships of the township was a sloop belonging to Thomas Ridgway, Sr., who bequeathed it to his son John in 1724. John Mathis, Sr., owned a vessel commanded by his son Daniel which plied the West Indies routes. Sometime after the Revolution a large ship, the brig *Loranier*, was built at Tuckerton and the brig *Argo* at Bass River.

Bays and inlets offered another occupation, the gathering and harvesting of clams and oysters. This was a profitable endeavor, and seafood from the area soon became popular in Philadelphia and New York. It was hauled over dusty trails in vehicles known as Egg Harbor wagons, a version of the Jersey Wagon, a flatbed contrivance with canvas covering.

During the fight for independence, saltworks in the vicinity supplied the colonists and the Continental Army with that much-needed commodity. Privateers used Little Egg Harbor Bay as anchorage. During the administration of President George Washington, the district of Little Egg Harbor became a port of entry to the United States. Ebenezer Tucker was named collector of the port.

The first schools of Little Egg Harbor were built and controlled by the Quakers. A schoolhouse located on land belonging to Oliver Parker is said to have been the initial one in the township; it was demolished in 1872. A new school was erected by the Quakers on land .belonging to Captain Anthony Atwood; within a few years this burned to the ground. John F. Jones sold land to a group who erected a school in the neighborhood of Down Shore. This was the first over which the Quakers had no control. Crude schoolhouses were also located at Bass River and Mathistown. The latter community was on the farm of Samuel B. Headley, and received its named from the Jeremiah Mathis branch of the family. Jacob Willits set up a tavern there and operated it for several years.

The settlers of Little Egg Harbor were predominantly Quaker. A graveyard adjacent to the Friends Meeting House, erected in 1704, was the only burial grounds in the township for more than a hundred years.

Little Egg Harbor Township today retains its salty flavor in its many boatyards and marinas. It has a land area of 45 square miles and includes West Tuckerton, Parkertown, Atlantis, Mystic Islands, Holly Lake Harbor, Deerfield Park, Tuckerton Gardens, Spring Valley Lakes, and a part of Warren Grove. Estimated year-round population is 3,210, swelling to about 7,000 in the summer months, when pleasure-boating and fishing activities are at their height.

TUCKERTON, SALT AND PRIVATEERS

Tuckerton dates its history to 1699, when Samuel Jennings acquired a grant of more than 550 acres on the east side of Pohatcong Creek and offered parts of it for sale. Edward Andrews of Little Egg Harbor Township purchased a large tract and built a sawmill and a gristmill, operations which attracted settlers. In 1702 Jacob Andrews established a Quaker Meeting. Reuben Tucker, arriving from New York in 1765, acquired what became known as Tucker's Beach; his son Ebenezer also bought considerable acreage. These holdings comprised what is now the center of Tuckerton.

The town's Revolutionary War history is closely knit with that of Chestnut Neck in Atlantic County. Both harbors were hangouts of coastal privateers. To eliminate the drain on British shipping caused by the operations of these men the British termed "blasted pirates," an armed force was sent from New York to wipe them out. Captain Patrick Ferguson, in charge of the raiding party, landed troops at Chestnut Neck and burned docks and shipping there before bringing his barges into the mouth of Bass River. Making fast to the docks of Eli Mathis, the raiders burned the Mathis dwelling, barns, and other buildings. A small saltworks, sawmill, and twelve houses of the village were also put to the torch.

General George Washington, learning of the raids, dispatched Brigadier General Count Casimir Pulaski and picked troops to the scene. On the evening of October 8, 1778, Count Pulaski and his legion arrived at Middle of the Shore, as Tuckerton was at that time known, following a forced march from Trenton. Camp was made on the farm of James Willits.*

Count Pulaski's command was composed of three companies of light infantry, a detachment of light artillery, equipped with a single piece, and three troops of light horse. From the Willits farm the commander had a good view of British vessels in the harbor. A few hundred yards from his doorway were the mounted troops, artillery, and part of the infantry. Nearer the lowlands, in an untenanted farmhouse belonging to Jeremiah Ridgway, was a picket post occupied by about 50 infantrymen commanded by Lieutenant Colonel Baron de Bosen, second in rank to Pulaski.

Lieutenant Gustav Juliet, who joined Pulaski after deserting from the ranks of the Hessians a year previously, again switched allegiance and got to the British with complete information on Colonial positions, men, and arms. Juliet also told British commander Captain Ferguson that Pulaski had given orders that, should their forces meet, there would be no quarter given.

The turncoat's information convinced Captain Ferguson that a successful raid could be staged upon that part of Pulaski's troops stationed on the road leading to Osborn's Island.

An hour after midnight on October 14, 1778, Ferguson, accompanied by Juliet, left the fleet with 250 men detached from British regulars and Jersey Loyalists. They rowed in galleys ten miles to the island and landed about four o'clock on the morning of Thursday, October 15. Ferguson raided the home of Richard Osborn, Jr., and forced Osborn's son Thomas to direct his men to the American outpost.

Marching across the island they came first to a narrow defile and then to a bridge on Big Creek. Ferguson left fifty men there to cover his planned return to the sea. Proceeding silently to-

* The Willits family came to South Jersey from New England settling in what is now Ocean County and spreading to upper Cape May County and Haddonfield. Another branch relocated at Morristown. There is a wide variation in the spelling of the family name ranging from Wyllis and Willis to Willets and Willitts. Even maps, marriage records, death notices, and Quaker Meeting minutes (three different Meetings) do not agree. Lea Blackman, Ocean County genealogist, noted in 1880: "It is impossible to say what is the correct spelling. They were miserable spellers."

ward the Pulaski outpost, the invaders overcame an outer sentry before an alarm could be sounded, then rushed the three houses containing the picket guard.

The men, taken by surprise, hastily seized weapons and attempted a defense. With pistol in one hand and sword in the other, de Bosen led the fight. He was spied by Juliet, who shouted, "There he is! Kill him!" De Bosen went down, pierced by many bayonets. Historians later discovered there was a personal feud between the two stemming from de Bosen's advice to Pulaski that Juliet could not be trusted and it would be well to get rid of him. Unfortunately for Pulaski's troops, the advice was not followed.

The outnumbered garrison cried for mercy but were cut down to a man; the wounded were also bayoneted. About forty, including de Bosen and Second Lieutenant Joseph de la Borderie, died in the early morning massacre.

It all happened quickly, but the sound of flintlocks being fired roused the main force of Pulaski's troops. The general dashed to the scene too late, the invaders having beat a successful retreat to their boats, blowing up the only bridge over Big Creek.

While Captain Ferguson was making his withdrawal he was informed that another force under Colonel Thomas Proctor was rushing to the Forks of the Mullica and was only two miles to his rear. Ferguson hoisted sail for New York. As the ships were passing over the bar, the flagship *Zebra* went aground. Troops were transferred to the *Vigilant* and *Nautilus,* and the *Zebra* was fired.

Young Thomas Osborn, the reluctant guide, upon emerging from his hiding place, was seized by the soldiers, tied to a tree, and would have been flogged to death save for the intervention of officers. Osborn and his father were taken to Trenton for trial, found not guilty of conspiracy, and returned under a safe conduct pass signed by Pulaski.

Traitor Juliet did not fare too well in the hands of the British. According to a letter dated Newport, Rhode Island, January 11, 1779 (reported in Vol. IV of *Historical Magazine*), he went back to New York with the Ferguson forces and was placed under arrest.

In 1950 the Ocean County Board of Chosen Freeholders erected a marker at the site of the 1778 massacre. It reads: "The Pulaski Monument, commemorating the October 15, 1778, massacre of a portion commanded by Brigadier General The Count Casimir Pulaski of the Continental Army at Little Egg Harbor in the American Revolution."

After the end of the war, Ebenezer Tucker, first collector of the port of Tuckerton and later its first postmaster, was honored when the village dropped the names "Middle of the Shore" and "Clamtown" for Tuckerton.

A stagecoach line linking Tuckerton and Philadelphia was established in 1816. In 1853 the United States mail stage was making triweekly trips to Tuckerton via Freehold. The Tuckerton Railroad built a spur line, sometimes referred to as the "clam line," practically to the pier, providing the baymen fast rail transportation for their clams. In 1886 the railroad was rerouted, bypassing Tuckerton.

As the rails remained, baymen secured a flatcar, rigged it with a mast and sail, and used what became known as the Clamtown Sailcar to get their clam baskets to the railroad's new main line.

This solved a serious shipping problem, and once again the clam business flourished. It is said that the sight of a flatcar under full sail gliding across the meadows made many a guzzling veteran swear off. This unique device performed its task for several years, until some pranksters crashed it into a ditch. It was never resurrected.

Tuckerton separated from Little Egg Harbor Township in 1901, forming the borough of Tuckerton. Today the town has a year-round population of more than 2,000 and a mayor-council form of government. It is still a big boating and fishing center for sportsmen.

THE AFFAIR AT TOMS RIVER

Salt was important in the American colonies to preserve meat and fish. When supply lines from the Azores and the Canary

Islands were cut by the British blockade, the colonists were forced to start their own salt industry. Saltworks were established at several places along the South Jersey coast, mostly on meadows opposite an inlet, as extracting salt from the ocean was the only method of production known to the settlers.

On June 24, 1776, the Pennsylvania Council of Safety voted 400 pounds to Thomas Savage to build a saltworks in the vicinity of Little Egg Harbor. He chose a site at Shelter Cove, outside the present municipality bounds of Toms River. On November 2, 1776, an officer and twenty-five men were sent to the saltworks by the Pennsylvania Council to defend it in case of attack. The Continental Congress requested Governor William Livingston of New Jersey to provide additional men, and exemption from military duty for those working in the salt industry was sought by the legislators. But Governor Livingston replied that this was inconsistent with the laws of the state.

In response to a request from Savage, the Navy Board of Pennsylvania sent the armed boat *Delaware*, in command of Captain Richard Eyre, to patrol the waters off Cranberry Inlet.

Salt from other operations along the coast was stored at Toms River, and a blockhouse was built to protect the warehouses.

A group of New Jersey Volunteers under Colonel John Morris made a march on the saltworks late in 1777 but, upon arriving, failed to molest the plant, allegedly because an *R* was painted on the wall. This *R* was a code letter which meant that at least part of the works was owned by Royalists, favorable to the crown—in this case noted Tory partisan General Cortlandt Skinner.

The operation was not so fortunate when on April 1, 1778, another British force of 135 men, mostly Royalists under command of Captain Robertson arrived in South Jersey and proceeded to systematically destroy saltworks at Toms River, Squan Beach, and Shark River. In December of 1779, following the death of Thomas Savage, the Toms River saltworks, rebuilt after the 1778 attack, was bought by John Thompson of Burlington County for $15,000 Continental money. The works thus came under the protection of New Jersey troops.

The final raid upon the saltmakers occurred when fighting

was for the most part over. Cornwallis had surrendered at York-town on October 19, 1781, but the treaty of peace had not been formally signed. A boat belonging to William Dillon, a British spy living on Dillon's Island (Island Heights), was captured off the Jersey coast by privateers and sold at auction at Freehold on March 16, 1782. In retaliation Dillon persuaded the Board of Associated Royalists, presided over by William Franklin, the Tory son of patriot Benjamin Franklin, to send a force to destroy the "Toms River pirates."

On March 20 the raiders left New York under convoy of the armed brig *Arrogant*. Unfavorable winds delayed the action. Eighty men commanded by Lieutenant Blanchard finally crossed Cranberry Inlet in three armed whaleboats during the night of March 23, 1782, and early the next morning attacked the blockhouse at Toms River.

The garrison of twenty-five men was commanded by Captain Joshua Huddy. When the British force attacked, some townsmen rushed to the aid of the defenders, but Royalists kept others at their homes at bayonet point. Captain Huddy's men held the blockhouse until their powder gave out and the invaders swarmed over the ramparts. Nine of the defenders were killed and the remainder, including Captain Huddy, were taken prisoner. Before they left the village the attackers burned every house, save two owned by Loyalists, who cheered them on.

Huddy was taken aboard a British prison ship off the coast, but at ten o'clock on the morning of April 12, 1782, Captain Richard Lippincott, a British officer and former neighbor of Huddy, acting under orders of the Board of Associated Royalists (or so he claimed), demanded the prisoner. Huddy was taken to Gravelly Point, where a gallows had been hastily constructed. Lippincott's men rebelled at pulling the rope so the British lieutenant did the job himself, creating an uproar which eventually involved General Washington, Sir Henry Clinton, the British commander, King George III, and the king and queen of France.

Washington demanded Sir Henry Clinton surrender Lieutenant Lippincott to the American forces for trial. While Clinton and his successor Sir Guy Carleton both admitted Huddy's death was murder, they refused to turn over the officer. Instead Sir Henry placed Lippincott on trial. The latter hid behind alleged orders from William Franklin and the Associated Loyalists and won acquittal.

Angered, Washington and a council of twenty-five officers decided to hang a British officer in reprisal. Lieutenant Charles Asgill of the Foot Guards, then a prisoner of the Continentals, was chosen. Asgill was the son of Lady Theresa Asgill of London, who appealed to King George III, who interceded to the extent of ordering Lippincott surrendered to the Americans; the order was never obeyed. Lady Asgill also secured the intercession of the king and queen of France. Asgill was spared and returned to England a hero.

The Huddy hanging was never avenged. The location of his grave is today unknown. Papers in the affair are recorded in the New Jersey Archives; Huddy's will is in possession of the New Jersey Historical Society.

A small island east of the bridge at Toms River was named for Captain Huddy. In 1907 a park was created there. On March 29, 1928, the state legislature approved erection of a monument to Huddy, and a small plot was deeded to New Jersey for the purpose. The move bogged down during the depression days in the 1930s, and the monument was never built. But in connection with the New Jersey Tercentenary in 1964, a replica of the Toms River blockhouse was built to scale from native pine logs and placed in Huddy Park, with four corner cannon mounted on swivels like the originals in 1782, as a memorial to the stand of Captain Huddy and his men.

Most early historians accepted the story that Toms River was named for early settler Captain William Tom of Delaware, who was said to have come to Toms River in 1673. Captain Tom arrived in America in 1664 with Sir Robert Carr, agent for the Duke of York, and settled in New Castle, Delaware, where he died in 1678. There is no proof that Tom ever resided in the Dover Township (Toms River) area.

Another bit of tradition is that the town was named for "Indian Tom," a member of the Lenni-Lenape nation who lived in a dugout on the river at what is now Island Heights. The story is not substantiated by fact.

After a painstaking search of existing records, Mrs. Herbert F. Miller, a Toms River historian and president of the Ocean County Historical Society, discounts both these stories. Toms River, she claims, first received its name in 1712 when a road was laid out following a path from the Metedeconk area crossing of the river where the Toms River bridge is now located. Before that time the river was called Goose Creek.

Toms River, states Mrs. Miller, was actually named for Thomas Luker, who arrived in the area about 1700. Luker married an Indian chieftain's daughter, Princess Ann, and erected a wigwam at the bend of the river. He took on the ways of the Indians, dressed like one and lived at the river's crossing.

Today Toms River retains its colonial red-brick atmosphere while serving as the seat of Dover Township government and the county seat of Ocean County. The original courthouse built in a cornfield in 1850 is still used although newer structures have been added. Township Hall is located on Washington Street. Dover Township is the site of the Ocean County College and Ocean County's Vocational-Technical School. The Toms River Chemical Corporation is the largest industry of the county, occupying 1,240 acres off Route 37. Toms River and Dover Township have a 32,000 year-round population.

LONG BEACH ISLAND

"Thar' she blows!"

This whaling cry was commonplace on Long Beach Island when whalers from New England followed the great mammals down the coast to Delaware Bay and established a colony on the island. A communal watch was maintained from a lookout built on stilts. When a whale was sighted, an alarm was given and whalers raced to the beaches, launching their small boats to give chase.

During the early seventeenth century there were a number of whaling units on the island. One was Harvey's Whaling Quarters, located at what is now Harvey Cedars. As far as is known the whalers were the first people on the island. Whaling was practiced by island inhabitants as late as 1820.

Many naval engagements were fought by British and American ships on the waters surrounding the island during the days of the Revolution. Most of the battles stemmed from the activities of privateers attempting to steer prize cargoes into Cranberry Inlet.

Details of these encounters were printed in Isaac Collins's *New Jersey Gazette,* the state's first regular newspaper, which supported the patriot cause during the Revolution. Collins detailed one story of a sloop from Jamaica, laden with a rich cargo of rum and sugar, brought into Little Egg Harbor Inlet after a group of American prisoners being sent to New York took over the ship as it left Jamaica harbor and sailed it for the Jersey coast.

On August 1, 1778, the British ship *Love and Unity* was beached and the Dover Township militia (many of whom were registered privateers) went aboard, floated the ship, and took it into Cranberry Inlet. It proved to have a prize cargo, which was later sold by Marshal John Stokes of Toms River. The purchaser of the ship renamed it the *Washington.* On September 18 in a surprise raid the British recaptured the vessel; its American captain and officers escaped in whaleboats to the mainland of Ocean County.

On August 29, 1779, the sloop *Susannah* (eight guns and thirty-five men) met the British armed sloop *Emerald* (ten guns), which was conveying two merchantmen. A battle followed. The merchantmen ran up the beach to safety, and the *Emerald* followed after inflicting losses to the *Susannah* which caused her captain to head back to port.

A little less grim sea story of this period concerns Captain Edward Giles of Philadelphia, master of the schooner *Shark* built on the Jersey shore. Captured by a British sloop, Giles and his crew were made prisoners. A prize crew was put aboard the vessel to sail it to New York. Giles showed the British crewmen his rum stores and soon had them drunk, retook his vessel and, with the Britishers as prisoners, sailed back to Little Egg Harbor Inlet.

On October 25, 1782, about a mile south of Barnegat Inlet, a crew under command of Captain Andrew Steelman of the privateer *Alligator* unloaded goods from a British ship which had run aground on a sandbar. By nightfall the weary crewmen stretched out on the sand and slept. A Tory discovering the men sent word to Tory outlaw Captain John Bacon, who was encamped upon the mainland. Under cover of darkness Bacon and his men massacred all twenty-six of the sleepers. Bacon escaped pursuit from hastily formed units of patriots, but he was caught and killed in a tavern between West Creek and Tuckerton the following spring.

During the War of 1812 British troops looking for provisions landed on Long Beach Island. The soldiers killed fifteen head of cattle and took them aboard their ships. Owners were told to "submit bills to the crown and you will be paid." There is no record anyone did so.

One of the legends of Long Beach Island is how the municipality of Ship Bottom received its name. Mayor Frank Klein filled me in on the story the natives like to tell.

Captain Stephen Willits of Tuckerton, master and owner of a sloop plying the coast from Little Egg Harbor in the year 1817, was known among his fellow sea captains as a religious man who lived by the Good Book's admonishment to help a neighbor in distress.

Following an especially violent storm in 1817 he took to sea and headed in the direction of Barnegat Inlet. Near the midway point on Long Beach Island he spied the hull of a ship, bottom side up. He ordered a boat lowered to investigate the wreck.

When the men reached it they heard a tapping inside the hull. They chopped an opening with an ax and pulled out a young woman, still alive but exhausted. She spoke a foreign tongue believed to have been Spanish. The seamen chipped in and put her aboard transportation for New York, one of the men having believed he heard the girl say the name of that city.

The spot where the incident occurred was generally referred to by the natives as *Ship Bottom,* which eventually became its official name.

When Ocean County was separated from Monmouth County in 1850, Long Beach Island was divided among the various mainland townships. Residents felt they had nothing in common with mainland neighbors and sought independence of action and development. Eventually six municipalities emerged: Long Beach Township, Beach Haven, Ship Bottom, Surf City, Harvey Cedars, and Barnegat Light.

Joseph Horner's Guest House, near the center of the island, catered to most of the first visitors. It was said to have been constructed for "good cheer," leaving the impression there was not much in the way of conveniences. Since most of its guests were fishermen, they did not care, as long as there were substantial meals and something with which to wash them down. Horner supplied both as well as the usual pile of help-yourself oysters in the back yard.

Rates at Horner's were $5 a week for room and board. Meals consisted of chicken and whatever seafood the guests caught. Twenty-five cents a day was charged for use of a boat for in-channel fishing and for boat rides to Tuckerton. In 1851 Horner sold his house to Captain Thomas Bond, who changed the name to Bond's Long Beach House. Captain Bond was especially concerned with shipwreck victims, for whom he built a "House of Refuge" near by.

A U.S. Mail Stage run was inaugurated between Manahawkin and other shore points in 1853. It carried passengers to New York in one day, a boon for the island's growing visitor trade. By 1855 there was a wider choice of accommodations: the Ashley House near Barnegat Light operated by John Brown, the Club House near Harvey Cedars operated by James James, and the Harvey Cedars Hotel operated by Captain Sammy Perrin. The Mansion of Health was located in the Great Swamp (now Surf City) and employed an oxcart to take lady guests and invalids to the beach.

The budding resort life of the island was given a substantial boost in 1871 when a railroad line was established between Philadelphia and Tuckerton. A year later A. R. Pharo of Tuckerton talked the railroad into building a spur to the bay, where passengers could take his steamer to the island. In 1885 a viaduct was built across the bay and tracks laid out on the island from Beach Haven to Barnegat Light. (The line was abandoned in 1923, and an automobile road from Manahawkin now provides access to the island.)

On May 1, 1897, the ship *Francis* caught fire and ran aground off Long Beach. The crew was rescued by the Long Beach Life Saving unit. Later the *Francis* began to break up and casks of port, sherry, and Burgundy began to bob all over the inlet waters. Thirsty townsmen organized their own rescue parties, and legend has it that the whole village went on a spree.

Long Beach Island today is a series of resort communities with a winter population of 2,000 and an estimated summer one of well over 50,000. Boating and fishing are still top summer pastimes.

TUCKER'S ISLAND

Tucker's Island, off the southernmost tip of Ocean County, is today a sandbar. However, when fishermen attempted to establish a colony there in the mid-1700s it was known as Short Beach.

According to historical records, Ephraim Morse built a frame shack on the beach sometime prior to 1745. A winter storm swept the house into the sea, and Morse was glad to sell his island to sportsman Reuben Tucker, Sr., who came to the area from New York state. Tucker erected a one-story structure and invited some fishermen friends to share it; others learned of its existence and began to use it as headquarters in fishing trips to Ocean County. In 1765 Tucker decided to meet expenses by renting rooms, giving rise to the lore that Tucker's Island was southern Jersey's earliest seashore resort, a tale disputed by Cape Island (Cape May City), which bases its claim as the first resort on a hotel advertisement placed in the *Pennsylvania Gazette* of June 26, 1766, by Robert Parsons.

Tucker used his boardinghouse in summer only, residing the remainder of the year at West Tuckerton. Following his death his widow conducted the establishment. It was subsequently operated by Joseph Horner, Thomas Cowperthaite, Rebecca Rogers, and John Horner. A fire in 1848 ended the Tucker enterprise.

In the same year the Little Egg Harbor lighthouse, a 50-foot tower whose kerosene light could be seen twelve miles at sea, was built on Tucker's Island. Eben Rider was the first keeper. The beacon was abandoned in 1859 and not reactivated until 1965 (as an automatic device).

In 1869 the Little Egg Harbor Life Saving Station was constructed on the island and Rider's son Jarvis put in charge. Congress authorized salaries for members of the newly organized service. (Prior to this most of the lifesaving chores were performed by volunteers.) Crewmen and families moved in and additional structures were erected, including a small schoolhouse which was financed by a series of clambakes. The one-room building opened on December 9, 1895, and served the community as school, church, and social center until the early 1920s.

By that time the sea was eroding the sand island, and most of the families who had originally settled there moved to the mainland. By 1927 only the old lighthouse structure and the lifesaving station remained. The station itself was closed in February 1933 and was swept into the sea during a storm in 1935. The sea now covers the island at high tide.

THE GREAT JOHN MATHIS

"The Great" John Mathis, who became Bass River's most distinguished citizen, built his first home in the Little Egg Harbor area in 1729 on the east side of Bass River about a hundred feet from where the house, a decaying ruin, now stands.

Together with his brother Charles, John Mathis emigrated to this country as a young man, settling at Oyster Bay on Long Island in 1690. The family name was originally Matthews, which John shortened to Mathis. In company with William Birdsall and Moses Forman, Mathis acquired 250-acre Biddle Island (also known as the Daniel Mathis Island) at Bass River from Daniel Leeds of Springfield, New Jersey, in 1713. Within a year the two partners sold their holdings to Mathis, who used the purchase as a foundation upon which to build a land empire.

In 1716 John Mathis married Alice Higbee, widow of John Higbee and oldest daughter of Edward Andrews of Tuckerton. The couple lived on Biddle Island until 1729, when Mathis bought 813 acres on the east side of Bass River. There he built the place today known as the Great John Mathis house.

This house, or what is left of it after having been the victim of vandals over the years, is located about a hundred feet from the present Bass River Marina and is almost hidden by trees and heavy underbrush. It was moved from its original location to higher ground in the late 1950s in an attempt to preserve it.

In 1961 a move was started to save the old dwelling and restore it as a museum for the lower part of Ocean County. To this end the Great John Mathis Foundation was formed, but because of lack of financial support the proposal fell through. In 1966 Mrs. Harold H. Mathis of Tuckerton, a member of the foundation, made a gift of what remained of the home to Mr. and Mrs. Fred Noyes of the restored Towne of Smithville in Atlantic County. At that time it was planned to move the structure to Smithville to become part of a collection of old South Jersey houses. This plan also failed to materialize. Many feel the house has deteriorated past the point of restoration.

When I first went through the structure some years back it contained a beautifully carved hidden stairway, but by my second visit in 1969 this and other examples of its original design had disappeared. Loose boards were scattered about and it was a depressing pile of old, rotting timbers.

Besides being a farmer and land holder, Mathis was also a builder of ships. He was the first to construct a vessel on Bass River. He lent considerable sums to the struggling American government for the conduct of the Revolution. Because of these aids and in accordance with a custom of the time, he was referred to in official documents as "The Great . . . ." The title was strictly honorary, with no formalities involved. Ocean

County's historical societies continued use of the title in all references to the man.

Following the Revolution the financially shaky government paid back the John Mathis loans in Continental paper scrip which proved worthless. Mathis found himself money poor but continued to keep his land holdings.

Many still living in the Little Egg Harbor area trace their ancestry and land to the Great John Mathis. His offspring seem to have been industrious and prosperous.

At an early date there were Matthewses or Mathises who settled in Cape May County. A Thomas Mathews was among the early settlers of Burlington. A Matthews was governor of the province of Virginia. All are believed to be relatives of the Great John Mathis.

SAVING LIVES ON THE BEACH

The idea of an organization trained to aid shipwreck victims was conceived on the night of August 13, 1839, by Dr. William A. Newell of Manahawkin, Ocean County. Just out of medical college, Dr. Newell was standing on a Long Beach Island sand dune watching the crashing waves and bracing against the gale winds that seemed bent on the destruction of the island.

Near midnight the brig *John Minturn,* out of control, its rudder gone, and sails cracking like pistols, struck a shoal. Above the winds the young doctor could hear cries for help, then silence. Dr. Newell rushed to the water's edge and out into the breakers in the hope of helping those who might be tossed ashore; but the sea gave up only dead bodies, fourteen of them.

With the coming of the first streaks of dawn the wreck of the brig was visible, only three hundred yards from shore. Dr. Newell never forgot the picture. Returning home, the physician found he could not concentrate on his medical practice. A mere three hundred yards, the difference between life and death, haunted him. He began experimenting with what he called a lifeline. His theory was that if a line could be shot to the distressed ship and made firm on the beach, those aboard the sinking craft could be pulled to shore by means of a sling or breeches buoy. He tried many means of casting the line and finally settled for a mortar shot as the most practical.

Meanwhile Dr. Newell's career turned into political channels, and he was elected to Congress in 1846. He continued knocking on doors in the interest of doing something about the increasing loss of life along the Jersey coast due to shipwreck. On August 3, 1848, Dr. Newell delivered in the House of Representatives a stirring plea for attention to this problem. He described in detail some of the pitiful scenes he had witnessed on Long Beach Island following storms at sea.

A bill was about to go through the House for additional money for lighthouses. Dr. Newell was successful in attaching a rider to the bill providing for "surf boats, rockets, carronades, and other necessary apparatus for the better preservation of life and property from shipwrecks on the coast of New Jersey, between Sandy Hook and Little Egg Harbor, ten thousand dollars; the same to be expended under the supervision of such officers as may be detached for this duty by the Secretary of the Treasury."

As an initial result of this measure passed on August 9, 1848, eight boathouses were erected along the Jersey shore. They were crude shacks, scantily equipped; but it was a start. Captain Douglas Ottinger of the Revenue Marine Service was assigned to carry out the project. Each shack was equipped with "one metal surfboat with air chambers and cork fenders, seven oars, two Indian rubber bailing buckets, one metal life-car with cord or Indian rubber floats and fenders and rings and chains each end, one manila hawser, one crotch and ten shots fitted with spiral wire, powder canister and four pounds of powder for same, twelve blue lights, five rockets and a box of fifty quick matches."

Unfortunately Dr. Newell's rider contained no provisions for staffing these stations. Captain Ottinger was obliged to leave the key to the equipment in the hands of someone in the vicinity who would volunteer to take over operations in an emergency. This system proved unsatisfactory, although there are records of some rescues having been made by the volunteers.

Congress appropriated more money for maintenance during the period 1849 to 1853. A bill passed in 1854 for the first time provided for the appointment of boatkeepers. The issue soon became a political football. By 1871 the service had deteriorated so much that a complete overhaul was ordered. Better equipment was provided, and eventually trained men were sent to replace the political appointees. Many valiant rescues were credited to the infant service.

One of the most notable of the early uses of the Dr. Newell lifeline and breeches buoy was in January of 1850, when they contributed to the rescue of 201 persons from the sinking immigrant ship *Ayrshire* off Squan Beach. The lifeline was shot to the *Ayrshire* and the bucket buoy drawn back and forth through the breakers until everyone aboard the ship was safe on the strand. The *Ayrshire* was grounded only a few hundred yards from the spot where nearly three hundred had perished only four years earlier in the disaster of the *John Minturn*.

While Dr. Newell must be credited with the first use of a lifeline to rescue shipwreck victims, the technique was further improved by the invention of a closed lifeboat by Joseph Francis of Toms River. Francis's boat had a canvas top and strong supports which made it workable in seas which would have swamped an ordinary open boat.

In 1915 the lifesaving service was merged with the Revenue-Marine to form the U.S. Coast Guard.

What happened to the man from Ocean County who started it all? Dr. Newell was elected governor of New Jersey in 1856, reelected in 1858. He returned to Congress in 1865 and continued his efforts to make coastwise navigation safer. He headed the New Jersey State Board of Agriculture in 1875. In 1880 he was appointed governor of the Washington Territory by President Rutherford B. Hayes. Dr. Newell served four years in the territory before returning to private practice at Allentown, New Jersey. He died on August 8, 1901, a few months before his eighty-fourth birthday, having seen his dream of a lifesaving service well on its way.

OLD BARNEY

The square rigger, loaded to the rails with a West Indies cargo, plowed through the evening mists. Suddenly there was a light to port. "Old Barney!" shouted the lookout. The helmsman made a slight adjustment and reported: "All's well. We'll hit New York harbor on the nose."

Sails changed to steam, the wireless came into use, sea lanes along the Jersey coast were plainly marked and patrolled, but until its demise in 1927, Old Barney, the name given the Barnegat Inlet Light by seamen, was a most welcome sight.

Today Old Barney stands alone on a sand and rock formation off the end of Long Beach Island where Barnegat Inlet connects the Atlantic Ocean with Barnegat Bay. It has long since been out of service, yet the old light draws several million visitors yearly.

Once doomed because of the sea threatening its base, Barnegat Light was saved by the citizens of Long Beach Island, who taxed themselves to raise money to keep the old light intact until the state finally accepted it as a historic site and assigned it park status.

Old Barney's life has been hectic. The original lighthouse, a 40-foot beacon about seventy-five feet from the present structure, was built in 1834. It toppled into the waves on the evening of November 2, 1856, after tides and storms ate away three hundred feet of sand between the inlet and the light.

The new light was designed by Lieutenant George Gordon Meade, who later (as a general) commanded the Union forces at Gettysburg. In his memory a bronze bust was placed at the entrance of the lighthouse park. Lieutenant Meade's lighthouse, built in 1858, was the pride of the island, rising 172 feet above its base with a 17-foot chamber for a light. Twenty-seven feet across at the bottom, the lighthouse tapers upward in graceful fashion to 18 inches at the top. Its walls are 10 feet thick. As additional protection against sway in storms, Lieutenant Meade

The present Barnegat Light, built in 1858, served navigation until 1927, when it was so threatened by erosion that a lightship was put in service eight miles offshore. Old Barney continued with a reduced beam until the blackout of the coast during World War II. (New Jersey Department of Conservation)

had a heavy iron pipe installed from top to bottom. The stairway is not anchored to the walls, as one would suppose, but hangs independently on this pipe. From the balcony just below the light visitors today can enjoy a 20-mile view of Long Beach Island.

Barnegat Light was turned on without ceremony at sunset on January 1, 1859. Keeper James Fuller simply climbed the 217 steps to the top and ignited the lard-oil lamp. His assistants followed to wind the lens, which revolved by means of heavy weights on long cords. On stormy nights the light was operated by hand, the keeper and his assistants sharing lonely watches.

While Barnegat Inlet had many wrecks due to ships hitting the shifting shoals, its faithful lighthouse saved many vessels and gave their crews new hope on a stormy night.

The sea was Old Barney's worst enemy. Within ten years of its construction the seventy-five feet of sand between inlet and lighthouse were nearly gone. Two hundred tons of stone were dumped at its base in 1866, by the federal government. The next year 331 tons of stone were brought in, followed by another 1,220 tons in 1868.

Each year the report was the same: "Erosion threatening Barnegat Light; more stone needed." By World War I the government was tired of trying to keep Barnegat Light in operation, and a lightship was proposed, much to the distress of Long Beach Islanders. But progress does not stop for sentiment, and the lightship was put in operation eight miles offshore in 1927. At the same time the Barnegat Light was reduced from 80,000 candlepower to 11,000.

Because of German U-boat activities in World War II the War Department ordered a blackout of the coast, including navigation aids. Old Barney was turned off along with other beacons and has not returned as a navigation instrument.

Today a small museum at the base of the light contains the original kerosene light-crown composed of 1,024 prisms assembled into 24 bull's-eye lenses. Although the assembly is said to weigh five tons, it was so delicately balanced by designer Henri Lepaute of Paris that it could be rotated by hand.

The great storm of 1962 caused the evacuation of island residents, and the island itself suffered major destruction. Old Barney weathered the storm and today is a sentimental symbol of a salty past. The lighthouse is located in the borough of Barnegat Light, which until 1948 was known as Barnegat City. The town itself was made a separate municipality in 1904.

Keepers of the light were as follows: James Fuller, Burch Brown, Jack Kelly, Captain Yates, Joshua Reeves, Thomas Bills, William Woodmansee, Clarence H. Cranmer, Andrew E. Applegate, Robert E. Applegate, and William E. Rothes.

IRON AND HEALTH IN THE PINES

Lakewood began existence as a rough and ready bog iron town, a far cry from its present status as a popular health resort.

Jesse Richards was twenty-seven years old in 1809 when he took over management of the Batsto iron village from his father William Richards, who had retired to Mount Holly. The War of 1812 proved a boom to Batsto and fired Jesse's ambition to annex other holdings. Hearing that a new bog iron deposit had been found in what was then Monmouth (now Ocean) County, he made a preliminary investigation. The survey convinced him this new ironfield could be profitable. Together with partner William Irvin, Jesse entered a contract with James Skidmore, one of three brothers who arrived in South Jersey during the Revolution and built a mill at a spot which became known as Three Partners Mill. On June 12, 1814, with legal transfers completed, Jesse set about building a furnace near the mill site. He changed the name of the community springing up around the enterprise to Washington Furnace.

Although experienced and able, Jesse Richards was forever in financial difficulties. In the case of Washington Furnace he blamed it on the poor quality of iron deposits; others blamed his management. By 1818 Richards had abandoned the undertaking.

The property lay idle until April 12, 1830, when it was purchased by William Remsen of Dover Township. Remsen turned his holdings over to Joseph W. Brick of Burlington County on

September 30, 1833. Brick was a former Richards employee at Batsto who rose from hired hand to clerk of the works, according to the Batsto books.

The new owner rebuilt Washington Furnace and renamed it Bergen Iron Works. By 1844 the Bergen Works community had a population of two hundred and a post office. In his book on forges, Charles Boyer places the exact location of this town as "just below the present South Branch of Metedeconk River about where the old road from Toms River to Squankum crossed the stream."

Log houses, homes of men who worked in the Brick enterprise, stood on what is now Clifton Avenue between Main and First streets, Lakewood; another row existed between the lakes. The foundry was located north of the present electric light plant.

After Brick's death in 1847, the property went to his five children. A son took over the management and moved the operation to where the Lakewood YWCA now stands.

On July 4, 1865, the oldest of Brick's daughters came of age. To mark the occasion and also to honor Brick, citizens of Bergen Iron Works voted to change the name of the town to Bricksburg. The lake was named for Brick's daughters Caroline, Sarah, and Josephine. By uniting the names in abbreviated form, the word *Carasaljo* was coined. The lake still carries this name.

The iron works had its own general store and printed its own company money. Six-team wagons were used to haul products of the blast furnace down to the river at Bay Head, where transfer was made to schooners for the trip to New York.

In 1865 Riley Brick built a tavern facing Main Street. He called it Bricksburg House and, according to town historians, brought the first New York visitors to this spot in the pines.

The iron foundry was later sold by the Bricks to Campbell and Pharo, who moved the business to Perth Amboy, ending ironmaking in Bricksburg.

In 1866 the Bricksburg Land and Development Company was formed and launched a town development plan. Streets were laid out and lots advertised for sale in New York papers. The area was billed as "especially beneficial to throat and lung," thus giving the community its first boost as a health resort.

The Bricksburg House, later (1880) the Laurel House, was the first major hotel to be built in Lakewood. It stood on the north side of Main Street between Lexington and Clifton avenues and soon became the favorite vacation spot for many prominent in the social and business world of the times, the register containing such names as the Astors, Rhinelanders, Vanderbilts, and Tilfords. Oliver Wendell Holmes was one of the early guests. According to old-timers he was induced to recite his famous poems while standing before one of the giant fireplaces. Rudyard Kipling stayed there three years as did the Rev. S. Parkes Cadman, Harvey Fisk, and S. S. Childs of restaurant-chain fame.

Early land promoters felt they had a liability in the name Bricksburg, which they claimed sounded more like an industrial town than the health resort they were trying to sell. On March 20, 1880, the name of the community was changed to Lakewood, more descriptive of a place which boasted beautiful Carasaljo Lake, as well as smaller Manetta Lake, named for Mrs. Brick.

No two men had more to do with Lakewood's fame as a health and vacation resort than Albert M. Bradshaw, Army captain by appointment of President Abraham Lincoln, and Charles H. Kimball, for whom Kimball Hospital is named. Captain Bradshaw came to Bricksburg in 1865, when he was mustered out of the 127th New York Volunteer Infantry. He purchased the Bergen Iron Works store. After operating this for two years he established a real estate business and devoted the rest of his life to selling the merits of Lakewood. He died on September 3, 1915.

Kimball, a Wall Street banker ill of a throat infection which had taken his voice, stopped at Lakewood on his way south in 1878. He found his health so improved after one visit in the pine air that he returned. Together with Captain Bradshaw he formed a company for the promotion of the Jersey Pines town.

The new group bought the holdings of the Bricksburg Land and Improvement Company as well as the Bricksburg House. Kimball also built a boys' school on Sixth Street. In 1890 Kimball formed the Forest Hotel Company and purchased a site overlooking the lake on which in April he began erection of Laurel-in-the-Pines. This 300-room hotel was officially opened in December of 1891, and the *Lakewood Times and Journal* of December

19, 1891, called it "the best hotel of the times." Laurel-in-the-Pines was the victim of several fires and was completely destroyed in March, 1967, bringing to an end an era of elegance.

Another individual who left his imprint on Lakewood was Francis P. Freeman, an associate of Commodore Vanderbilt. He established his home in Lakewood and among other tasks acted as treasurer of Laurel-in-the-Pines.

One of Lakewood's early visitors, George J. Gould, son of millionaire railroad owner Jay Gould, built an elaborate estate along the north shore of Lake Carasaljo. It was finished on January 18, 1896, and named Georgian Court. A 170-foot bridge, 32 feet wide, crossed the gully in front of his property. Gould was a lavish entertainer and brought trainloads of people to Lakewood; in May of 1899 he introduced his Lakewood polo team to play on one of four polo fields he constructed. When George Gould died in 1923 his estate was divided among his sons and daughters. They did not want the responsibility of upkeep. So in June of 1924 the estate became an exclusive school for young ladies known as Georgian Court College.

No history of Lakewood would be complete without a mention of another prominent citizen, John D. Rockefeller, Sr., who acquired an estate within the town limits off Ocean Avenue early in the century. He spent summers in Lakewood until his death.

One of his favorite Lakewood activities, old-timers recall, was a daily ride in his open Lincoln automobile during which he wore paper vests to keep out the wind. These were purchased personally in a Lakewood store. Rockefeller also kept a dairy herd and distributed free milk to his friends in and about Lakewood. When death came to the financial giant at Ormond Beach, Florida, on May 23, 1937, at the age of ninety-eight, he was preparing to return to Lakewood, and a reception was planned by the townsfolk.

Three years after Rockefeller's death, his 600-acre estate was given to Ocean County, which maintains it as a park. His mansion, an elaborate showplace of its time, has been demolished, the county feeling it too costly to maintain.

Much of the old splendor and glory of Lakewood remains today in its fine residential areas. Lakewood Township, which grew out of the original Bricksburg and was established on March 23, 1892, is governed by a township committee of five elected members plus a city manager.

Some of the old charm of Lakewood is maintained in its horse-drawn sleighs during the snowy period and horse-drawn carriages during the spring and summer months.

EELGRASS—FORGOTTEN INDUSTRY

Eelgrass is a species of seaweed thrown against the shores of Jersey coastal islands by action of the sea. It is a nuisance today and is carted away to keep beaches clean, but around the turn of the century the gathering of eelgrass was one of the principal occupations of the inhabitants of Long Beach Island, for it brought fancy prices on the Philadelphia and Boston markets.

The islanders worked for the B. J. Kinsey Sea Moss Company of High Point, a place now known as Harvey Cedars. One who recalls this industry well is Mayor Reynold Thomas of the Cedars, who has good cause to remember, having been an eelgrass gatherer for his "Uncle Bo" Kinsey.

Uncle Bo was an island character who believed in taking advantage of what the sea offered, and eelgrass was one thing it supplied in plenty. What possible use could be made of eelgrass? Uncle Bo could name many uses, strange to us today but commonplace in the early 1900s. Funeral directors and coffin makers used eelgrass to line coffins. The grass has two things in its favor; it is bugproof and fire resistant. These factors also made eelgrass of prime importance to steamship companies, which used it for "steerage mattresses." These mattresses were of the cheapest possible manufacture and were discarded after one crossing of the Atlantic Ocean. Some prisons also used seaweed for mattresses. Another of its many uses was for upholstery in Model T Fords.

While High Point was the center of the eelgrass industry on Long Beach Island, there were other seaweed stations at Loveladies, North Beach, Surf City, Ship Bottom, and Brant Beach. A station usually consisted of a storage barn, a horse press in which horses walked around a capstan, drying fields, stables, scows, wagons, and dump carts. The common method of seaweed collection was by wagons along the bayfront. Automobiles later replaced the wagons. Loads of seaweed, heavy with water, were carted to open fields and spread out for drying. During this process the weed was given a wetting with well water to wash away the salt. After being thoroughly dried the seaweed, weighing much less, was put in the horse press. It was then packed into bales for shipment to metropolitan centers on a spur line that once ran the length of Long Beach Island.

Another favorite gathering method was by scows. The parent company would lend scows to baymen who collected the seaweed from the many islands in Barnegat Bay. This was piecework, at so much per scowload, usually about $6. Baymen were a breed in themselves, existing entirely on the treasures of the sea—fish, oysters, clams, and eelgrass.

The gathering of eelgrass continued as a prosperous business until around 1929, when a blight hit the growth and it disappeared from the waters. Although eelgrass made a comeback in recent years as insulation, the industry as such is just another memory of the colorful past of the Jersey shore.

TUCKERTON TOWER

In the midst of the sprawling Mystic Islands home development near Tuckerton stand three concrete blocks, 20 feet in the ground and 24 feet above. They and a concrete blockhouse are all that remains of one of the tallest telegraphic towers in history, one which allegedly played a part in the destruction of the British passenger liner *Lusitania* by a German U-boat and the entrance of the United States into World War I.

During the early 1900s wireless telegraphy was in its infancy. Although the Marconi Company is credited with discovering the principles of wireless communication, it was Dr. Rudolph Goldschmidt, a German scientist, who did much toward its initial advancement. Dr. Goldschmidt conceived the idea of transocean wireless, choosing the Jersey coast as one terminal of his experiments. Hickory Island, three miles south of the community of Tuckerton and commanding an unobstructed view of the Atlantic Ocean, was picked because of its isolation. There were no roads to the spot, only a dirt trail.

On May 21, 1912, construction was begun on what became known as the Tuckerton Tower. The tower was originally assembled in Germany, then disassembled, brought across the ocean on a freighter, loaded on flatcars in New York, finally arriving at its destination by horse-drawn vehicles across soggy meadows.

A number of engineering firsts were involved in the construction of the tower, which was supported by four cables on each of the three sides. These cables were attached to three concrete, steel-reinforced blocks, 20 feet in the ground. Each of the blocks, weighing approximately 1,100 tons, was located 600 feet from the base of the tower.

The station maintained the highest voltage of any radio tower in the world. Standing on a solid steel ball, supported by six columns of glass, the base was thoroughly insulated. Secrecy was maintained by the company although local labor was used. Construction bosses and engineers were Germans; they boarded with Tuckerton residents during the 1912–14 period. These residents seemed little inclined to be curious. They were told the station was a commercial experiment.

When the Tuckerton operation got under way in 1912 a similar project was begun at Eilvese, near Hannover, Germany. The Jersey station was not completed until March 31, 1914, though some messages were sent on a limited-range basis as early as January 27, 1914.

According to available records, the first official notice of the venture by the United States government seems to have been on May 5, 1913, when William M. Smith of the Bureau of Yards and Docks requested an inspection of the operation by the U.S. Navy Department. Under orders from the Navy, D. M. Mahood, Chief Superintendent Electrical Inspector, made a check on the station on May 18, 1914. The government apparently found no cause for alarm and gave the station official call letters WGG.

President Woodrow Wilson sent birthday greetings to Kaiser

Wilhelm II on the latter's fifty-fifth birthday via the Tuckerton wireless. The *New Jersey Courier* (Toms River) on January 30, 1914, reported the Kaiser answered Wilson expressing hope the station would become "a new link between our countries."

When war in Europe erupted on July 28, 1914, the Tuckerton tower was still an unrestricted operation. In the early fall of 1914 there were charges that the station was being used for war purposes by the government of Germany. There were official protests by both France and England.

President Wilson issued a message of neutrality on August 5, 1914, and wireless stations were forbidden to contact ships at sea. Disregarding the order, Tuckerton wireless communicated sailing information to the German cruisers *Dresden* and *Karlsruhe* in the North Atlantic.

On August 6, the U.S. Navy moved in on the Tuckerton wireless with a censorship team headed by Ensign Comfort B. Platt. The Navy men had authority on operational output, but no power to take over equipment.

Censorship was tightened by order from Secretary of the Navy Josephus Daniels to the effect that no cipher or code could be transmitted from any installation in the United States except ciphers to and from American officials. This ruling cut off Germany from wireless communication with her embassy here.

Operational takeover of the Tuckerton station was further strengthened by order of President Wilson on September 5, 1914. Navy Lieutenant Felix Gygax took charge on September 9; Ensign Platt continued duties there. Nine enlisted men were assigned. Station manager Emile E. Mayer was allowed to continue in his capacity, even though it had been proven that he was a member of the German Army Reserves. German employees remained in charge of maintenance; the navy handled all transmissions.

Despite this supposedly strict censorship, there were continued charges that military messages were getting through to Germany.

On May 1, 1915, American metropolitan newspapers printed this Imperial German Government warning: "Travelers intending to embark on the Atlantic voyage are reminded a state of war exists between Germany and Great Britain; that the zone of war includes the waters adjacent to the British Isles. Vessels flying the flag of Great Britain, or her allies, are liable to destruction in those waters."

Six days later after Lieutenant Schweiger, commander of the Imperial German submarine *U-20*, received the message "Get Lucy," allegedly sent from the 862-foot wireless tower at Tuckerton, the liner *Lusitania*, of British registry, was torpedoed with a loss of 1,198 lives, including 124 Americans, as she neared the British coast. A single shot at the unarmed vessel was all that was required, according to Lieutenant Schweiger's notes of the affair in his diary, which was secured by the U.S. government from the Imperial German Navy following the Armistice.*

On February 8, 1917, the U.S. government, under war powers, ordered all German nationals employed by the station to leave. Some took up residence in town; others tried to secure passage home. A company of U.S. Marines commanded by Lieutenant E. A. Richtenstein moved in. The United States declared war on Germany on April 6, 1917. On April 7 Secret Service men came to Tuckerton and placed the German staff, as many as they could find, under arrest, including Emile Mayer. All had been proved members of the German Army and were held as prisoners of war. There were no spy charges. The men were sent to a war camp in Virginia for the duration of the conflict.

The tower was operated by the U.S. military throughout the rest of the war. Following the peace it was transferred to French ownership for a 15-day period before it was turned over to the Radio Corporation of America along with other foreign wireless stations operating on these shores. RCA continued use of the tower for several years.

During World War II the tower was again used by the military for antisubmarine service. It was closed in 1949. Meanwhile, the property on which the tower was located passed into the hands

---

*At no place in the diary does Lieutenant Schweiger discuss receipt of the "Get Lucy" message. His notes are dated May 7, 1915. There is no real evidence the message was ever sent although the story has been repeated in print many times and is still a matter of strong debate among Tuckerton natives. The story was neither confirmed nor denied by the U.S. government.

of the Mystic Islands Corporation, a home community development firm, and a decision was made to demolish the structure following a check with the Defense Department, which stated the operation had outlived its usefulness.

Demolition experts moved in. On December 28, 1955, acetylene torches were applied to the cables, and the big mast came crashing down. It was then cut up for scrap, yielding approximately 800 tons of steel, not to mention two miles of 2-inch cable.

Today the spot is marked by the original concrete anchors and a concrete engine house so solid they cannot be removed without the use of explosives, according to engineering experts. Streets detour around the anchors.

ANNAPOLIS OF NEW JERSEY

A visitor to Pine Beach on Toms River, Ocean County, will find a scene similar to that of Annapolis, Maryland—sloops, sailing craft, motor launches, and navy training ships all in neat anchorage. In the early evening, colors are lowered with traditional ceremony. The Admiral Farragut Academy, the first school in America offering college preparation in an atmosphere of naval tradition, is in many ways a replica of its big brother, the U.S. Naval Academy.

In 1932 Admiral S. S. Robinson, USN (Ret.), and Brigadier General C. S. Radford, USMC (Ret.), became convinced that, just as private schools with military training facilities served the army, so could a private institution with naval training serve the navy. Through their efforts a site overlooking Toms River at Pine Beach was selected and the Admiral Farragut Academy opened in September 1933 with an enrollment of fifty-six cadets. Facilities of the academy were located in a rambling hotel later christened Farragut Hall.

The Academy was named for Admiral David Glasgow Farragut, who, after a brilliant career in the United States Navy, was commissioned as the first admiral of the navy by a special act of Congress in 1866.

A new dormitory and classroom building was completed at the Academy in 1936 and named for Admiral Samuel Francis du Pont. It catered to the needs of the corps, by then grown to 175 cadets. The Academy was designated an Honor Navy School by Congress in 1941.

Farragut prepares its students for admission to colleges and the United States academies. Today's corps averages 300. The current fleet of the Academy includes Marconi-rigged Barnegat Bay sneak boxes, a 40-foot launch, and a 63-foot flagship, in addition to whaleboats and motor launches.

The municipality of Pine Beach was founded in 1909 as a summer resort. It became a borough in 1925 after separation from Berkeley Township. The year-round population is 1,232.

HOME OF THE DIRIGIBLES

The sprawling Lakehurst Naval Air Station, in the borough of Lakehurst, Manchester Township, Ocean County, today goes quietly about its mission of helicopter training and experimentation, a contrast to the days when, as a center for lighter-than-air activity, it was frequently in the national headlines.

Prior to World War I the area which is now the naval station was used as an ammunition proving ground for the Imperial Russian government, and then as a test area for U.S. chemical warfare training. Later the U.S. Army operated the site as Camp Kendrick. It was commissioned a naval air station in 1921, the year the Bureau of Aeronautics was established.

Among the history-making events occurring at Lakehurst was the start and finish of a round-the-world trip by the German dirigible *Graf Zeppelin* in 1929 under command of Dr. Hugo Eckener, then employed by the German government (later by the United States).

For years Lakehurst was the home of the huge airships *Akron, Macon, Shenandoah,* and *Los Angeles.* It was also the American base for the *Graf Zeppelin* and the *Hindenburg.* Tragedy trailed nearly all the big ships. The *Akron* broke up in 1933, and 73 people perished. The *Macon* went down off the California coast in 1935 with a loss of 83 crewmen. The *Shenandoah* was wrecked with a large death toll. The *Los Angeles,* built in Germany in 1924 and flown to this country as part of the German war debt, proved one of the most sturdy of the lot. It was finally retired to Lakehurst and dismantled in 1939. The *Graf Zeppelin* also escaped a violent end.

No event in history was so faithfully recorded as the death of the *Hindenburg* at Lakehurst on May 6, 1937. Reporters and cameramen representing every major wire service were on hand for what was always an exciting event, the landing and securing of the trans-Atlantic giant. Roads to the field were solid with sight-seers. Hundreds of amateur as well as professional cameramen were merrily clicking away.

The *Hindenburg,* one year old and on her eleventh round trip between Germany and the United States, was about to land. Headwinds over the Atlantic had slowed her down, forcing skipper Captain Max Pruss to set a new landing time of 6 P.M. instead of the scheduled 6 A.M. As the big ship approached Lakehurst, she was two hours ahead of the revised schedule. Although landing conditions were favorable, Captain Pruss ordered the ship to cruise down the Jersey cape to consume time.

A cold front passed Lakehurst about 4:30 P.M. and continued for about an hour, bringing with it heavy showers. The station advised Captain Pruss to wait out the temporary front. At 7 P.M., with the air cleared, the ground crew resumed stations as the *Hindenburg* returned, maneuvered into position, and dropped rope and cables of steel to the ground.

There was a hush as the awesome craft hovered over the landing mast. Then, without warning, there was a burst of fire, and the hydrogen-filled bag was a mass of flames. Explosions ripped the framework as the skeleton of the big ship settled to the ground before horror-stricken onlookers. In minutes the "Queen of the Skies" was a charred tomb.

During World War II Lakehurst served as a base for the naval antisubmarine patrol which used small blimps for that purpose. These proved inadequate, and most of the patrols were entrusted to the Civil Air Patrol antisubmarine units, one of which was

On May 6, 1937, just one year after it had begun the first commercial transatlantic air service, the hydrogen-filled German dirigible *Hindenburg* burst into flames as it prepared to dock at its American base, Lakehurst Naval Air Station. Thirty-six of the ninety-seven passengers and crew perished. (Courtesy of Lakehurst Naval Air Station)

stationed at Bader Field, Atlantic City. Planes from the naval installation at Millville also took part in this mission.

The huge dirigible hangars of Lakehurst still dominate the other buildings on the grounds, but they no longer house the air giants of yesteryear. Although the primary mission of Lakehurst is fleet support, it is a biservice installation with nine tenant commands representing a broad cross-section of navy and army aviation.

An interesting place to visit on the installation is the Cathedral of the Air, erected in 1932 by the New Jersey Department of the American Legion. Regular services are held there each Sunday.

A bronze plaque marking Lakehurst Hangar No. 1 as a national historic landmark was received from the National Park Service in November of 1968 and put in place with appropriate ceremonies presided over by Captain M. A. Esmoil, Jr., USN, commanding officer of the station.

The hangar, completed in August 1921, was the largest span building ever erected, measuring 807 feet in length, 268 feet in width, and 172 feet in height. It was initially the home of the big blimps. Today part of the hangar houses a half-scale model of a carrier flight deck where navy personnel are trained to operate catapults and arresting gear found on the latest type aircraft carriers.

APPENDIX
Town Names Past and Present

ATLANTIC COUNTY

Present Name	*Earlier Names*
Absecon	—Mount Eagle, Peter White's Plantation, Ragtown, Absecum, Lower Island
Atlantic City	—Further Island, Leed's Plantation, Absecon Beach, Absecon Island
Bargaintown	—Cedar Bridge
Brigantine	—Baremore's Plantation, Atmoonica, Brigantine Beach
Corbin City	—Champion's Landing
Chestnut Neck	—Egg Harbor, Chestnut Ridge, John Adams' Landing
Egg Harbor City	—Gloucester Furnace, Gloucester Landing
Elwood	—Colville
Folsom	—New Germany
Hammonton	—Coffin's Mill, Hammondtown, Coffin's Glass Factory, Hammond's
Leeds Point	—Leeds
Linwood	—Leedsville, Pearville, Steelmanville
Longport	—Sand Hills Beach
Margate	—South Atlantic
Mays Landing	—The Landing, Iliff Town, May's Place, May's Landing
Northfield	—Bakersville, Dolphin
Oceanville	—Tanners Brook, Toadtown

Present Name	*Earlier Names*
Pleasantville	—Risleytown, Adamstown, Lakestown, Smith's Landing
Pleasant Mills	—Nescochague, The Mills, Sweetwater (lower part)
Pomona	—Doughty Station, Cedar Bridge, Swamp Siding
Port Republic	—Wrangleboro, Union, Uniontown, Unionville, Clark's Mills
Smithville	—Galloway Cross Roads
Somers Point	—Somers Plantation, Job's Point, Somerset Plantation, Somers Ferry

BURLINGTON COUNTY

Atsion	—Atsyunk, Atsiung, Fruitland
Bass River	—Bass River Hotel
Batsto	—Batstowe, Five Forks, Batsto Furnace
Beverly City	—Dunk's Ferry, Churchville
Birmingham	—Brumahin, New Mills
Bordentown	—Bordings Town
Browns Mills	—Brown's Mills Lake, Biddles Mills, Mirrow Lake
Burlington City	—New Beverly, Bridlington, Borlington
Centerton	—Bougher
Chatsworth	—Chesilhurst, Chamong, Shamong, Shamong Station
Chesterfield	—Recklesstown
Cinnaminson	—Westfield, Lower Chester
Columbus	—Black Horse, Encroaching Corners
Crosswicks	—Crossweeksung, Crosswicke
Florence	—Florence Heights, High Bank
Georgetown	—Fooltown
Green Bank	—Sooy's Inn
Harrisville	—McCartyville

Present Name	*Earlier Names*
Hog Wallow	—Haines Bog
Indian Mills	—Edgepillock, Brotherton
Kresson	—Bordon's Mills, Pendleton, Milford
Lazy Point	—Leasy Point, Lassa Point, Wingerworth Point
Medford Lakes	—Ballinger's Mills
Moorestown	—Moorfield, Chestertown, Rodmantown
Mount Holly	—Mounthalli, Bridgeton, Crips Mount
Mount Misery	—Mount Relief
Riverside Township	—Progress, Goattown
Smithville	—Parker's Mills, French Mills, Shreveport
Vincentown	—Vincent's Town, Brimstone Neck, Quakertown, Weepink
Wading River	—Bridgeport

CAMDEN COUNTY

Berlin	—Long-a-Coming
Blackwood	—Blackwoodtown
Blenheim	—Mechanicsville
Camden	—Cooper's Ferry, Coopersville, Wrightsville
Chews	—Chews Landing, Abraham Roe's Landing, Hodgson's Landing
Cherry Hill	—Delaware Township
Clementon	—Newman's Mills
Collingswood	—Newton Colony
Fairview	—Yorkship Village, Yorkship
Gloucester City	—Gloucester Town
Haddon Heights	—Baker's Corner, Borton's Hill
Kresson	—Barton's Mills, Pendleton, Milford
Mount Ephraim	—Ephraim's Mount, Crossroads in the Town of Gloucester
Pennsauken	—Pennsoakin

Present Name	*Earlier Names*
Sicklerville	—Waretown
Westmont	—Rowandtown

CAPE MAY COUNTY

Avalon	—Seven Mile Beach, Leaming, Piermont
Beesley's Point	—Goldin's Point, Stites Point, Willets Point
Burleigh	—Gravelly Run
Cape May City	—Cape Island
Cape May Court House	—Shamgar Hand Plantation, Rumly Moch, Romney Marsh, Middletown
Cape May Point	—Stites Beach, Seagrove
Cold Spring	—Centerville
Dias Creek	—Dyers Creek
Dennisville	—Dennis Creek
Erma	—Swaintown
Fishing Creek	—Fisher's Creek
North Wildwood	—Anglesea
Ocean City	—Peck's Beach, Pete's Beach, Pet's Beach, New Brighton
Petersburg	—Littleworth
Rio Grande	—Hildreths
Sea Isle City	—Ludlam's Beach, Strathmere
Swainton	—Townsend's Inlet
Tuckahoe	—Head of the River, Williamsburg
Town Bank	—Portsmouth, Cape May Town, New England (Village), Falmouth
Wildwood	—Holly Beach, Five Mile Beach

CUMBERLAND COUNTY

Present Name	*Earlier Names*
Bridgeton	—The Bridge, Cohansey Bridge, Bridgetown
Cedarville	—Cedar Creek
Dividing Creek	—Strongtown, Mincetown, Dragston, Turkey Point
Greenwich	—Manor Town
Mauricetown	—Mattox Landing
Millville	—Shingle Landing, Maurice River Bridge
Port Norris	—Dallas Ferry
Roadstown	—Sayre's Corners, Cross Roads, Roads Town
West Creek	—Jacak's

GLOUCESTER COUNTY

Almonesson	—Lambtown, Jenningsville, Young Fox Place
Aura	—Union, Union Cross Roads, Unionville, Union Meeting House
Barnsboro	—Lodgetown, Barnesborough
Billingsport	—Roder Udden, Mantua Hook, Byllynges Point
Bridgeport	—Raccoon Lower Bridge
Cecil	—Coles Mills
Clayton	—Fislerville, Fislertown
Colonial Manor	—North Woodbury
Franklinville	—Little Ease
Glassboro	—Glass Town, Glassworks
Grenloch	—Tetamekon, Spring Mills, Bateman's Mills

Present Name	Earlier Names
Hardingville	—Red Lion
Harrisonville	—Coles Mills, Coles Town
Janvier	—Baums Pond, New Denmark, Tallow Hill, Ellens Ridge
Jefferson	—Cox's Hill, Allenboro, Lawrenceville, Lazy Lawrence
Mantua	—Smith's Landing, Carpenter's Landing, Henessey's Landing, Easleys Landing, Eastlacks
Mount Royal	—Sandtown, Berkley
New Brooklyn	—Marshalls Mill, Seven Causeways
Paulsboro	—Crown Point
Pineville	—Pine Tavern
Plainville	—Hopeville, Woolfordtown
Richwood	—White Horse, Five Points, Mount Pleasant, Campbell's Crossroads
Salina	—Bees Corner
Sewell	—Chewville
Swedesboro	—Raccoon
Thorofare	—Flyatem Town
Westville	—Buck Tavern
Williamstown	—Squankum, Squankum Neck, Squankum Village, Squankum Settlement
Woodbury	—Woodbury Creek, Ye Shelter, Piscozackasing Kill

OCEAN COUNTY

Browns Mills	—Biddle's Mills
Harvey Cedars	—High Point
Indian Mills	—Brotherton
Lakewood	—Bricksburg, Washington Furnace
Laurelton	—Burrsville
Toms River	—Goose Creek, Town of Dover

Present Name	Earlier Names
Tucker's Island	—Short Beach
Tuckerton	—Clamtown, Middle of the Shore
West Creek	—Westeconk, Mannahocking

SALEM COUNTY

Alloway	—Thompson's Bridge, Allowaystown
Elmer	—Pittstown, John Pym's Place, Ticktown
Finn's Point	—Fischer's Point
Fort Mott	—Finn's Point Battery
Pedricktown	—Pedrick's Town
Penns Grove	—Helm's Cove
Pennsville	—Obisquahassit, Kinseyville, Craven's Ferry
Pole Tavern	—Champney's Corner
Quinton	—Quinton's Bridge
Salem	—Fenwick's Colony, Salem Town
Woodstown	—Pilesgrove, Millbrooke

SELECTED BIBLIOGRAPHY

No bibliography would be complete without reference to the people without whose help much of the most useful material would not have been available. I have cited them in the Acknowledgments in the front matter.

MANUSCRIPT SOURCES

Atsion
  Account books, Burlington County Historical Society, Burlington
Batsto
  Batsto Committee, Minutes, 1958–71, Batsto
  Dedication program, May 15, 1964, McMahon collection
  Hartman papers, New Jersey State Department of Historic Sites, Trenton
  J. A. Starkey personal notes, McMahon collection
  Washington papers on Batsto firebacks, Library of Congress
Berlin
  Borough records, Borough Hall, Berlin
Catawba
  Deeds, Atlantic County Surrogate's Office, Mays Landing
  Deeds of the West family, Gloucester County Surrogate's Office, Woodbury
Camden and Atlantic Railroad
  Handbills, McMahon collection
Cumberland County
  Notes of Frank Butler, McMahon collection

Admiral Farragut Academy
  Academy records, Tom's River
Finn's Point-Fort Mott
  Records, New Jersey Department of Conservation, Trenton
"The Goldschmidt Wireless"
  Roy M. Nunn, thesis, Albright College, Reading, Pa. (1967)
The Great John Mathis
  Letters of S. C. Loveland, Jr., McMahon collection
Harvey Cedars
  Records of Thomas Reynold, his home, Harvey Cedars
Land grants
  Deeds, House of Proprietors, Burlington
Dolly Madison
  Dolly Madison will, Camden Historical Society
Colonel John McKee
  Deeds, Atlantic County Surrogate's Office, Mays Landing
  Deeds, Cabell County Clerk's Office, Huntington, West
    Virginia
  Deeds, Gloucester County Surrogate's Office, Woodbury
  Notes of the McKee Foundation, Catholic Historical Society
    of Pennsylvania, Philadelphia
  Will and statistics, Philadelphia Bureau of Vital Statistics
Martha Furnace
  Account books, Camden County Historical Society
  Martha Furnace diary, Camden Historical Society, Burlington
    County Historical Society
Ocean County
  Jack Lamping files, Ocean County Court House, Toms River
Port Republic-Chestnut Neck
  Dedication program of monument, Oct. 6, 1928, McMahon
    collection
  Records, Saint Paul's Methodist Church, Port Republic
  Union Chapel, Records, Port Republic
Raccoon
  Records, Swedish Lutheran Church
Salem County
  Notes of Frank Butler, McMahon collection
  Records, Quaker Meeting

Sea Isle City
  Notes of William J. Haffert, Sr., McMahon collection
  Notes of Vincent LaManna, McMahon collection
Smithville
  Notes of J. A. Starkey, McMahon collection
Railroads of South Jersey
  Pennsylvania Railroad Archives, Philadelphia
Swedesboro
  Notes of J. E. Pfeiffer, McMahon collection
Toms River
  Notes of Mrs. Herbert Miller, Toms River Historic Restoration
    Committee
Tuckerton Tower
  Report, U.S. Navy Superintendent of Radio Service (1914),
    Ocean County Public Relations Office, Toms River
Wharton Tract
  "Historic Aspects of the Wharton Tract," summary report by
    G. Edwin Brumbaugh, New Jersey State Department of
    Historic Sites, Trenton

Historical Society Files

Barnegat Historical Society, Barnegat City, N.J.
Burlington Historical Society, Burlington, N.J.
Camden Historical Society, Camden, N.J.
Cape May County Historical Society, Cape May Court House, N.J.
Cumberland County Historical Society, Greenwich, N.J.
Forked River Historical Society, Forked River, N.J.
Gloucester County Historical Society, Woodbury, N.J.
Haddonfield Historical Society, Haddonfield, N.J.
Hammonton Historical Society, Hammonton, N.J.
Millville Historical Society, Millville, N.J.
New Jersey Historical Society, Newark, N.J.
Ocean County Historical Society, Toms River, N.J.
Pennsylvania Historical Society, Philadelphia, Pa.
Salem County Historical Society, Salem, N.J.
Stratford Township Historical Society, Stratford, N.J.
Vineland Historical Society, Vineland, N.J.

Industrial Company Files

Welch Grape Juice Company, Westfield, N.Y.
Ball Brothers, Muncie, Ind.
Consolidated Fruit Jar Company, New Brunswick, N.J.
Glass Container Manufacturers Institute, New York, N.Y.
Museum, Ford Company, Dearborn, Mich.
RCA-Victor Company, Camden, N.J.
Campbell Soup Company, Camden, N.J.
Pennsylvania Railroad Company, Philadelphia, Pa.
Associated Realties Company, Atlantic City, N.J.

PRINTED SOURCES

Alexander, Robert C. *Music of Old Cape May.* Privately printed, 1964.

Andrews, Frank D. *Bibliography of Vineland Authors and Writers.* Centennial edition. Vineland Historical Society, 1961.

Bancroft, Raymond Mitchell. *Collingswood Story.* Privately printed, 1965.

Barber, John W., and Howe, Henry, eds. *Historical Collections of the State of New Jersey.* S. Tuttle, 1844.

Barraud, Francis. "His Master's Voice." *Strand,* London, August 1916.

Barrett, Charles, and Scull, Kenneth N. *Tall Pines at Catawba.* Privately printed, 1968.

Batsto Citizens Committee. *Holdings of Jesse Richards.* Privately printed, 1965.

Beck, Henry Charlton. *Forgotten Towns of Southern New Jersey.* Dutton, 1936.

———. *Jersey Genesis.* Rutgers University Press, 1963.

———. *Roads of Home.* Rutgers University Press, 1956.

Biographical, Genealogical and Descriptive History of Southern New Jersey. 2 vols. Lewis Publishing Company, 1900.

Bisbee, Henry H. *Place Names in Burlington County.* Privately printed, 1970.

Blackman, Leah. *History of Little Egg Harbor Township.* 1888. Reprint. Great John Mathis Foundation, 1963.

Bole, Robert D., and Walton, Edward H., Jr. *The Glassboro Story.* Maple Press, York, Pa., 1964.

Bowen, F. W. *History of Port Elizabeth.* Lippincott, 1885.

Boyer, Charles W. *Annals of Camden: The Civil and Political History of Camden County and Camden City.* Vol. 4. Privately printed, 1922.

———. *Early Forges and Furnaces of New Jersey.* University of Pennsylvania Press, 1931.

———. *Legends of Old Gloucester.* Camden County Historical Society, 1960.

———. *Old Inns and Taverns of West Jersey.* Camden County Historical Society, 1962.

———. *Span of a Century: History of the City of Camden.* Camden County Historical Society, 1928.

Brown, Helen R. *Long-a-Coming: A History of Berlin, New Jersey.* Privately printed, 1964.

Brydon, Norman F. *Of Time, Fire and the River.* Privately printed, 1970.

Burgess, Paul C. *Annals of Brigantine.* Privately printed, 1964.

———. *Colonial Scrapbook.* Carlton Press, 1971.

Butler, Frank. *Book of the Boardwalk.* Privately printed, 1952.

Camden County Historical Society. *Bulletins.* Vol. 5, No. 3 (June 1970); Vol. 6, No. 2 (March 1971).

Carnsworthe, —. *Atlantic City, Early and Modern.* Privately printed, 1868.

Chambers, T. F. *Germans in New Jersey: Their History.* Dover, Del., 1895.

Craig, C. Chester. *Council of Proprietors of West Jersey.* Camden County Historical Society, 1922.

Cumberland County. Privately printed, 1964.

Cushing, Thomas, and Sheppard, C. E. *Histories of the Counties of Gloucester, Salem, and Cumberland.* Philadelphia, 1883.

Delker, Thomas B. *Hammonton—Atlantic County, New Jersey.* 1912.

*Descriptive History, First Congressional District of New Jersey,
1900.* Lewis Publishing Company, 1900.

Egg Harbor City. Privately printed, 1930.

Elmer, Lucius. *Elmer's History of Cumberland County.* 1869.

English, Al. *History of Atlantic City.* Privately printed, 1884.

Ewing, Sarah. *Hancock Family History.* Privately printed, 1967.

Ewing, Sarah, and McMullin, Robert. *Along Absecon Creek.*
Bridgeton, N.J., 1965.

Federal Writers Project. *New Jersey: A Guide to Its Present and
Past.* Hastings House, 1939.

Fichter, Jack. *History of Pennsauken Township.* Privately printed,
1964.

Fifty Years: New York Shipbuilding Corporation. Privately
printed, 1949.

Fleetwood, Jean G. *Where Divided Waters Flow.* Cumberland
County Historical Society, 1964.

Gloucester County Historical Society. *Foraging.* 1929.

Godfrey, Carlos E. *Origin of Old Gloucester.* Gloucester County
Historical Society, 1922.

Gordon, Thomas F. *History and Gazetteer of the State of New
Jersey.* 2 vols. D. Fenton, 1834.

Gowens, Alan. *Architecture in New Jersey.* Van Nostrand, 1964.

Green, Charles F. *A Place of Olden Days.* Privately printed, n.d.

Haddonfield Historical Society. *This Is Haddonfield.* 1963.

Hall, John F. *Daily Union History of Atlantic City and County.*
Atlantic City, 1900.

Hammonton Printing Company. *Hammonton News Almanac.*
Hammonton, N.J., 1940.

Hand, H. Wilbur, and Hand, W. B. *Illustrated History of Town
of Hammonton.* Hammonton, 1889.

Heston, Alfred M. *Absegami: Annals of Eyren Haven and Atlantic City, 1609 to 1904.* 2 vols. Privately printed, 1904.

———. *Jersey Wagon Jaunts.* 1926.

———. *South Jersey: A History, 1664–1924.* 4 vols. Lewis Historical Publishing Company, 1924.

Industries and Resources of New Jersey. Pennsylvania Publishing Company, 1891.

Jones, Carmita de Salma. "Batsto and the Bloomaries." *Pennsylvania Magazine of History*, Vol. 47, No. 3 (1923).

Kobbé, Gustave. *The New Jersey Coast and Pines*. Short Hills, N.J., 1889.

Leaming, Aaron, and Spicer, Jacob. *The Grants, Concessions and Original Constitution of the Province of New Jersey*. Philadelphia, 1758.

Lee, Francis B., ed. *Genealogical and Memorial History of the State of New Jersey*. Lewis Publishing Company, 1910.

———. *New Jersey as a Colony and as a State*. Publishing Society of New Jersey, 1902.

Lee, Harold. *History of Ocean City*. Ocean City Historical Society, 1965.

Mathewson, Craig C. *Post Offices of Cape May County*. Laureate Press, 1970.

Miller, Pauline S. *Early History of Toms River*. Privately printed, 1967.

Mints, Margaret L. *Dallas Ferry*. Cumberland County Historical Society, 1964.

Mullica Township Centennial Committee. *Mullica Township, 1838–1938: From Eric Mullica to the Present*. 1938.

Nash, Charles. *Lure of Long Beach*. Privately printed, 1936.

Nelson, William. *History of the New Jersey Coast*. Lewis Publishing Company, 1902.

Peterson, Charles J. *Kate Aylesford: A Story of the Refugees*. T. B. Peterson, 1855.

Pomfret, John E. *New Jersey Proprietors and Their Lands*. Van Nostrand, 1964.

Prowell, George R. *History of Camden County*. N.p., 1886.

Reeves, Augustus. *Early Settlement of Old Gloucester County*. Vol. 1. Camden County Historical Society, 1908.

Salem Tercentenary Committee. *Fenwick's Colony*. 1964.

Sawn, Walter. *Sea Isle City: A History*. Privately printed, 1964.

Sharp, Robert L. *Concise History of Colonial Bridgeton*. Privately printed, 1963.

Shinn, Henry C. *History of Mount Holly*. Mount Holly Herald, 1957.

Slade, J. E. *Pioneer Days of Aviation in Jersey.* Privately printed in Mannheim, Germany, 1964.

Smith, Samuel. *Fight for the Delaware.* Freneau Press, 1970.

Snyder, John F. *Story of New Jersey's Civil Boundaries.* New Jersey Bureau of Geology and Topography, 1968.

Souder, H. J., ed. *Who's Who in New Jersey.* Atlantic County edition. Gazette-Review Company, 1925.

Steelman, Robert B. *Cumberland's Hallowed Heritage.* Cumberland Mutual Fire Insurance Company, Bridgeton, 1965.

Stevens, L. T. *History of Cape May County.* Cape May City, 1897.

Stewart, Frank H. *Notes on Old Gloucester County.* Camden County Historical Society, 1917.

Van Doren, Carl. *Secret History of the American Revolution.* Viking, 1941.

Wallitsch, Al. *Early Bridgeton.* Heritage edition. Atlantic City Press, 1964.

Weiss, Harry B. *Early Sawmills of New Jersey.* New Jersey Agricultural Society, 1941.

———. *Early Woolen Industry.* New Jersey Agricultural Society, 1958.

Wharton Subcommittee. *Management Policies of the Wharton Tract.* 1956.

White, Margaret. *Decorative Arts of New Jersey.* Van Nostrand, 1964.

Wilson, Harold F. *History of Pitman, New Jersey.* Borough of Pitman, n.d.

Woodward, Major E. M., and Hageman, John F. *History of Burlington and Mercer Counties.* Lippincott, 1883.

Woolman and Rose. *Atlas of the New Jersey Coast.* 1878.

Wortman, C. Byron. *The First Fifty: History of Seaside Heights.* Privately printed, 1963.

Zich, Gerald E. *Fertile Furrow: History of New Jersey Agriculture.* New Jersey Department of Agriculture, 1966.

Newspapers

Atlantic City Press
Batsto Citizens Gazette

Camden New Republic
Gloucester City News
Hammonton News
New Jersey Courier (Toms River)
Ocean County Daily Times
Philadelphia Bulletin
Salem Standard and Jerseyman

INDEX

Leeds, Robert B., 246
Leeds, Thomas, 246
Leeds, Titan, 211
Leeds Point, 197, 210–11, 212–13, 246
Leektown, 115
Leggett and Company, Francis H., 194–95
Lehman's Mill, 37
Lenni-Lenape Indians, 3, 4, 38, 56, 71; in Atlantic County, 197, 215–17, 231–32, 233, 242; in Burlington County, 80, 81, 83, 95, 97, 104, 105, 106, 108–13, 117n; in Camden County, 276, 277, 278, 281, 283, 285; in Gloucester County, 137, 140, 141–42, 145; in Ocean County, 297–98, 306, 307
Lenox China Company, 242
Lepaute, Henri, 319
Levine, Leo, 42
Lewis, L. R., 34
Lewis, Samuel, 101
Liberty Boys, 19, 61
Liberty Shipbuilding Company, 43
Liepe brothers, 242
lighthouses, 249, 315; in Cape May County, 9–11, 25, 50; in Ocean County, 310–11, 312, 317–19
"Light on Old Cape May, The," 9
Lincoln, Abraham, 13, 38–39, 84, 322
Lincoln, Mary Todd, 39
Linden Hall, Bordentown, 91
Lindenwald, 259
Linwood, 237–38
Lippincott, James, 99
Lippincott, John H., 262
Lippincott, Nathan, 262
Lippincott, Richard, 305–306
Little Egg Harbor Inlet, 308
Little Egg Harbor Life Saving Station, 312, 315–16
Little Egg Harbor lighthouse, 312
Little Egg Harbor River, 144, 197, 203, 245. *See also* Mullica River
Little Egg Harbor Township, Ocean County, 296, 297–300, 304
Little Timber Creek, 277
Livingston, William, 23, 64, 203, 304

log mining, 7
Long-a-Coming (Berlin), 124, 258, 281–82
Long Beach Island, 6, 307–11, 314–19, 324–25
Long Beach Township, Ocean County, 310
Longfellow, Henry Wadsworth, 259
Loranier (vessel), 299
Los Angeles (dirigible), 330, 331
Loveladies, New Jersey, 324
Lovett, Samuel, 82
Love and Unity (vessel), 308
Lower Bank, 114, 124, 144
Lower Penns Neck Township, Salem County, 55
Lucas, Nicholas, 55, 56
Lucas, Simon, 207, 208
Ludlam, Alex R., 32
Ludlam, Anthony, 25, 36
Ludlam, Charles, 30
Ludlam, Isaac, 32
Ludlam, Joseph, 25, 36
Ludlam, Joseph, Jr., 36
Ludlam, Richard S., 13
Ludlam's Beach, *see* Sea Isle City
Ludlam's Island, 25
Luker, Thomas, 307
Lusitania (vessel), 325, 328
Lutherans, 141–42, 153
Lyle, A. C., quoted, 41–42
Lyons, Russ, 7

McCarty, William, 121
McCollum, Hugh, 205
McCowan, J. M., 160
McCullum, Patrick, 202
MacFadden, Fred R., Jr., 212
McGlade, Charles, 249
McGregor, Samuel, 61
McGuire Air Force Base, 81
McKee, John, 242–45
McKee City, 242–45
McKenzie, Alan, 48, 50
McKnight, William, 97
Macon (dirigible), 330, 331
Madison, Dolly Payne (Mrs. James Madison), 264
Madison, James, 264
Madole, James, 62

ABOUT THE AUTHOR

William McMahon has been senior music critic, columnist, and feature writer at *The Press* (Atlantic City). He is the author of numerous books on South Jersey history and has received awards from the Association for State and Local History, the New Jersey Association of Teachers of English, the Atlantic Community Concerts Association and Stockton State College. He is currently a freelance writer.